THE NATURE AND LIMITS OF AUTHORITY

THE NATURE
AND LIMITS
OF AUTHORITY

Richard T. De George

UNIVERSITY PRESS OF KANSAS

Published by the University Press of Kansas (Lawrence, Kansas 66045),
which was organized by the Kansas Board of Regents and is operated and funded
by Emporia State University, Fort Hays State University, Kansas
State University, Pittsburg State University, the University of Kansas,
and Wichita State University

Library of Congress Cataloging in Publication Data

De George, Richard T.
  The nature and limits of authority.

  Bibliography: p.
  Includes index.
  1. Authority. I. Title.
BD209.D4   1985   303.3   85-8128
ISBN 0-7006-0269-0
ISBN 0-7006-0270-4 (pbk.)

Printed in the United States of America

Contents

Preface

The sustained, widespread, and sometimes violent attacks on authority that characterized the year 1968 have long subsided. But the erosion of authority has quietly continued. Frequently those who uphold authority have been no more clear in their defense than those who attack it have been in their protest. A large number of recent works have dealt with particular aspects of authority. The classical analysis of Max Weber has been subjected to a thorough critique. The sociologist Robert Nisbet has described the "twilight of authority," and Stanley Milgram has dramatically portrayed some of the pernicious psychological aspects of "obedience to authority." Yet there remains a need for a comprehensive philosophical analysis in order to get clear what authority as such is, what its forms are, which of its functions can be justified, and when it should be challenged and resisted. This book is an attempt to fill that need.

Authority is assumed by many to mean political authority, or the right to command, together with the concomitant obligation of those who are subject to it to obey. Clearly there are other kinds of authority. The authority of most professors as experts in their field, for instance, does not include any right to command. The analysis I undertake in these pages is not restricted to political authority; it seeks to clarify the nature and status of authority in its myriad forms.

My ideas have developed over the years since I started writing on authority. This book's present shape is different from what I orginally envisaged and different from what I previously presented in many places in lectures and papers. I have sought to handle what I considered serious difficulties raised by those who voiced objections to my analysis, though I am sure some of my critics will remain unsatisfied.

My first attempt to clarify the nature of authority resulted in an article, "The Function and Limits of Epistemic Authority," *Southern*

Journal of Philosophy (1970), which appeared in revised form, together with an extensive bibliography on authority, in *Authority* (University of Alabama Press, 1976). In 1974 I published "Authority and Morality" in *Authority* (Nijhoff). These were followed by "Freedom and Authority," *ACPA Proceedings* (1976), and "Anarchism and Authority," *Anarchism* (New York University Press, 1978), two invited papers that I presented to professional organizations. Another of my papers, "The Concept of Authority," appeared in *Power and Authority in Law Enforcement* (Charles C. Thomas, 1976). I have incorporated, often in greatly changed form, much of the material from those pieces into the present work.

Keeping this volume within tolerable limits was a continuing difficulty. The chapter on epistemic authority invited the presentation of a complete theory of knowledge; the one on political authority could have been a book of its own, as should, perhaps, some of the other chapters. I have attempted to be systematic rather than historical. Yet historical positions and figures frequently lurk in the background of my discussions of particular issues.

My work for this volume has been supported by a variety of sources. I gratefully acknowledge support by the National Endowment for the Humanities in the form of Fellowship Grant no. H69-I-125 and Project Grant no. R-6424-72-402, which I held while being, respectively, a research fellow at Yale University and a visiting fellow at Stanford University. I completed a draft of this study while holding a Rockefeller Humanities Fellowship. The University of Kansas has continuously helped support my work on this and other projects through University Research Grants. My thanks go to them all. Their support, of course, in no way implies their endorsement of the ideas, views, or positions contained herein.

Whether or not this book is an authoritative account of authority, I have attempted not to make it dogmatic. The last thing a book on authority should be is authoritarian.

1

Introduction

Authority is a fact of social life. Most often it is simply accepted. When abused, it turns into authoritarianism. Although authoritarian regimes can reign for a long time, societies seldom thrive under them. Eventually those kept subservient react to such authority. The desire for freedom, when smothered by authoritarianism, sometimes manifests itself in the opposite extreme—anarchism. Societies seldom thrive under conditions of anarchy either, nor are such conditions stable and long-lived.

The theme of this book is that acceptance of a certain degree of authority—which those subject to it regard as more or less legitimate, which they accept more or less easily, and which they challenge only exceptionally—is the normal state of affairs. Legitimate authority is bounded by the extremes of anarchism and authoritarianism between which it vacillates and against which it must guard. The norm of authority is rationally defensible within certain specifiable limits. The justifiability of any specific use of authority can be assessed. But as the norm, authority need not be constantly defended. Rather, challenges to it are what require defense. Such challenges are most successful when they demonstrate abuses of the norm rather than when they attack the norm itself.

Authority is typically and mistakenly equated with political authority. Assuming political authority as the paradigm with which one begins makes it difficult to provide the conceptual apparatus adequate for rationally evaluating and resolving conflicts that involve various kinds of authority in such realms as education, religion, and the family.

Because of the mistaken equation between authority in general and political authority, various standard roadblocks must be cleared before we can approach the many issues that are intertwined with attacks on and defenses of authority. One such claim is that every position on authority is an ideological one and hence is neither neutral nor objective. A second, related claim is that analysis, when applied to authority, simply masks one's predispositions and commitments. Since I shall attempt a neutral and objective analysis of authority, I shall face these charges right at the start, clearing the way for the substantive tasks of the chapters to follow.

IDEOLOGY AND AUTHORITY

We cannot easily dismiss the claim that every view of political authority represents some class position or group interest, that everyone must be ideologically committed to one side or another, and that neutrality in practical affairs is a sham, a cover to hide deep-rooted feelings, or a case of self-deception. If made without sound arguments to back them up, such judgments provide a dogmatic means of silencing, dismissing, attacking, or ignoring a position with which one disagrees. As a tactic, such an approach may prove effective; as a means of achieving clarity, it leaves much to be desired.

In the days of prescientific and prephilosophical thought, myths were a typical kind of conceptual scheme used to justify authority. A myth consisted usually of a fable, a story, or an allegory; it accounted for the origin of the world, explained some natural phenomenon, or justified some aspect of social life, such as authority. The myth fulfilled an explanatory or justificatory function.

In time these fables and myths gave way to conceptual schemes of a more sophisticated kind. Though more abstract, inclusive, and perhaps consistent, these latter conceptual schemes still have the same function as myths of old, namely, explanation and justification; they help understanding and perhaps guide action. They include descriptions about the way things are, as well as statements about the way things should be. A teleological scheme presents the justification of an end, and political authority may be justified in terms of the end to be achieved. A moral conceptual scheme presents a defense and/or explanation of a set of values, of which acceptance of authority may be a part. A metaphysical scheme presents a total view of reality, in which authority may be central. Conceptual schemes aid understanding; they also facilitate manipulation. In some cases the scheme is a model; in other cases, a hypothesis to be verified or falsified. Some are ideologies.

2

Ideology, at its simplest, is a conceptual scheme that has been generally adopted or accepted by a specific group and that serves as the official basis and justification for its social action, its social structures, and its systems of authority. Such ideologies catch the "consciousness" of a group. Liberalism is one such ideology; communism, a second; fascism, a third. Each has as its basis a view of reality that supplies its justification. For its adherents the view serves not as a hypothesis to be tested but as a framework and set of values to be held. Each justifies certain forms of authority.

The distinction between the conceptual schemes that we call science, myth, philosophy, and ideology is not always clear-cut. Psychoanalysis, Keynesian and Marxist economics, and similar theories are conceptual schemes that aim to supply certain types of explanations and that act as limited guides to action. The same conceptual scheme may be treated as a hypothesis by some or as a dogmatic tenet of belief and basis for action by others. What differentiates an ideology from other conceptual schemes is not what it says but how it is held and by whom, as well as how it is used— officially or individually.

Each period or age reviews its social conceptualizations, its ideologies, its myths, and its beliefs concerning authority in the light of its own experience and needs, and evaluates them accordingly. A number of different kinds of claims exist within each conceptual whole and within the corresponding social framework. We can properly examine arguments for or against certain uses or functions of authority not only for the validity of the argument but also for its adequacy within the total conceptual scheme. In the absence of scientifically determined sets of norms and goals, a makeshift attempt at achieving a coherent conceptual scheme is frequently superior to no attempt at all. In the absence of any scheme only ad hoc decisions guide our actions; and such decisions tend to multiply counter-finalities and to obstruct later ad hoc decisions. In this case our myths or hypotheses can provide only a weak justification—if any—for authority.

Any existing social order is difficult to maintain without some justification for its values and authority structures. Social myths often make social order and intercourse possible. Their justification is pragmatic—and in part psychological—insofar as they aid action. They supply the basis for the functional ideologies necessary to mobilize a people for social improvements—the building of a "Great Society" or the constructing of a society that realizes social justice.

3

Yet social myths and ideologies should be analyzed and clarified. If they are wanting in their structure, insight, argument, or results, they should be either repaired or replaced.

Society once believed that all authority proceeds from God. Today many hold that political authority comes from the people. Each is part of a larger theoretical system and cannot be understood apart from it. Each coheres better with the beliefs of a certain group at a certain time, with its view of what man is or should be, with the group's felt needs and values. Each may be more or less adequate for its time; and the arguments given in support of it or any of its parts may be deficient—invalid, inadequate, misleading, or based on false beliefs.

Any evaluation of authority, however, faces a major difficulty. Since it must be made from a certain point of view and within a certain conceptual scheme, it cannot be entirely neutral or ideologically free. While the perspective of reason is neutral with respect to the validity or invalidity of arguments, an argument's premises often contain claims or values that are not simply true or false, and they operate in contexts and within conceptual schemes that are not value free. Critics may show the inadequacy of a theory to handle certain experiences or data. They may claim that the conceptual schemes, the justificatory myths, or the value systems that are espoused by certain views of authority no longer answer the emotional or intellectual needs of the people. Or they may say that they lead to undesired results and therefore should be abandoned. The anarchist makes this sort of claim about all authority. It is easier to criticize, however, than to catch the consciousness of a people and to give voice to their feelings, aspirations, and nascent beliefs by advancing a new conceptual scheme.

The claim that any defense of authority is ideological often comes from Marxists. However, Marx, Engels, and Lenin did not attack authority as such—Engels has a classical defense of authority—but authority as found in "bourgeois" institutions and societies. They attacked both the institutions and the defenses that were given of them. In the Marxist view the economically dominant class defends its position and authority through the legal system and governmental forms and through the religion, art, philosophy, and morality that it imposes on all of society. All these are aspects of the ideology of the ruling class that it disseminates through its schools, churches, and courts and through its newspapers, films, TV, and other media of mass communication.

4

The dominated class, however, can be duped for only so long. Ultimately it sees that the ideology of the rulers is simply a means by which they defend their position, that the ideology it is taught does not conform to its needs and aspirations. It comes to view reality differently. Marx attempted to present the view of the proletariat, to give voice to its needs and aspirations. He claimed to articulate the view of a classless society in which no man would dominate any other, in which all men would be free to develop themselves fully, and in which all would have what they need. It was an ideology for the overwhelming mass of society; it was to be the ideology of the future; and it would be the ideology of everyone in the future classless society.

Despite its many shortcomings, Marx's critique was a potent weapon. His insight that the Establishment develops and uses social institutions and other ideological forms to defend its vested interests and political authority remains true. The revolution he envisaged, however, has never taken place; and the revolutions that have taken place in his name have led to societies, such as that in the Soviet Union, which are at least as far from achieving Marx's ideal as are the United States and the countries of western Europe. The authority assumed by the Communist Party was not envisaged by Marx, who presented no clear scheme for running a large, complex society.

If authority is equated with state power and with the institutions of a society and if these are not responsive to the people, the people sooner or later will feel alienated from them, subservient to them, and dominated by them. They accordingly reject the legitimacy of such authority. The notions of "shared authority" and "participatory democracy" are attempts to conceptualize authority in nonhierarchical ways, in ways that are more compatible with the basic equality of all and with the inappropriateness of any group's dominating any other.

People at various times and in various societies have adopted and lived by many different models of authority. To be effective, the conception or model must cohere with other components of the social beliefs and values of the society. If a view of authority is to speak to members of contemporary society, it must cohere with such contemporary views as the equality and dignity of all and the right to equal opportunity and self-development.

Some views of authority are more or less adequate to the needs of a society, and some cohere with the attitudes and values of that society better than do others. The arguments supporting a particular view may be defective, and the presuppositions from which a person starts may be acceptable to one society at one time but not to the same or another society at a different time. Although the view that all authority comes from God was convincingly used for a time to justify the divine right of kings, it fails as a justification for the authority of the president of the United States. It served adequately to justify the authority of popes and bishops on a hierarchical model of Christianity; it serves less well when a church is viewed as a community of all its members.

This view of conceptual schemes, constructs, models, myths, and ideologies is not a completely relativistic one. It does not say that any view of authority is as good or adequate as any other. It holds that some are better defended by argument than others, that some cohere better with certain beliefs than others, that some respond to the needs and aspirations of certain people at certain times better than do others. If there is one best means of organizing society, one best set of human values, one best way of viewing man, then there may well be one best view of authority. No one has yet found it.

Hence the charge that any examination of authority must be ideologically tainted is not a very telling one. Although partially true, it does not invalidate a study of the structures of authority or of the way in which various kinds of authority cohere with or fail to correspond to social needs. Conceptually, moreover, we can turn the charge back on itself. Is the claim that any evaluation of authority is ideological in itself ideological? If so, then the question is whether some ideologies are better—perhaps truer—than others and how this is to be decided. If the claim is not ideological, then it is not clear why other statements about authority cannot also be nonideological. In either case the best reply to the objection is to present as objective a study of authority as possible and then to let the reader judge its success.

ANALYSIS AND AUTHORITY

The second attack criticizes any analytic investigation of authority. The critic maintains that attempting to clarify the concept of authority misses the point, that examining the validity of arguments given in its defense is a means of fighting a delaying tactic, and that distinguishing limits for its possible legitimate use is an unconscious defense of the establishment.

The critic is again at least partially correct. Appeals to reason, in some instances, are a polemical means of preventing action. They frequently concentrate on the rational side of man, ignoring his emotions. They often result in lengthy and inconclusive investigations, while conditions that demand attention and change are kept the same. The ''reason'' that they employ may be suspect. How, it is asked, can one legitimately speak of reason in a world gone mad? Rational beings who wield great political authority calculate the megaton equivalents necessary to destroy a city of two million inhabitants concentrated in an area twenty miles square. Reason is used as a tool of political authority in a context that makes no sense to anyone who has any human feeling.

True, reason can be corrupted, but it need not be corrupt; it can inhibit action, but it can also promote it; it can squelch feelings, but it can also promote them and do them justice. Theoretical considerations are in themselves neither revolutionary nor conservative. They can guide both sorts of enterprises. A rationale can always be devised for preserving the status quo in terms of history, convenience, or practical necessity; and a rationale can always be devised for changing an imperfect society. The degree and rate of change are the questions at issue.

The charge that analysis masks one's commitments takes too narrow a view of analysis. Analysis can operate within any conceptual scheme. Analysis need not be an ideology, and it may be used by both those who wish to attack and those who wish to defend authority. Analysis, as a logical operation, is neutral with respect to the content upon which it is turned. It can clarify concepts. In examining a concept in relation to the conceptual net of which it forms a part, analysis can expose inconsistencies, lacunae, infelicities, and previously unnoticed connections. In the evaluation of arguments, analysis can either strengthen a position by showing that the arguments being used to support it are valid or undermine a position by demonstrating that the arguments being used in its support are unsound. Analysis can uncover the presuppositions of a position and evaluate them for consistency and rigor, clarity, and applicability. It can also consider the viability of a conceptual scheme as a whole, its overall coherence, its ability to handle and account for pertinent data or experiences.

Analysis, as a tool, is thus inherently neither conservative nor radical. Having no specific content, it is not true or false; rather, it is valid or invalid, acute or gross, penetrating or superficial, trivial or

7

important, useful or useless, depending on one's purpose in employing it. Nor is analysis a unique kind of endeavor. It may be logical or conceptual, quantitative or qualitative, phenomenological or empirical. A rational analysis of authority can have a valid nonideological use, which is neutral amidst competing claims, conceptual schemes, value systems, and ideologies. The analysis of given structures of authority may bolster but may also undermine them. Whether it does one or the other depends on the particular form, use, and justification of the authority under consideration.

An analysis of the meaning of authority and of its concrete social embodiments is a study of both theory and practice. Logical and conceptual considerations can go only so far. If they are to be pertinent to social conditions and needs, they must grow out of the uses of and difficulties posed by authority. The clarifications, distinctions, arguments, and procedures that emerge from an analysis of authority should be applicable to specific situations and should be useful in evaluating various types of action or inaction.

The analysis of authority involves both empirical and conceptual data. It includes both institutionalized practices and the theoretical frameworks within which they operate. It measures empirical practices against desired goals and in the context of some conceptual scheme. We construct conceptual schemes and nets to unify disparate elements within a whole so that we can grasp them and use them successfully.

Analysis shows the confused thinking that is still prevalent in many realms involving authority. But if the objection is that life demands action, it is correct. We cannot wait until all our concepts are clear and analyzed, until all our arguments are logically sound, or until all our values are solidly grounded. We must often act on the best possible available data. This is evident in moral and political judgments. We must do the best we can in unclear circumstances, and we must generalize on the basis of our common experience and moral insight. In the absence of sufficient knowledge, a developed conceptual scheme often supplies some justification and understanding and also fosters continued action. It may be more or less adequate to the needs at hand. Even when it reflects the common consciousness of the people, however, it should undergo scrutiny. The doctrine of the divine right of kings gave way to doctrines of social contract and of the natural rights of man, which formed the basis for much of the theory behind both the American and the French revolutions. Many people no longer hold these views with the steadfastness of earlier times. They seek reformulations that will be better able to support the superstructure of which these views were the theoretical underpinning.

The best answer to the attack on an analytic approach to authority—like the answer to the attack on any justification of authority as ideological—is to admit it is partially true, to indicate why it is partially false, and then to produce an analysis that is to be judged on its merits.

AN APPROACH TO AUTHORITY

I shall begin with an analysis of the concept of authority. I shall develop models for the most important types of authority and consider the justifiability of those types and the appropriate limits on their use.

Much slippage exists between a conceptual model of authority and any actual implementation of that model; just as much slippage occurs between the institutions as established and their everyday operation in specific instances. So long as the model is adequate to the society, however, it can serve as an ideal against which to test the institutions of a society and their actual operation.

Authority is found in many different forms throughout society. The study of authority cuts across many disciplines—philosophy, education, psychology, political science, law, religion, and theology, among others. There is no a priori reason to think that any one form of authority is primary. Careful analysis alone determines whether the concept of authority is univocal, equivocal, or analogical.

We can view the institution of authority in general, its structure in particular fields, and its exercise in individual instances. The justification of individual instances usually depends on some general justification of the pattern or institution that it exemplifies. Since the theory can only be tested in terms of its individual exercise, the three levels are mutually interrelated.

In my analysis of authority I shall concentrate on theory. I shall consider what people say about authority, how they conceive it, what they regard as its function, the models they choose, the arguments they use to support or attack it, the claims they make for it, and the means they employ to evaluate or react verbally to its use. Authority, in any given instance, may function differently from the way in which it is conceived. I shall note general misfires of this type. But I shall not pursue the validity of the authority used in any individual historical instance.

Authority is always part of a social fabric and setting. Hence the study of the institutional facts or frameworks within which the various forms of authority operate should accompany conceptual and linguistic analysis. Yet we can start by asking: How do people use the word 'authority'? Are the different uses reducible to certain basic types? How do these types interrelate? How do we ascertain if any of them are primary? Ordinary usage is often vague, inconsistent, and inadequate for handling the complexities to which a consideration of authority gives rise. The use and development of the term in the more technical discussions of philosophers, lawyers, political scientists, and theologians may also help clarify the nature of authority and its relation to the other terms and concepts used in handling the institutions of authority—such as power, obedience, right, or command.

This study will consider the various models that have been constructed to understand authority and the arguments that have been presented to justify, defend, or attack it. The validity of arguments to defend the institutions of authority should be distinguished from the value of the models that they are intended to justify.

Some anarchists claim that no type of authority is legitimate and that all exercise of authority is corrupt and fails to respect the human individual in his freedom and autonomy. Can adequate grounds and justifications for authority be found? Can the exercise of authority ever properly be absolute, and if not, what principles can be established for its limitation? In case of conflict, can we determine any a priori ranking of the types of authority that take precedence?

Authority is operative in a variety of social domains, including government, religion, and education. Authority infuses both the public realm and areas that are generally considered the private realm. Attacks on authority have produced changes in our attitudes and in our institutions over the past generation. Some were positive and overdue; others were pernicious and raised new problems in their wake. A reasoned examination of the many kinds, uses, justifications, and limitations of authority will help us to revise what should be changed and to preserve what should be kept in the continuing public and private scrutiny of authority in our society.

PART 1

The Nature of Authority

2

The Concept of Authority

Authority pervades society. It is embedded in the ordinary family structure, it is part of the business world, and it is the mainstay of the political realm. Ordinary usage of the word 'authority' reflects the wide range of what can be called the authority experience in all its fuzziness and ambiguity. A theory of authority can start with the ordinary usage of the term. But it must go on to organize and account for that experience in both its diversity and its unity. Since all forms of authority are called by the same name, common sense suggests that they have something in common. Political theory frequently asserts and assumes that political authority is basic and that other forms are derivative. Is there some common element in all forms of authority? Is there some basic form on which all the other forms of authority depend? These are topics for investigation and not for dogmatic pronouncement.

What are some of the ordinary uses of 'authority'? We speak of someone being an authority on a certain topic, as when we say, "Professor Gilles is an authority on high-temperature chemistry." We also say, for example, that "crime should be reported to the authorities." Being an authority in a field of knowledge is different from being an authority in public life, though in both instances we refer to people as authorities. We also sometimes point to a set of rules as being "the final authority" in a game; and we cite "the authority of the Bible." In all of these cases someone or something *is* an authority.

A cluster of other uses draws our attention to the fact that people or things not only are authorities but that in some instances they *have* authority. Thus a justice of the peace can say, "By the authority vested in me by the State of Kansas, I now pronounce you man and wife." Though we do not usually speak of law as being *an* authority, we do speak of "the authority of the law." These instances suggest that authority is something that can be possessed. It can also be exercised, at least in some cases. A different but related use occurs when we say that someone speaks or acts "with authority." To speak with authority does not imply that one is an authority or that he has authority in any of the senses we have already mentioned. We can describe someone who speaks with authority as speaking authoritatively, or we might refer to the statement as authoritative. Other derivative forms of 'authority' suggest other approaches. People who have authority sometimes have been authorized to do something, and we can call someone "an authorized representative." Though we might be reluctant to say that "an authorized dealer" is an authority, we can say he has the authority to speak or act within the limits set by the parent organization.

The distinctions and nuances embedded in ordinary language are useful and instructive. These few illustrations show that any account of authority must consider the difference between a person or thing that is an authority and the authority—that is, the quality or power—that he has or exercises. Furthermore, a person may be an authority in at least two different ways, namely, he may be an authority in a certain field of knowledge, or he may occupy a certain position which carries with it certain rights or powers. This already suggests that an analysis of authority which considers only political authority, or the right to command, spreads its net too narrowly.[1]

In many cases although we use the word 'authority,' we can use another word or expression equally well. We might call Professor Gilles an expert on high-temperature chemistry as well as an authority on that topic, and we might speak of "the person in charge" instead of the one in authority. A final authority might be a last court of appeal. And a person who has the authority to perform some action might frequently and just as correctly be said to have the power or the right to perform that action. We are not interested simply in the word 'authority' but in those practices, actions, states of affairs, and conceptual schemes that can be appropriately described

---

1. Thomas Hobbes, in his *Leviathan* (ed. Michael Oakeshott; Oxford: B. Blackwell, 1957, p. 106), lays the foundation for this approach when he says, "By authority, is always understood a right of doing an act." He is followed by many up to the present day. See, for example, R. S. Peters, "Authority," *Proceedings of the Aristotelian Society,* supplementary vol. 32, p. 207, who starts from Hobbes's definition; and Robert Paul Wolff, *In Defense of Anarchism* (New York: Harper Torchbooks, 1970), p. 4: "Authority is the right to command, and correlatively, the right to be obeyed."

as involving authority, even though some other word or phrase might be substituted for the word 'authority' in any of its forms or in any of its derivatives.

Do all forms of authority share certain characteristics? The answer can be established only after we have found and clarified a number of the kinds of authority. My initial approach will suggest a working model of authority which handles the more obvious cases. It will then be expanded, refined, revised, and corrected as needed.

A WORKING MODEL

As an initial formulation: someone or something (X) is an authority if he (she, or it) stands in relation to someone else (Y) as superior stands to inferior with respect to some realm, field, or domain (R). Thus Professor Gilles is an authority for his students in the field of high-temperature chemistry; the captain of a ship at sea is an authority for the others on board the vessel; and the office manager is an authority for the office secretary in regard to which letters in the office are to be typed first.

In each of these cases we are clearly specifying some sort of relational quality. I shall call X (the person or thing who is an authority) a bearer of authority, whether or not he should properly be said to have or to exercise authority. I shall refer to all Ys over whom or for whom authority is exercised or for whom someone else is an authority as those subject to authority.

Just as the term 'father' specifies a relation to a child, so to be an authority specifies a relation. This is evident in the political realm. Political authorities are authorities with respect to the members of the society in which they are authorities, in which they hold an office or a certain position. Because they are authorities, they can do certain things, make certain decisions, give certain commands. Similarly when we say that someone is an authority on a certain topic, we also relate him in certain ways to others for whom he is an authority and to a certain body of knowledge. To say that Professor Gilles is an authority on high-temperature chemistry is to say something not only about his knowledge but also about his knowledge in relation to others. To be an expert on high-temperature chemistry involves having a great deal of detailed and systematic knowledge on the topic. To be an authority seems to say more: that is, not only does Professor Gilles have a great deal of knowledge on his topic, but he has this knowledge in a social context in which he knows more than others for whom he serves as a source of knowledge. The authority relation is, moreover, one of inequality, the authority being the superior, and those subject to authority being the inferiors.

Consider a typical sixteen-year-old native speaker of English in New York. Other New Yorkers would hardly consider him an authority for them on proper English usage. He does not have more knowledge than they have about English, and his view of what sounds right would be taken as no more authoritative than that of most other native speakers of the language. Take the same New Yorker, however, with the same knowledge of English, and place him in Paris, Rome, or Moscow. In those cities he may well be considered an authority on English by many people who are struggling to learn the language. What sounds right to his ear would carry weight with them; his statements about what is correct and what is not would likely be believed. If the amount of his knowledge is constant in the two cases and if we would not ordinarily call him an authority on English in the one case but we would do so in the other, then what makes him an authority is not simply his knowledge but his knowledge in relation to a certain class of people.

Consider, secondly, a castaway on a deserted island, who comes to know the topology of the island, its flora and fauna, but who dies before being found. If we call him an authority on the island's geography or vegetation, we imply not only that he knew a great deal but that he *would be* an authority for others on those topics. For someone to be an authority implies that there is at least potentially someone for whom he can be an authority. Even if this is not always the case, my initial model plausibly takes the notion of someone's (or something's) being an authority to be a relational one; for it is evident that there are many instances in which this is the case.

The model specifies a realm because the superior/inferior relation between people is not absolute. No one, with the possible exception of God, is an authority in general; and even God, strictly speaking, is not authorized to do those things for which he must be elected, unless he is elected. One is an authority with respect to only a certain field of knowledge or only in a certain area in which he is authorized to act.

There are two aspects to the specification of the realm in which X is an authority for Y. If X is an authority for Y in a certain realm, then X is (or is considered by Y to be) superior to Y in that realm. But what constitutes superiority in a realm may, and frequently is, specified by the nature of the realm and the conventions attached to it. These may be either formal or informal, institutional or not. The authority relation is limited not only by the realm but also by a context. We can make this explicit by saying that X is an authority for Y in realm R and context C, although in most instances, if the context is equivalent to the realm, the context is left implicit. Sometimes the realm determines a system of authority; sometimes the context does; sometimes both together do.

We have already seen that an authority might be not only a person but also possibly a thing, such as a book or the law, and in such instances it is not inappropriate to say that the person stands in an inferior relation to the thing. We speak appropriately about obeying the law and about a certain dictionary's being the authority on the spelling of a word. Those subject to authority, on the other hand, are not things.[2] We own things; we have dominion over them; we may have the authority to use them or to dispose of them. But they constitute, in these instances, the field over which authority extends, not those subject to authority. The case of animals is ambiguous. We give animals orders, and well-trained ones respond appropriately. Whether we wish to call such responses authority responses and whether we wish to say that animals are subject to authority depends on one's view of animals as well as on one's characterization of authority. Nonetheless, usually those subject to authority are persons, and most, if not all, of the kinds of authority are characterized by human social contexts. Human authority can be objectified and embodied in human products—books or laws, tradition or institutions. The realm or field over which authority can be exercised is indefinitely large.

What is exercised is clearly different from the person who exercises it; and though sometimes a person is called an authority because he exercises authority over others, this is not necessarily the case. If our inhabitant of the desert island had been rescued before he died, he would have been an authority for others on matters having to do with the island without exercising authority over others, or

---

2. The claim that things are not subjects of authority is not a logical but is an empirical claim. Thus, in the New Testament, Christ's followers can intelligibly say that Christ has authority over the wind and waves when they obey his command, and the boatswain in *The Tempest* intelligibly says: ''If you can command these elements to silence, and work the peace of the present, we will not hand a rope more. Use your authority.'' Such cases, however, are peripheral and need not concern us.

without exercising authority at all. It is difficult in this case even to say that he *has* authority rather than to say that he *is* an authority. By contrast, the captain of a ship might both be an authority and have authority, which he does not necessarily exercise. In general, an authority on a topic need not either have or exercise authority, while an authority with the power or right to act in a certain way—whom I shall call an executive authority—is an authority because of the authority he possesses.

Executive authority is the right or power of someone (X) to do something (S) in some realm, field, or domain (R), in a context (C). When S is an action that X does to someone (Y), then Y is said to be subject to authority and X exercises his authority over Y. When S is an action that X does for someone (Y), then Y is subject to X's authority if Y is properly bound by the action, unless X is simply acting as Y's agent.

In some of its forms, authority is a power; in some, a right; in some, neither. We speak of Congress's having the power or authority to declare war. But in the same way we also speak of Congress's having the right to declare war. When the words 'power' and 'right' are interchangeable, authority is either a right or a power. In other cases the words are not interchangeable. If someone has the authority to do something but not the power to do it, he has a right that is empty, ineffective, powerless. Not all kinds of authority are types of power, and not all types of authority are the same as a right—that is, a title to do certain acts. The case of influence is similar. When the president puts his influence behind something, it is sometimes appropriate to say that he puts his authority behind it. But again, not all instances of authority are the same as exercising influence. Kurt Baier distinguishes between authority, influence, and power by saying that power is necessarily grounded, influence is necessarily effective, and authority is not necessarily either one.[3] Although the distinctions are useful, they are insufficient: if authority is grounded, it is not necessarily the same as power; if it is effective, it is not necessarily the same as influence; and it is certainly not the case that it is authority only when it is neither grounded nor effective. Baier, of course, does not claim that it is. But unless we are stipulating our definitions, the distinctions are not always neat, and the concepts

3. Kurt Baier, ''The Justification of Governmental Authority,'' *Journal of Philosophy* 69 (1972): 710.

sometimes overlap. Some authority is an exercise of power; some is an exercise of influence; some is an exercise of a right to do a certain action. Yet each of these, in the abstract, is not very enlightening. Part of the difficulty is that we cannot introduce more precision until we find out what kinds of authority there are. For if we proceed as if all kinds of authority are the same, as if they all have the same relation to power or right, to influence or to force, we would presume much of what has yet to be discussed and displayed. Authority may be greatest when the least force is required; the less the authority, the greater may be the need for force and coercion. But this presupposes that authority involves getting people to act in certain ways, that it is related to commands or obedience, which is not necessarily the case.

In society, certain people are authorities for others. Let us call X a de facto authority if he is recognized as such by some Y who acts appropriately in response to X. What constitutes an appropriate response can at this stage be left purposely vague.

To call X a de facto authority vis-à-vis Y is simply to affirm a relation common in our ordinary experience. To speak of X as a de facto authority is to speak of him as an authority in the weakest sense. By starting with this notion of authority, we can avoid begging the question of whether being an authority is a value term that has certain prescriptive elements built into it. Thus, when I speak of some X as a de facto authority, I wish to leave open the question of whether it is ever right or justifiable—according to some criterion or other—for one person to be an authority for another. Yet an ambiguity remains, since some people may feel that someone—for instance, a learned sage—is de facto an authority on a certain topic, whether or not he is recognized as such by anyone else. Similarly, one might hold that de facto the heir to the throne is the king, even if he is not recognized and if a pretender is sitting on the throne. The proper heir is the de facto king in one sense, and the pretender is the de facto king in another sense. I shall avoid the ambiguity by stipulation. I shall not build legitimacy into the notion of de facto authority, because I wish to be able to identify someone as exercising authority even if he does not hold it legitimately. I shall refer to someone as a "valid authority" if he fulfills some additional criterion (CR) that is specified as necessary and sufficient in order for someone to be an authority in a strong or prescriptive sense. Thus if someone claims that having knowledge (CR) constitutes one as an authority, then using my terminology, X is a valid authority if he fulfills CR, whether or not he is recognized by others and whether or not he functions as an authority in relation to them. Again using this terminology, X may be a de facto authority even if he is not a valid authority. The model that I am proposing allows the addition of a criterion but also allows us to handle instances of people who act as authorities even if there be no such thing as a valid authority.

Another ambiguity should be cleared up. Various justifications have been given for people's being authorities. The justification consists of reasons that are given in order to defend practices or institutions or particular individuals as authorities. We can speak of the source of authority, or the basis from which it springs (e.g., God or consent of the governed), though we do not speak of the source of *an* authority. We can call the argument or justification that is given in defense of authority or an authority as the grounds for authority or for X's being an authority. There may be good grounds for authority or for an authority, though the grounds may not be made out or the case may be poorly presented. I shall call an authority a legitimate authority if he is a grounded authority, though whether any X is a grounded authority is at this point still an open question. If X's authority is not grounded, he is an illegitimate authority. X is a de jure authority if he holds his position of authority and exercises his authority in accordance with a certain set of rules or specified procedures, which are frequently legal (these may in some cases be considered a CR). Hence, using my terminology, X may be a de jure though not a legitimate authority, and vice versa.

A similar distinction holds for the authority one exercises. Authority may be de jure but not grounded (and hence not legitimate) if the legal framework or other set of rules is not grounded or justified; and it may be grounded but not de jure if its exercise is justified though contrary to the rules or laws. Both the terms 'de facto' and 'de jure' and the pair 'legitimate' and 'illegitimate' are necessary, because there are two different distinctions to be made. De facto authority may be either legitimate or illegitimate. De facto authority may also be de jure; but legitimate authority can never be illegitimate, or vice versa. Legitimate and illegitimate are opposites, while de facto and de jure are not.

X is a de facto authority if he is recognized as an authority by some Y who acts appropriately in response to him. He may be formally recognized according to some procedure—be it a voting or a licensing procedure or the granting of a diploma or an honorary degree—or he may be informally recognized—for example, by friends, students, or neighbors. The authority he exercises may also be formal or informal. It may also be effective or ineffective (as he may be an effective or ineffective authority). X is an effective authority if there is an end or goal for which he is an authority or for which his authority is exercised and if that end is achieved in an appropriate manner. He (or it) is ineffective if there is such an end but it either is not achieved or is not achieved in an appropriate manner.

The bearer of authority exercises or wields his authority in certain ways, and these can be called the instruments or means of the exercise of his authority. Even if X has legitimate authority, the means of its exercise may be illegitimate. The actions or reactions of those who are subject to authority when acting as subjects can be called their "authority response." We would expect the authority response to an ineffective authority to be different from the response to an effective authority, just as we would expect different responses to differing means of the exercise of authority.

As we describe X's de facto authority, we can distinguish between its extent and its intensity. The extent of his authority is a function of the number of persons for whom he is an authority. A parent may be an authority for his child, a professor for his class, a president for all the citizens of a country. The extent of the authority of the professor is greater than that of most parents and less than that of the president. Intensity refers to the degree of acceptance of the authority by those subject to authority. Suppose that someone's authority were in a given case a function of his knowledge and that his being a de facto authority involved having others believe his assertions. Then a parent's authority over his young children would be more intense than a professor's over his students if the children believed firmly what was said to them by their parents just because they said it, while the professor's students were inclined to believe what he said, but not very firmly. If authority involves obedience, then intensity might be a function of whether those subject to it obey quickly and eagerly or with reluctance or only under threat of force.

The scope or range of a person's authority refers to the realms or fields in which he is an authority or over which he exercises authority. A president might exercise a greater range of authority. His authority has greater scope than the authority exercised by a policeman. A very learned person might be an authority in several branches of learning; the scope of his authority would therefore be greater than that of someone who was an authority in only one of those same branches. An authority in only one branch of knowledge might have deeper and more acute knowledge than someone else. We might say that his authority in that case is better grounded than that of the other, even though the scope of their authority and also the intensity of their authority might be the same. The scope or range of authority is generally limited. If it is considered to be unlimited, then the bearer of such authority might be said to have or to exercise supreme authority; such a person would be a universal authority or would exercise universal authority.

Authority is sometimes a function of a system. The legal system creates and defines the authority of the judges who operate within it. In the absence of the system they would have no judicial authority. A system obviously does not create executive authority as such, but only particular instances of it. Legal authority without a legal system would make no sense. Systems involve certain structures which specify who (or what positions) will be bearers of authority, the field or scope of that authority, and the instruments of its exercise; similarly they may designate who will be subject to that authority and what will be the proper authority response. A person may belong to a number of systems of authority: he may be a bearer of authority in one, but a subject in another. He may experience a clash between what authorities in different systems command. Within any realm an authority is ultimate if there is no higher authority. To the extent that each state considers itself sovereign, it holds its authority ultimate, or the highest in the realm of its system of law or government. Authority is absolute if there is none higher and if in any clash of authorities it reigns supreme. Whether there is any such thing as absolute authority or an absolute authority remains to be seen. Since the bearer of authority may be more than one person, systems do not preclude the possibility of speaking of collective authority or of shared authority.

TYPES OF AUTHORITY

What are the types and kinds of authority? The answer depends on the criterion or criteria used for distinguishing them. We noted that ordinary usage suggests a division between an authority in the realm of knowledge and an authority who holds a particular office. We can use any of the elements that make up authority to divide it into types and kinds. We can thus divide authority on the basis of the bearers or of the sources of authority, those subject to authority, the fields in which authority is exercised, the reasons for the acceptance of authority, or the justifications given for authority. Classifications are

21

not right or wrong; they are more or less useful, clear, or complete for specified purposes.

The model I have presented gives no priority to any particular kind of authority or to any criterion of division. I have suggested that X is a de facto authority for Y if they stand in the relation of superior to inferior with respect to some realm (R) and if Y acts or reacts in certain appropriate and specifiable ways with respect to X in R. Additional conditions may be added for validity, legitimacy, source, purpose, or reasons for acceptance. Since ordinary usage distinguishes two ways in which X might be an authority, we can characterize the appropriate authority response for Y in each case. Thus X is a de facto authority with respect to some field of knowledge if Y believes what X says in that domain or holds it to be true (or false) with a greater degree of certainty as a result of X's having said it. X is a de facto executive authority for Y if simply as a result of X's having given an order, Y does what X has commanded. These rough characterizations correspond to the two ways of being an authority which are distinguished by ordinary usage. R. S. Peters catches some of this distinction when he speaks of in-authority and an-authority.[4] J. M. Bochenski divides authority into two basic kinds: epistemic and deontic.[5] The basic division I shall suggest is close to these but is not identical to either of them, for the first does not lend itself to distinctions we have already made which will prove useful in our later analysis, and the second canonizes too quickly the distinctions we found in ordinary usage.

I shall adopt a basic division according to types, between executive authority on the one hand and nonexecutive authority on the other. The division is neat, even if there may be some instances of authority which fall clearly on neither one side nor the other. Each can be further divided into kinds by using any of the distinguishing criteria mentioned earlier. In general, an executive authority has the right or power to act for or on someone else. A nonexecutive authority does not. The distinction is important because so much that is written about authority applies only to executive authority.

An epistemic authority is an authority in a field of knowledge.[6] He is a nonexecutive authority, but he does not exhaust that type.

4. Peters, "Authority," pp. 86–89.

5. J. M. Bochenski, *Was ist Autoritaet? Einfuehrung in die Logik der Autoritaet* (Freiburg: Herderbuecherei, 1974), pp. 53–54.

6. Following Bochenski's nomenclature.

The leader of an art movement who attracts imitators is another kind of nonexecutive authority. He serves as an example for others, and he can be called an exemplary authority. The realms in which such authorities function can further subdivide these kinds. Someone in the artistic realm who, because of his knowledge in that realm, serves as an authority for someone else is an aesthetic epistemic authority or an epistemic authority in the realm of art; someone who serves as an example of artistic practice for someone else is an aesthetic exemplary authority or an exemplary authority in the artistic realm. The realm may thus divide either categories or subcategories of authority. An epistemic authority can, by extension, be said to have epistemic authority, which refers to the relation that exists between him and those Ys who hold him an authority in a particular realm.

We shall deal in a later chapter with the questions of whether moral authority is a separate kind of authority and, if it is, whether or not it is a kind of executive authority. The answers to those questions will help us clarify other aspects of the nature of authority.

Political authority is the most widely discussed kind of executive authority. It is exercised by a state and its officials through government, laws, organs, and agencies. The legitimacy of any government depends on the possibility of its authority being grounded and justified. An anarchist claims that this is in principle impossible. If political authority can be grounded and justified, this does not of course mean that any particular government is justified; and even if a particular government is justified, this does not justify all of its actions or laws.

The sources of political authority frequently suggest subclasses of authority. Some writers thus distinguish natural authority from conventional authority.[7] The former is that authority which accrues to a person because of natural qualities, such as leadership, strength, or personal magnetism. Conventional authority, on the other hand, derives from a particular position: the office of president, of a judge, or of a legislator. S. I. Benn and R. S. Peters make a similar distinction but use the terms 'personal authority' and 'rational-legal authority'.[8] Obviously, the same person may have both kinds of authority.

---

7. Based respectively on what are called natural societies (i.e., the family and the political society) and what are called conventional societies (i.e., all others). See, for instance, John L. McKenzie, *Authority in the Church* (New York: Sheed & Ward, 1966), p. 8.

8. S. I. Benn and R. S. Peters, *Principles of Political Thought* (New York: Collier Books, 1964), pp. 211-15.

23

Another division according to source differentiates authority depending on whether it comes from nature, God, men, or reason. Thus if nature decrees that some are born slaves and others are born masters, the latter have natural authority over the former. If authority comes from God, then all authority is divine in origin. This historically has led not only to the divine right of kings but also to the claimed supremacy of religious over secular authority. If authority comes from men, then some sort of contract theory explains and justifies authority. Reason decides which kinds of authority are necessary in forming social groups and which are necessary in order to achieve common ends. Divisions according to source are closely related to divisions, as Max Weber puts it, "according to the kind of claim to legitimacy typically made" by each type of authority.[9] He classifies them into legal-rational authority, traditional authority, and charismatic authority.

Parental authority in its pristine form is the authority of parents over their minor children. By extension it is the authority of anyone standing *in loco parentis* over minors or over those who are in some way or other not completely competent to care for themselves and to accept the responsibility of adults.

Operative authority is that which is vested in any designated leader or officer of a group that has freely formed for the purpose of achieving some common end. Corporations, businesses, clubs—all involve operative authority. It can be further subdivided in a variety of ways: for example, by considering the field or by considering the end that the group wishes to achieve.

Is there a particular type of authority called religious authority, or is this reducible to some other type or types of authority? This question will remain open at this point, as will a consideration of the authority that comes from custom, public opinion, tradition, or competence.

This brief initial classification is compatible with designations that others have made of kinds of authority and has as its purpose, not excluding plausible candidates, but highlighting certain kinds of authority that raise some of the problems that I shall consider in later chapters. My list will not, either now or later, make any pretense of

---

9. Max Weber, *The Theory of Social and Economic Organization*, trans. A. M. Henderson and Talcott Parsons, edited with an Introduction by Talcott Parsons (New York: Free Press, 1964), p. 325.

being exhaustive, for there is an indefinitely large number of fields. It should also be clear that the types and the kinds of authority I have mentioned so far are in no instance exclusive, since the same person may exercise both types of authority and several kinds of each. Parents may exercise parental authority over their children in virtue of their children's position, biological relation, and need; and the parents may also have legal authority over their children by virtue of the law. A leader of a state may have duly constituted political authority and may exercise charismatic authority as well.

The relation of authority to power, obedience, law, freedom, coercion, and respect varies according to the type and kind of authority, the system in which they are found, and similar factors. Different types and kinds of authority, if they result in different conceptual nets and are found in different social practices, will result in different systems of authority, each with its own structures. The structures and systems may intertwine or conflict. If they conflict, we must consider ways of resolving such conflicts.

Just as different types and kinds of authority lead to different structures, the justification for different kinds of authority need not be the same. The justification for epistemic authority, for example, is different from the justification for political authority. In each case we can look at the source of the authority, question its legitimacy, and ask which possible principles of limitation appropriately apply to it. The relation among the various kinds of authority is clearly a question that we can fruitfully address only after we are clearer about the nature and status of the different kinds.

How the various kinds of authority operate within different social settings depends not only upon their purported function and supposed justification but also upon the institutions in which they are found. A general analysis of the concept of authority can therefore go only so far, and general principles of justification and of limitation can throw only partial light on complex social problems.

3

The Authority of Knowledge and Competence

Nonexecutive authority does not involve any right to command or to act on or for another. Although frequently ignored or considered secondary, such authority plays an important role in social life. It makes possible complex society, as well as the transfer of knowledge, skills, and culture. And the possession of such authority is frequently the basis for conferring executive authority on an individual.

Epistemic authority is an example of nonexecutive authority. To say of someone that he is an epistemic authority is to make some claim about him based on or related to his knowledge. This claim may be expressed in a number of ways.

That someone is said to be an authority on a certain topic usually means that he is very knowledgeable about that topic. If we find that he has very little such knowledge, we might conclude either that he is not an authority after all or that the person who called him an authority knows so little about the field as to be impressed by anyone who has the slightest knowledge of it. This reaction rests on an implicit definition of an authority as someone with a certain depth of knowledge in a given area. It assumes that X is an authority in R only if he has a great deal of knowledge in R; if he does not have such knowledge, he is not an authority in R, even if he is thought by others to be one. According to this view, only a valid authority is an authority, and the degree of knowledge is the deciding criterion. Anyone who has the required amount of knowledge is an authority; anyone who does not is not an authority. But how much knowledge is necessary, and who decides how much is enough and when the designation is appropriately attributed?

A second way of expressing what it means for someone to be an epistemic authority emphasizes the relative knowledge of an authority with respect to others. An authority is defined as someone who has either more knowledge than normal about a certain topic or more knowledge about it than do certain other people. Someone might be an authority for one group though not for another. But this approach, like the previous one, starts with a normative view of an epistemic authority by building in a criterion for deciding in advance who is an authority. It encounters similar difficulties to those of the first approach, since the requisite kind and degree of necessary knowledge cannot be specified in advance.

I shall follow a third approach, initially defining an epistemic authority in terms of those for whom he is an authority. We thus consider those who are in fact taken as authorities by anyone else. Any adequate interpretation of authority must be able to give an account of this known nonempty class. This approach allows for differences of opinion about who is an authority. It emphasizes the relation of an authority to those for whom he is an authority, and so it underlines the functional aspect of being an authority. Finally, since it does not build in any evaluative element for proper attribution, it allows us to raise the questions of the grounds for such authority and the empirical parameters we can use in discussing, weighing, and investigating a person's authority.

DE FACTO EPISTEMIC AUTHORITY

A person is a de facto epistemic authority if he is considered to be an authority by another or by others with respect to some field or area of knowledge. Thus X is a de facto epistemic authority if there is some Y who considers X an authority for Y in some realm (R). With respect to that realm, Y considers X his superior in knowledge. Now it would be odd to consider X an authority in R and yet not believe anything that X has said (or written, etc.) in R. If this were the case, we might try to make sense of the situation by saying that although Y calls X an authority on R, Y does not really believe that X is one; or if Y seriously calls X an authority, Y might mean only that other people consider X to be an authority. For Y to consider X a de facto epistemic authority for Y means that at least under certain conditions and at least to some extent, Y is willing to believe what X says in R. Thus we can say that X is a de facto epistemic authority if there is some Y who, because of Y's belief in X's greater knowledge of R, holds some proposition (p), which X has enunciated (or which Y believes X has enunciated) in R,

27

to be true or more probably true than Y did before Y believed that X enunciated *p*.

Several aspects of this characterization deserve amplification. X may of course be a person. But Y may also treat some written document as an authority: a dictionary, a reference book, an encyclopedia, a textbook, a newspaper. Y may take a dictionary as an authority on the meaning of a word, or he may take a map as an authority on the location of an island. Since books, maps, and newspapers are all human products, in the last analysis it is the author of the book or the compilers of the dictionary who are authorities on certain topics. Nonetheless, since people tend to believe or do believe to a greater or lesser extent what they find in certain books, these books are de facto epistemic authorities according to our characterization.

X might also be some tradition, oral or written, whether it be in one place or diffuse or attributable to one person or to many persons or even to many generations. X might be a group or a certain class of people. Even more vaguely, some anonymous "they" might be taken as an authority. Thus, some Y might believe what "they" say or what Y thinks "they" say, even if Y cannot identify who "they" are. The problems raised by these kinds of substitutions for X are more complex than if X is taken as a single individual. But to the extent that tradition is a de facto epistemic authority in some field, we should consider the conditions, if any, under which tradition (or custom or "they") can be a legitimate epistemic authority, and we should realize that these conditions may be different from those which apply in the case of a single individual.

One of the results of this scheme is that according to it, some people will be authorities who are not usually thought to be such. Thus, if a child is brought to a doctor who pushes the child's abdomen and says, "Tell me when it hurts," the doctor acknowledges that the child is an authority as to the location of his own pain. When the child says, "It hurts there," and the doctor believes him and acts accordingly, the doctor acknowledges the child as an epistemic authority in the realm of the child's pain. This makes all of us at least potential authorities on certain aspects of ourselves; we may be thought to be the best authority on some of these aspects. But we all become de facto epistemic authorities whenever anyone believes what we say simply because we say it.

It would be unusual for both the bearer (X) and the one who is subject to authority (Y) to be the same person. In most cases I am not an authority for myself, because I do not believe what I say simply because I say it. But I might believe what I once said simply because I said it. Thus, if I remember having arrived at some conclusion but have forgotten the reasons, or if I remember having recounted some event but have forgotten experiencing the event, I might believe what I had said simply because I said it. My status vis-à-vis myself in these instances would be similar to the status of someone else vis-à-vis me, though in a sense I believe what I said because I said it.

It is both a necessary and a sufficient condition for X's being a de facto epistemic authority that there be some Y who believes what X says. If there is no such Y, then no matter how great X's knowledge, X is not a de facto epistemic authority. The de facto label refers neither to X's having knowledge nor to X's being someone whose word on a certain topic can or should be accepted or believed at least to some extent by some Y. There may be no good grounds for Y's acceptance or belief. Nonetheless, Y makes X a de facto epistemic authority by Y's belief.

This initial characterization does not deny that others may designate X an authority in a field of knowledge, even though X is not an authority for them. A school principal may introduce a new teacher to a class as an authority. According to my characterization the teacher is not a de facto authority unless to some extent the students believe what he says when he teaches. When the principal introduces the teacher as an authority, what the principal means is not that the teacher is believed by others but that he is knowledgeable in his field and is worthy of being believed by the students. The principal designates the teacher as a valid authority. In one sense of de facto, if the teacher is a valid authority, he is a de facto authority. But I have given de facto authority a weaker meaning and have restricted it to cases in which what X says is believed by some Y. Not every de facto authority (in my sense of de facto) is valid or legitimate. Whether anyone is a valid or legitimate epistemic authority is still an open question.

Is this a backwards characterization of a de facto authority? We do not usually think that we make someone a de facto authority by believing what he says. Rather, we encounter someone who holds a certain position or title or who speaks knowledgeably about a topic, and because of his position or title or apparent knowledge, we believe him. Children do not make their first-grade teacher an authority by believing what he says, but they believe what the teacher says because they think he is an authority.

This describes our experience. But to account for this experience we must clarify the logic behind our acceptance. Filling an institutionally defined role can make one a legitimate epistemic authority within a system, and having appropriate knowledge can make one a valid epistemic authority in some realm. These statements are compatible with being a de facto authority in my weak sense of the term. Since an ordinary experience takes place in a society which is already structured and in which authority is already constituted, our experiential encounter with authority differs from its logical structure. In our ordinary experience we assume the legitimacy of authority which my characterization of de facto authority allows us to question.

In that characterization, Y must be a person, assuming that only persons are capable of having beliefs and of responding to statements by believing them. Y may, however, be some class of persons or a multiplicity of persons. We can and do judge the extent of someone's epistemic authority by the number of persons—actual or, by some reasonable scale, potential—for whom he is an authority.

Extent is not always easy to measure. What an Einstein (E) says on some esoteric topic in physics to a group of physicists (G) may be taken by them as being more probably true than before he made his statement. The particular proposition might be understood only by a small number of trained physicists. The physicists may in turn repeat to others (O) what Einstein says. These others accept what Einstein says because someone they accept as an authority in physics accepts it. But though we may be tempted to say that if E is a de facto epistemic authority for G and if G is a de facto epistemic authority for O, then E should be a de facto epistemic authority for O, this may not be the case in fact. Suppose a well-known physicist (A), whose word is widely accepted, meets an obscure but brilliant fellow physicist (B). A believes—for whatever reason—B's statements in some esoteric realm of physics and then publishes those statements as A's own. They are in turn believed because A said them. The scope of A's de facto epistemic authority may be very wide. If the obscure savant (B) says the same thing, he may be believed only by the professor (A) in question. The extent of B's de facto epistemic authority might thus be limited to one. Even if the proper extent of epistemic authority might be considered to be a factor of the transitivity of valid epistemic authority, it may not be a factor of de facto epistemic authority.

In my initial scheme I have added a condition to Y's acceptance of *p* as uttered by X: namely, that Y believes that X has greater knowledge of R than Y has. To be an epistemic authority implies some relation to knowledge. If Y believes what X says, even though Y does not believe that it involves some area of knowledge, then Y would not be considering X an epistemic authority. Not every case of belief involves epistemic authority, as we shall see later.

The characterization of "greater" knowledge need not, however, be construed narrowly. A historian who has very wide knowledge, and who in most senses has greater knowledge than his graduate student, may nonetheless believe what that student says on some particular point within the subject of the latter's dissertation. In this instance the student is an epistemic authority for the professor, though on many other issues the professor may be an epistemic authority for the student.

Thus the range or scope of R might be very large or very small, depending on X's knowledge, Y's belief about X's knowledge, and Y's knowledge. The scope of X's de facto authority is a function of the areas in which, or the topics on which, X is accepted as an authority by others; and this scope need not be measured only by the specific accepted statements that X has made. The scope of X's authority can be assumed to extend to other statements within the area. The reason for this is that Y believes X to have greater knowledge than Y in R, and Y's basis is the same for believing a great many different statements in the field, providing they are intelligible and do not contradict or conflict with Y's other beliefs. A parent may be an epistemic authority for his small child on a broad range of topics. In weighing the scope of the parent's authority in order to decide how impressive it is, we might want to consider the extent of the knowledge of the Ys for whom X is an authority, as well as how many other similar Xs there are who would be authorities for Y. Most parents, for instance, are epistemic authorities for their young children; and most adults are at least potential epistemic authorities for children in general, although what they say may not be accepted unless the person is a friend or is known to the child or holds some position that the child recognizes. A parent's being an epistemic authority for his own child over a very large area will not count for much because of the child's lack of knowledge and because most parents stand in comparable authority relations with their children.

If the realm R were without limit and included all knowledge, X might be claimed or believed to be a universal epistemic authority. If God is believed by Y to be an omniscient being, he is a de facto universal epistemic authority for Y. But even when broad knowledge is attributed to the king or ruler or ruling party, it is unlikely that he or it would be a de facto epistemic authority in all branches of knowledge. The field is ordinarily limited.

The realm of authority is usually some branch of knowledge. We thus speak of someone's being an authority on internal medicine or on early American history or on Greek philosophy. This implies that X is an authority on some objective branch of knowledge, which is systematically developed to form a branch of learning. To say that the branch of knowledge is objective means that it is in principle knowable by others and in ordinary ways open to their study.

Each person knows his own private thoughts, actions, and feelings. In certain circumstances we accept as true or believe what others tell us they saw or experienced. If they describe an event that they saw or in which they took part, we are more inclined to call them firsthand witnesses rather than authorities on the event. We probably would not call everyone who was involved in the French Revolution an authority on the French Revolution, nor even everyone who took part in the storming of the Bastille an authority on that smaller event. We might believe a participant's statement about the event, and we might say that he is an authority on his part in the event. But an authority on the storming of the Bastille or on the French Revolution would presumably have greater, more comprehensive, and more systematic knowledge than a simple participant would have.

The stringency placed on R's being a field of knowledge that is objective and systematic is not a matter of legislation. We do not usually say that each person is an authority on his own feelings and private thoughts. But if someone were to use the term 'an authority' to refer to each person whose statements about himself, his feelings, or his thoughts are believed by some Y, no harm would be done. In most cases we do not say that each native speaker is an authority on his native language while he is in his native country, even though, generally speaking, the subject matter is a systematic, objective body of knowledge. If everyone is an authority on the same topic, then it is unlikely that anyone will accept what someone says on that topic simply because he says it. If we disagree about our use of the word authority, for instance, I could believe that you use it in a slightly different way from the way in which I use it; but in ordinary usage, I would not say that simply because you are a native speaker of English, you are an authority *for me* on the meaning and use of English words, for I am also a native speaker of the language. Since we have this in common, it provides no basis for my accepting what sounds right to you rather than what sounds right to me, even though you are a de facto authority for me on *your* use of English when I believe, on your say-so, that something sounds right to your ear.

The working definition that I have proposed specifies that Y holds some proposition *p* to be true or more probably true than Y did before Y believed that X enunciated *p*. The term 'holds' can be taken to mean 'believes' or 'is inclined to believe' or 'accepts' or 'is inclined to accept'. The tenacity with which Y holds *p* or the degree of assent that Y is willing to give to *p* can vary from minimal acceptance to complete acceptance. The reaction of Y might be that if X says *p*, then it certainly bears looking into and may in fact be true, although Y did not think so before X said it. Or at the other extreme, Y may believe that *p* is true simply because X said it, even though Y previously believed non-*p* to be true. The degree of acceptance is an indication of the intensity of X's authority vis-à-vis Y. And again, if we wish to measure someone's authority, the greater is the propensity to accept X's statements as completely true in a field, the greater is the intensity of X's epistemic authority in that field. As before, however, we might wish to distinguish the level of development and knowledge of R that various Ys have when we consider the intensity of their belief. In general if Y is a mature discriminating adult, Y's acceptance will count more than if Y is a child or a gullible adult; and if Y is knowledgeable in the field, Y's acceptance might count more than if Y is a neophyte, even though it may be the case that Y would accept certain *p*'s on X's say-so, which a neophyte would not (e.g., some counterintuitive statements that the neophyte does not really understand or does not have the background to appreciate).

The proposition *p* can be any utterance or statement, oral or written, or even implied or suggested.

I added that Y needs only to *believe* that X enunciated *p* because people frequently get wrong what others say, though they believe the mistaken statement as readily as they would have believed the correct one. X is no less a de facto authority thereby, even though what X said, a particular *p*, is not what Y believes. The fact that Y believes that X said *p* and the fact that Y accepts *p* because Y believes that X said *p* are enough to make X a de facto authority. The truth or falsity of *p* does not affect X's being a de facto epistemic authority.

Finally, X is a de facto epistemic authority for Y if Y believes *p* primarily because X said *p*. If, for instance, X were teaching a class in geometry and gave a proof of a theorem, then presumably those members of the class who followed the proof and understood geometry would accept the theorem as true, not because the teacher enunciated it and not because it was written in the textbook, but because they understood the proof. Those in the class who did not follow the proof, on the other hand, might accept the theorem as true simply because their teacher said it was true, or simply because it was in the textbook (or for both reasons together). If, after completing that proof, the teacher simply stated another theorem which he said was true but which he did not have time to prove, most of the members of the class might well accept it as true. Since the students who understood the first proof did not have to accept the first theorem on the teacher's say-so, the teacher is not an epistemic authority for them in that instance, although he is in the second instance; he is an epistemic authority in both instances for those who accepted the theorems and did not follow the proof.

This model of de facto epistemic authority attempts to give due weight to the fact that people believe a great many statements simply because they have heard someone say them. An enormous amount of what most people believe comes from what they hear from others. Their response to what they hear or read is similar to their response to what a valid authority says: namely, they believe it. The people or books believed are, for this reason, de facto authorities. The fact that their statements are believed, of course, neither makes the statements true nor does it make the bearers of de facto epistemic authority valid authorities.

Almost everyone is a de facto epistemic authority in some small way for someone. For this reason we usually call someone an epistemic authority only if he is an authority in some particularly distinctive or eminent way. Yet the criteria that we should use in evaluating any individual epistemic authority is similar, whether the case be a trivial instance of de facto epistemic authority or the authority of an Einstein on physics.

LEGITIMATE EPISTEMIC AUTHORITY

Is anyone a legitimate epistemic authority? How, if at all, can such authority be grounded?

Since de facto epistemic authority involves Y's believing p simply because X enunciated p, whether X's authority is grounded depends both on the nature of p and the reason Y has for believing what X has enunciated. Y is justified in believing p if Y knows that p is true. If Y could be sure that what X said is true, that would be a good reason for believing what X says. Yet neither the truth of *p* nor Y's certainty that what X says is true is necessary for grounding epistemic authority.

If Y knows *p* to be true independently of X's enunciating *p*, then Y has no need of X as an epistemic authority with respect to *p*. Y may know that, with respect to *p*, X is worthy of being considered an epistemic authority by others and that, as certified or occupying a certain position, Y is a de jure epistemic authority. But the real concern is how a given Y is to know when some X is a legitimate epistemic authority for Y. If X is to be an epistemic authority for Y in some field, then X's utterances that are believed by Y must be such that Y does not know them to be true on independent grounds. To ask whether X's epistemic authority is grounded is to ask under what conditions it is *reasonable* for Y to believe what X says. Obviously the reply that it is reasonable whenever X is a valid and/or a de jure authority cannot be adequate. For we want to know how to identify someone as a valid authority, both that we might learn from him and that, if appropriate, he might be made a de jure authority—for example, by giving him a teaching position in a school or a university.

If X is to be a legitimate epistemic authority, then clearly it must be possible to attain knowledge independently of belief on the word of another. For X to be a legitimate epistemic authority in R, X must have knowledge of R; and if X's knowledge is based on the authority of someone else, then ultimately someone must have knowledge based on something other than authority—be it experience, logic, intuition, or some mixture thereof. For present purposes, *p* must be a statement, sentence, or proposition that is capable of being true or false, since Y's authority response consists in believing that *p* is true. But it makes no difference whether *p* be a matter of fact or a statement in logic or mathematics, whether it be theoretical or practical (i.e., knowledge of how to do things), and whether it be a priori or a posteriori.

Y's belief makes X a de facto epistemic authority. Yet such belief is not self-justifying. Several conditions are necessary in order to justify, or make reasonable, Y's believing *p* simply on the basis of X's uttering *p*. But the truth of *p* is not one of the conditions. X may be a legitimate epistemic authority in R, and Y may reasonably believe what X says in R, even if not all of X's statements in R are true.

For Y's belief in what X says in R to be justified, it is necessary that: (1) X have knowledge of R (the knowledge criterion); (2) Y have good reason to believe that X has knowledge of R (the inductive

35

criterion); (3) the *p*'s that Y believes fall within R or be so related to R that some aspect of X's knowledge of R is sufficient to justify accepting *p* (the relevance criterion); and (4) Y have good reason for believing that X is telling the truth or stating what X believes when X enunciates *p* (the trustworthiness criterion).

How can Y know that X has knowledge of R? The cases will vary of course. X can tell Y or assure Y that X has such knowledge. But then Y must consider whether Y should believe such assurances. In some instances such belief might be warranted. But a particular instance of such acceptance's being warranted has as its background a general argument for the reasonableness of accepting what someone says and, in general, also has as part of its background the custom, habit, or social institution of such acceptance. In the first instance we seek the ground for legitimate authority, and clearly this cannot rest only on anyone's claim that he has knowledge. In general we want to know when it is rational to accept such statements.

A general grounding of legitimate epistemic authority requires not only someone's knowledge but also some criterion for testing another person's claims to truth. If accepting what someone says is one way of attaining knowledge, it cannot be the only way. Someone must have attained what knowledge he has in some other way. The reason why *p* is true is not because X enunciates *p*; and though Y believes *p* because X enunciates *p*, if Y thinks Y's belief is justified, Y also believes that *p* is true independently of X's having said *p*.

We need not go into the alternate ways of knowing, so long as we admit that there are several such ways. All of them, assuming that they are valid, constitute part of the source of legitimate epistemic authority. The source of such authority should not be confused with epistemic authority itself. Though it is not common usage, one might speak of the authority of facts or the authority of reason, meaning that in some sense, human beings, in order to attain knowledge, must submit to or conform to reality, to facts, to the rules of logic, or to the power of reason. If we choose to describe such cases as instances of submitting to authority, we might describe such conformity as submission to ''ontological'' or ''logical'' authority. Submission to such ''authorities'' constitute some of the alternate ways of knowing that are prior to and presupposed by legitimate epistemic authority.

As a way of knowing, the acceptance of *p* on X's say-so is secondary. Legitimate epistemic authority is thus substitutional in nature. Its purpose is to substitute the knowledge of one person in a certain field for the lack of knowledge of another. It is in principle expendable and is open to challenge. X's knowledge of law or of medicine, of history or of physics, could, in principle, be acquired independently by Y, thus making the substitution unnecessary. Whenever one's belief is based on evidence that coerces belief or that constitutes it, then the belief is not based on authority.

As a social institution, epistemic authority arises from the dual recognition both that we and others have knowledge and that others have knowledge that we do not have. In order to establish that others have knowledge that we do not, we either have to understand the process involved in gaining knowledge and to realize that some people can and do pursue certain areas more than others, or we have to experience someone's saying something that we do not know but that we then come to know, realizing that he knew it before we did. In either way or in both ways combined, the fact that some people know what others do not is presupposed by legitimate epistemic authority. The acceptance of something on the word of another is a means of greatly expanding one's knowledge.

In general it is only because others can in fact or could in principle independently acquire the knowledge of an epistemic authority that he can achieve the recognition of the authority that he has. In order for X to be a legitimate authority in R, it must be possible for others to test X's claims to knowledge. If someone claimed knowledge in a field in which no one else had any knowledge, he could not legitimately be recognized as an authority in that field, since no one would be able to establish him as such. At least he could not be recognized directly. If knowledge forms a whole, then his claims might be in part established if what he asserts fits in with what else is known; or he might, by appropriate means, demonstrate enough about the field to establish the fact that he has knowledge of it. But unless he can do something like this, it would be difficult, except on grounds of his veracity, to find a basis for believing what he says and thus for establishing him as a legitimate authority in R.

Epistemic authority can be either first order or second order with respect to those who are subject to it. In first-order epistemic authority relations, Y accepts what X says in R, not because others certify X as an authority or testify to X's knowledge and not because X is generally truthful (all these are bases for second-order epistemic authority), but because, on his own, Y finds the ground and justification for Y's belief. For X to be a legitimate first-order epistemic authority for Y, Y must already know enough about R to know that X knows more about R than Y does. If Y knows nothing about R (as when a student starts the study of a new subject), then the ground for X's epistemic authority in R is most frequently that X has been acknowledged as an authority by someone else or by others who Y believes is or are trustworthy and knowledgeable in R so that they can testify to X's knowledge. In this case, however, Y simply takes it on the authority of someone else that he (Y) should accept X as an authority; and the acceptance of this claim made by someone else requires justification, just as accepting X's word does. If Y's acceptance of X as an epistemic authority is to be justified and is not simply blind acceptance (blind acceptance may be appropriate in a particular case, but not in general), then Y must have some knowledge upon which to base Y's acceptance of p as enunciated by X.[1]

The general justification of epistemic authority is based on the fact that people are unequal in ability, some being more capable intellectually than others; the fact that some people know more than others; the fact that some data are available only to certain persons who are appropriately located in space and time; and the fact that there is so much that can be known that no one can know it all. Some people know more than others about certain topics as a result of their individual study, research, thought, experience, or experimentation. The bearer of authority serves either as a guide or as a source for the person subject to epistemic authority who turns to the authority for information, guidance, or advice and who takes advantage of the bearer's superior knowledge. To the layman, a trained lawyer is an epistemic authority on legal matters; for the practicing attorney, a legal scholar or judge may be an authority. For the patient, the doctor is the authority in matters of illness and cure. For the student, the teacher is or can be an epistemic authority for a certain branch of knowledge. Reliance on authority is a way in which knowledge can be transmitted and shared so that more people may use this knowledge than would otherwise be the case. This, in brief, is the basis for the argument that epistemic authority is in general legitimate. The argument is a pragmatic one, and it claims that in some cases it is

---

1. In the case of knowledge of one's private experiences, which seems to be an exception to the rule that one needs some knowledge about the field, Y justifiably recognizes X as an authority only if Y knows from his own case the nature of private experience in general and either has reason to believe or no reason to doubt that X is truthful, a careful observer, etc.

reasonable and rational to accept the word of someone else that p is the case.

The truth of p is not a condition for the justifiability of Y's believing p, because although X may have a great deal of knowledge in R, it is possible for X to believe some things that are false. If X's knowledge of R is considerably greater than Y's, it is to Y's advantage to hold as true in R everything that X holds as true, unless and until Y has some reason for reconsidering or giving up certain of those beliefs. The justification of Y's belief is the advantage that Y gains by believing those who have superior knowledge. This advantage is somewhat diminished if Y believes some p's that are false. But if there are a large number of true p's that Y holds on the basis of authority, Y's overall advantage justifies Y's general belief and X's authority. The alternative would be to believe no proposition unless one also sees the proof of that proposition. Any such strict canon would preclude anyone's taking advantage of the experience of others. It would restrict our sharing in what people have learned and would limit our effective action accordingly. Descartes's radical epistemological independence is extreme and must be kept within bounds. It correctly tells us to trust our experience and our reasoning processes when the results conflict with statements by authorities; but it goes too far. Our knowledge of what constitutes our experience and of what constitutes valid reasoning, though not dependent for its validity on being taught, is in fact acquired through the teaching of others. Without social contact, we would not develop language, much less abstract reasoning processes. We find language already developed, and we learn to use it in many ways. We must be nurtured on current beliefs before we can begin to challenge them. The solitary thinker may realize that something that is taken by others as true is not in fact true. If his reasons are valid, others may come to the same conclusions. The process of developing knowledge is social, not an isolated individual exercise. Even the individual thinker, moreover, is bolstered in his beliefs when others whose opinion he respects agree with him and so reinforce his own belief.

I have concentrated so far on the first two conditions, the knowledge criterion and the inductive criterion, which must be fulfilled for Y's belief to be justified: namely, that X have knowledge of R and that Y have good reason for believing that X has such knowledge. These two conditions relate both to knowledge in general and to knowledge of a particular field. The third condition, the relevance criterion, concerns the specific propositions that X enunciates and Y believes. This condition states that p must be part of the field R or close enough to it so that X's knowledge of R is pertinent to Y's belief in what X says when X enunciates p. These three conditions have to do with knowledge.

The fourth condition, the trustworthiness criterion, has to do with character. Y must have good reason for believing that X is telling the truth or is stating what X believes when X enunciates p. Y's belief of p on X's say-so is reasonable only if all fair conditions are met. The trustworthiness criteria may be satisfied if there is no reason to doubt X's veracity when the general conditions of veracity serve as a backdrop. Not only good will is necessary, but good will joined with knowledge. Someone may always say what he believes, but that is not in itself sufficient ground for accepting what he says as correct. In a certain area he may be a simpleton who says what he believes but who believes a great deal that is not the case.

Our discussion thus far has considered the general grounds that justify accepting p on the basis of X's say-so. If these conditions are satisfied, they justify Y's belief in first-order epistemic authority relations. But if some individuals or some portion of society thus become epistemic authorities, they may in turn designate others as authorities, either by acknowledging them as authorities for themselves or by assuring others that they are knowledgeable in a field. Thus, if X is an authority for Y in R, and someone else (S) is an authority for X in R, then on X's say-so, Y may reasonably accept S as an authority in R. Y may also reasonably accept someone else (T) (e.g., X's student) as an epistemic authority if X, who is an authority in R for Y, says that Y should believe T in R, even though T is not an epistemic authority for X. These are second-order epistemic authority relations.

While first-order epistemic authority relations are often informal, society has found it useful to acknowledge certain classes of persons as authorities in certain fields and also to accept the formal certification of individuals by the leaders or teachers of those classes of persons or by their professional organizations. The general basis for acceptance of the institutionalization of epistemic authority is the general benefit that society as a whole, as well as its individual members, derive from knowing who in general is worthy of belief—that is, has knowledge—on a particular topic.

The ground for trusting, believing, or accepting the certification of any group or organization of those who have or claim knowledge in a field rests on a collective extension of the above-stated individual grounds. It is based on a collective induction. It is primarily pragmatic. Society's acceptance of such groups or organizations is properly a function of how effectively the groups or organizations demonstrate their knowledge: for example, in curing the sick, in building houses or bridges that do not collapse, in sending people to the moon. Acceptance is also legitimately a function of the organization's importance in fulfilling the needs of society.

An epistemic authority who belongs to a general class—a doctor, a lawyer, a professor—is often designated as an authority by those who have demonstrated knowledge of the field and who certify that a given individual has the appropriate knowledge which they verify and in virtue of which they award him a degree or title. Someone can thus be initially named as a valid authority by others who have appropriate knowledge: that is, as someone whose statements in a field are, in general, worthy of belief. Society often formalizes this, though it need not. Doctors and lawyers are certified as authorities by medical schools, law schools, and by state examinations, which are made up and graded by those who are competent in medicine or law. Similarly competent people check the work of a scientist or scholar before they certify him as an authority by conferring on him a degree or academic rank. So certified, X is usually not an authority for those who certify him, since they must generally have superior knowledge in order for their certification to be acceptable to others. Certification does not make X a de facto authority. It only supplies prima facie grounds for others to consider X as a valid authority in some field. Similarly, if someone holds a position—for example, a chair in a university department—he is a de jure authority in his field. That fact does not make him a valid authority in the field, but it is an indication that others consider him as such.

Since X is a de facto authority only if X is believed by Y, it is Y who makes X a de facto authority. Y may believe *p* when uttered by X because Y knows enough about the field to know that X knows a great deal and is trustworthy, an inference from past instances of X uttering *p*'s that Y has independently verified; or Y may accept *p* when uttered by X because Y trusts other Xs who have certified X. Y accepts their word because society in general does. And Y accepts what society in general does, because such acceptance seems to work.

Y's acknowledgment of X as an epistemic authority in R need not be an all-or-nothing matter. Y may hold *p* to be just slightly more probably true than before X asserted *p*; Y may hold *p* to be certainly true because X asserted *p*; or Y may adopt any intermediate position.

Y's position may also justifiably vary with respect to different p's, even though all of the p's lie within R.

Just as the general justification for epistemic authority does not guarantee that every p in R enunciated by X is true, so the general justification for certification does not guarantee that every X so certified is either trustworthy or knowledgeable. But belief of what a certified X says in R is likely to result in Y's believing something that is true. In general this is a valid way for Y to extend his knowledge, and in certain cases it may be the only practical means of doing so. This justification is compatible with acknowledging that there will almost certainly be times when by believing p on the word of X, one will believe what is false. The general justification does not maintain that any de facto epistemic authorities individually or collectively are infallible. Even if all were truthful and said what they believed, they might all believe something false. When all the authorities in the field believed that the earth was flat, it was reasonable for the ordinary person to believe this, even though it was false. But their collective belief did not make the proposition true. Belief based on authority does not constitute proof. Yet in the absence of counterevidence and arguments, the fact that some proposition is held by the authorities in the field constitutes a prima facie reason for holding it rather than its opposite. That it is reasonable to do so means that it is sometimes reasonable to believe what is false.

The general justification for epistemic authority is clearly tenuous. The knowledge attained may be mixed with some falsehood. Epistemic authority is substitutional; it also involves a certain amount of trust in the knowledge and veracity of the authority. When appropriate, reason and experience should challenge particular instances of epistemic authority. Formal certification does not guarantee the actual possession of knowledge, and the possession of knowledge does not guarantee the will and ability to transfer it effectively. Epistemic authority is always justified inductively. Although one may accept something as true that is in fact false, it is reasonable to accept some propositions as true on the basis of authority in certain cases. Hence epistemic authority can be legitimate as well as de facto.

COMPETENCE AND AUTHENTICITY

Epistemic authority is not the only kind of legitimate nonexecutive authority. Although the authority based on competence and the authority based on personal authenticity or excellence are closely related to epistemic authority, their dissimilarities can give some idea of how to characterize and justify different kinds of nonexecutive authority.

Competence is the ability to perform certain tasks. A person who is competent to do such tasks has the necessary knowledge to do them. Yet he does not necessarily make any statements or utterances. And if he does, his utterances are not necessarily propositions to be believed. They may well be instructions to be followed. Because of X's competence in R, Y may do some action (*a*) in the same way that X does it or that X says Y is to do it so as to achieve some end. X is a de facto competence authority for Y if, in some field R, Y is inferior in skill to X and Y either imitates X in R or does in R as X tells Y to do (though such telling is not to be construed as commanding).

For X to be a de facto competence authority, Y must know *what* X does, but not necessarily *how* X does it. For an apprentice, the master is a competence authority. The apprentice learns by observing, imitating, performing under supervision, and following instructions. For his patient, a doctor is an epistemic authority when he presents a diagnosis such as, "You have pneumonia," which the patient believes; he is a competence authority when he says, "Take two of these pills four times a day," and the patient does so as a means of getting well. Despite its imperative form, the doctor's prescription is not a command but is a hypothetical statement, telling the patient what he recommends that the patient do if the patient wants to get well.[2]

Though competence usually involves knowledge, the reason for distinguishing competence authority from epistemic authority lies in the differing authority responses that are characteristic of the two. Epistemic authority involves Y's doing something other than believing. If I buy a radio kit and assemble the radio myself according to the instructions in the kit, I follow the instructions. The instructions are not commands that I have any obligation to obey. The instructions may state no propositions that I have to believe. Yet my response to them, or to someone's telling me how to build the radio, is properly called a kind of authority response.

2. Some patients may, of course, take the doctor's imperative as a command to be obeyed. They make the doctor an executive authority. The justification, if one can be given, for the patient's giving the doctor the right to command him is different from the patient's simply doing as the doctor prescribes.

The relation of competence authority and epistemic authority can be viewed in two opposite ways. According to one view, epistemic authority is a broad type of authority, and competence authority is one kind of epistemic authority. The argument in support of this view holds that implicitly Y believes that X has the requisite knowledge in R to do *a*. Thus when the doctor says, "Take two of these pills four times a day," the patient believes that the doctor has knowledge of the pills' effect. The patient believes the proposition "If I take these pills four times a day, they will help me get well," which he believes the doctor implicitly stated. The patient wants to get well, and so he takes the pills. His action follows upon his belief of *p*, his desire to get well, and whatever else is necessary to fully explain his action. According to this view, competence authority involves the belief, implicit or explicit, of some proposition. In following the instructions for building a radio, I implicitly believe that by following them I will build a radio that works. In putting nut A on screw B as stated in the instructions, I believe that the nut belongs on the screw for the best and proper functioning of the radio.

According to the other view, competence authority is a broad type of authority of which epistemic authority is one kind. Thus someone is competent in R if he has knowledge of it. His knowledge may be theoretical or practical. If Y's response to what X says is simply belief in *p*, then we characterize X's authority as epistemic authority. If Y's response is to imitate X because of X's competence in R, then we can call X's authority paradigmatic. Sometimes the appropriate response to nonexecutive competence authority is belief; sometimes it is simply imitation or other action; sometimes it is imitation or other action joined with belief.

The justification for epistemic authority, which is of great importance in social life, is fairly clear and straightforward. Neither its intelligibility nor its justification depends on its including, being included by, or being distinct from competence authority. However that relation is construed, if Y imitates X or does as X suggests in R, Y's action and X's authority are justifiable if they fulfill the competence,[3] inductive, relevance, and trustworthiness criteria. Distinguishing the authority response of belief from that of imitation is often both appropriate and useful.

---

3. The competence criterion states that X has competence in R, just as the knowledge criterion states that X has knowledge of R.

The authority of authenticity might be described as competence in the art of living or as self-mastery and originality in any form of human endeavor. X is a de facto authenticity authority for Y if Y takes X's action in R to be an embodiment of an ideal that Y tries similarly to embody. If X is a competence authority for Y, then Y attempts to do what X does in the same way as X does it. If X is an authenticity authority for Y, then Y does not do as X does but as Y imagines X would creatively react under new circumstances. An authentic person is the author of his own life style and not the follower of another's. He is a master of his craft who sets his own style or trend. He dominates his material. He is a master of himself, and he realizes values to a preeminent degree. His actions become correct because he does them. Possessors of such authority are found in almost all areas.

Neither competence authority nor authenticity authority should be taken as any right or power to command. They are kinds of nonexecutive authority. Y may follow, imitate, emulate X. But X may not know of Y's existence, much less give Y orders. Christ, Buddha, the Christian saints—all have disciples and imitators. Great artists set trends and have followers, many of whom paint, compose, or play in the master's style. The master's way is for them authoritative, just as an epistemic authority's words are believed.

Since both competence and authenticity authority involve Y's following the example of X in some field, I shall consider them instances of exemplary authority. In general, Y's reaction of imitation and of emulation parallels Y's belief of X's utterances in epistemic authority. The reaction may be emotive and may lack cognitive content. Yet exemplary authority can be justified in a way that parallels epistemic authority, since it has a similar function.

Exemplary authority requires some belief in or response to the appropriateness of certain actions to certain ends. Y must have some competence in R or some feeling for the values X embodies or exemplifies in order to take X as an authority in R. The test of X's competence is X's ability to perform in R. The proof of X's authenticity is X's originality and self-mastery in R. The justification for Y's accepting X as an authority is both X's performance in R and the benefit that Y achieves by following X's example. Just as Y gains by believing X under appropriate conditions, so Y gains by following X's example or by imitating X under appropriate conditions. In both cases, Y's good is what justifies Y's making X an authority for Y. In so doing, Y can make faster progress in R than if Y had no one from whom to learn, no one to imitate, no one to inspire him.

LIMITATIONS ON NONEXECUTIVE AUTHORITY

I have argued that under certain conditions, some kinds of nonexecutive authority—in particular epistemic and some forms of exemplary authority—can be legitimate. Not all de facto instances of these kinds of authority are legitimate, and there are limits to legitimacy. Violation of the limits on nonexecutive authority helps erode the general justification of such authority and undermines the use of authority in the specific instances in question. What limits should those subject to either epistemic or exemplary authority place on their acceptance of others as such authorities?

We can set the limits to legitimate nonexecutive authority by considering the proper grounds of authority, the proper reasons for authority, and the proper use of such authority. When the proper limits are exceeded, authority is not legitimate. Violations of the limits tend to be of three kinds. (A) The first and broadest group consists of Y's acknowledging X as an epistemic authority without having rational grounds for doing so. The fault here may lie entirely with Y, who suffers the consequences of his intellectual error. (B) A second kind of violation of the limits occurs when X deceives Y or when X uses his epistemic authority for his own benefit at the expense of Y. (C) The third kind of violation consists of misconceiving the nature of nonexecutive authority by treating it as a type of executive authority.

With B and C, authority tends to turn into authoritarianism. In all three cases the violation of limits can take place on the individual level, on the societal or organizational level, or on both together.

A. Absence of Rational Grounds

Y should not acknowledge X as an epistemic authority unless the knowledge criterion, the inductive criterion, the relevance criterion, and the trustworthiness criterion are met. These constitute the justification for Y's acceptance of X as a legitimate epistemic authority. Y may accept X as an epistemic authority from a variety of motives—such as love, fear, or the hope of gain; but though such motives may explain Y's acknowledging X as an epistemic authority, they do not constitute legitimating grounds for such acknowledg-

46

ment. There are borderline cases and cases in which the facts are not clear. But many cases are not borderline.

The criterion of knowledge is violated when X does not have knowledge in R. He may not have knowledge because there is no knowledge to be had; or despite his having some knowledge, he may have a great deal of misinformation; or he may believe he has knowledge when he does not. The first type includes all of the so-called false sciences. Knowledge of how the stars determine individual destinies is simply not available if the stars do not determine individual destinies. People may claim to have such knowledge, and others may believe them. But their belief cannot be grounded if there is no such knowledge. The problem is how one is to know this. A complete answer requires a developed theory of knowledge. But even a few considerations of the development of knowledge to the present time provide some helpful rules.

Any purported knowledge that contradicts ordinary experience should not be accepted on authority. This applies both in individual and in collective cases. If what X tells Y contradicts what Y knows from Y's own experience, that is initially a good reason for not accepting what X says. Similarly, if some theory contradicts the general experience of members of a society, this is a good reason for them not to accept that theory on the word of the proponent of the theory. Individuals and members of a society may believe something to be true which is not. But if some claimed fact or theory contradicts ordinary experience, it is not reasonable to accept it on authority.

Similarly, if any proposition or theory enunciated by X violates what can be determined through logic or valid reasoning using premises based on ordinary experience, it should not be believed on the basis of authority. Since contradictions cannot both be true together, neither of two contradictory propositions uttered by X should be accepted on authority.

What constitutes knowledge for any given age varies from time to time. What may be believed to be true at one time may be found to be false at another. For centuries, people generally thought the earth was flat and believed that the earth stood still while the planets, sun, and stars moved in the heavens around it. This is what we naïvely experience. We revised our views as more and more facts were uncovered. But the roundness of the earth does not contradict our experience; it coheres or corresponds better with more of it than the view that it is flat. To have accepted the statement that the earth is round because someone said it at a time when everyone believed that it was flat, and when the data of experience seemed to confirm it, would have been to accept as true a proposition that was true; but given the weight of opinion on the other side, it should not have been accepted on authority.

Propositions may be accepted as true for good reasons other than authority. They may be logically true; they may accurately describe our experience; they may cohere well with other things we know; they may be demonstrated within a theory that has great explanatory power. Only because there are other ways of knowing is it reasonable to accept propositions on the basis of authority. Demonstration is a firmer ground for belief than is authority and appropriately should be accepted over authority. History shows, however, that generally held false beliefs are not easily overthrown. Demonstrating the truth of a proposition may be complex and may involve a new theory or reconceptualization of some realm. It may initially be understood only by a few people who have adequate background and knowledge. It filters down and becomes part of the generally held belief of an age through a process involving many levels of both demonstration and belief in the word of authorities.

So far I have argued that on the basis of the knowledge criterion, X cannot be a legitimate authority in R if there is no knowledge to be had in R and that Y should not believe p on the word of X if it goes counter to what Y knows and to what is generally accepted. We can add two more principles of limitation. In general, X's authority is better grounded the more developed the body of knowledge in R. There is good reason for Y to believe X, other things being equal, if p is a statement in a field in which knowledge has been developed, in which theories have been confirmed to a significant degree, and in which there is general agreement among those in the field. There is less reason to believe any X in a field in which knowledge is still tentative and theories are still awaiting significant confirmation. Knowledge in these instances is less sure than in better-developed fields. When great controversy exists among experts in a field, there is good reason not to accept any of them as authorities on the truth of p in the disputed area. The controversy indicates that knowledge in that area has yet to be grounded by ways that are independent of authority. Thus the pronouncement of a certified doctor concerning a fairly common and well-recognized ailment is more certain and should be given greater weight than his opinion concerning treatment in a disputed case. Even where there is great dispute, someone who is facing a forced option in an area in which he has no competence, however, is generally better off by accepting the opinion of a person who has some competence in the area. Though p may be false, the weight of an authority in the field still counts for something.

When knowledge in a field is grounded and when there is general agreement, it is more reasonable to believe those who one thinks have more knowledge in the field than those who have less knowledge. A young child may properly believe what his older sister tells him about a mathematical problem. He is more likely to believe what his mathematics teacher says than what his twin brother says, and rightly so. For the teacher has had more instruction and also has been certified by others who know or are supposed to know a great deal of mathematics. When his parents' statements conflict with those of his teachers, the child is often in a quandary, not knowing whom to believe. Applying the principle of conflicting authorities, he may suspend belief. His trust may be greater in the knowledge either of his parents or of his teacher, and so he may choose to believe one or the other on that basis. Or he may seek explanation, demonstration, or some sort of proof from either party. Each of these natural reactions has a basis in the principles of justification and limitation we have discussed thus far.

The inductive criterion is closely related to the knowledge criterion, because the justification of epistemic authority involves not only knowing that there is knowledge but also knowing who has it. This latter process is inductive and operates both on the individual and on the collective level. In general, the greater the number of independently verified statements that X utters in R, the more reasonable it is to accept X's other statements in R as true, other things being equal. The more correct and otherwise corroborated statements that X utters in R, the greater the basis for Y's belief of other statements that X utters in R. This inductive basis for Y's believing X provides a principle of limitation concerning the justification of Y's belief of X: a few cases of detected error can render X's epistemic authority dubious.

The members of society collectively use the inductive criterion to justify belief in the statements of classes of people in a given field or to accept the certification of some individuals by others in a field. This collective process in turn provides the grounds for Y's accepting X as someone to be believed in R, if X is certified in R. The process of certification is inductively justified. Since the whole process is based on induction, the results are never certain and are open to error. Yet despite this fact, the social process of acceptance of epistemic authorities, certification, and the like, makes it incomparably easier in many instances for an individual to know whom to believe, at least intially. Though each person can individually use the inductive process to determine whether it is reasonable for him to believe X, in most cases each person has a great deal of knowledge that he holds on authority, which he appropriately brings to bear.

Peers may certify a teacher, for instance, as an epistemic authority, and such certification, as well as the official teaching appointment, is generally sufficient grounds for a student initially to acknowledge the teacher as an authority in his field. The fact that past students speak highly of the teacher's knowledge and competence would be further grounds for the legitimacy of one's willingness initially to acknowledge him as an authority and to believe what he says in his field. However, indications from past students that the teacher did not merit their initial acknowledgment should temper one's eagerness to believe *p* simply on his say-so.

Despite the reasonableness of accepting what those in a field assert in that field, some of the great advances in knowledge have occurred because individuals have rejected what was held by the certified authorities in a field. For centuries Aristotle had great authority in the sciences because those who were qualified and certified in the field accepted what he wrote. However, his authority perpetuated his errors. Showing that Aristotle was in error on certain points required argumentation and demonstration based, not on authority, but on some of the primary ways of knowing. The weight of authority, morever, predisposes many not to accept demonstrations that show traditionally held beliefs to be mistaken. The reasons are both psychological and connected with the way in which we acquire and retain knowledge.

When we speak of *p*'s being true, we are usually concerned with *p* within some given context, framework, conceptual scheme, or tradition. It is possible to question the validity or adequacy of a whole conceptual framework or tradition. But even if we have arrived at our beliefs by reasoning or experimentation, we feel more secure in believing *p* if others, using the same means, arrive at the same results or conclusions. Such independent confirmation strengthens our belief that *p* is indeed correct; it does not constitute accepting *p* on authority. If a sufficient consensus builds up around the truth of *p*, then *p* does tend to be held because many have arrived at it by independent means. This refers not only to individual statements but to larger generalizations and theories as well. If they are generally held or widely held by those who are knowledgeable within a field, that consensus is a valid reason for holding or believing them. It is that broad background of authority, and not just the authority of a single individual scholar, that provides the ground for and justifies the belief.

A tradition in a field thus builds up a backlog of authority, based on the work and findings of individual authorities who may have long since died. If the weight of authority backs some *p* that is in fact false, then it is usually not a simple matter to prove that *p* is false. It is lamentable that it may be difficult for the individual thinker's claims or reasoning or experimental proof to get a fair hearing if his conclusions collide with generally accepted views or theories. Yet by following the principle that the authority of a tradition is more solidly founded than the authority of any individual, an initial skepticism towards the truth of a statement that contradicts a tradition is both rationally defensible and compatible with independent testing or analysis of such claims. It is often difficult to separate the claims of the genius from the claims of the crackpot, to know which is which, and to decide which views deserve serious examination. It is not practical to test every claim that runs counter to traditionally held beliefs, simply because someone asserts it. In the complex process of social acceptance of knowledge, the trustworthiness criterion also plays a role, and we shall return to this topic in discussing that criterion.

In general, children do well initially to believe what their parents or teachers tell them, because children know so little that they cannot help but learn a great deal that is true and useful from adults whom they trust, even if they assimilate some falsehoods in the process. Gradually they learn that not every adult is trustworthy and that not everything they are told is true. Most children, as they increase in age and experience, become more discriminating. Part of their education consists in learning to discriminate among authorities and among the utterances of their teachers, distinguishing fact from hypothesis, reasons from rhetoric. They learn to find things out for themselves, to reason about them, and to verify them on their own. If in university teaching the aim is to produce somewhat independent thinkers, then explanation, demonstration, and argument become more important than simply accepting what a teacher says because he says it. The ideal of the completely independent thinker, however, is a myth, for the backdrop of consensus and agreement over a large spectrum of areas helps define what is rational and acceptable. It is a necessary backdrop against which the few innovative thinkers stand out on specific issues.

Although the relevance criterion is frequently abused, it is also often acknowledged. The epistemic authority that is granted to a scholar should extend only to the area or field of his competence. If X is an authority in R, then when X asserts p in R, there is good reason to believe X. When X asserts some p in a field other than R, X's knowledge of R is not usually sufficient to justify belief in what X says unless the second p is in a field closely related to R or is otherwise connected to it. A noted chemist may wield great authority among chemists on topics connected with his research; but this does not make him an authority in history or in politics. Yet the transfer of knowledge into adjacent disciplines and the transfer of habits of scholarly care, tough-mindedness, and reluctance to make statements for which he has no evidence may be worth more than is generally realized.

The criterion of trustworthiness also applies in a common-sense way in everyday life. A known liar is not believed in difficult situations; a known exaggerator is not believed when the details sound unusual. If there is no reason to think that a truthful person has anything to gain by not being truthful, then there is good reason to believe that what he says is what he thinks is the case. His truthfulness does not guarantee the truth of what he says; but together with knowledge, it serves as justification for belief in what he says.

It is proper to inquire whether an epistemic authority can reasonably know what he claims to know and whether he has some purpose to serve by misrepresentation. But if X is known to be scrupulous and truthful and if X utters p claiming that he has good evidence for p, then unless Y has some reason for not doing so, Y is more likely to be believing something true than something false by believing p. Y can thus benefit by X's care, considered judgment, research, or study, even if p happens not to be in X's area of expertise.

The relevance criterion and the truthfulness criterion together can serve to extend the limits of justified belief in X's authority in some instances, even though in others they are irrelevant. If, for instance, I know that X is scrupulously honest and a careful thinker who has a mastery of R and has a certain skepticism for claims made in other areas for which X does not know the grounds and if X enunciates p which is in a field removed from X's area of expertise, assuring me that though he is not an expert in the general area, he has good grounds for believing p, then my trust in X's veracity, or in the qualities of X's mind, forms the legitimate basis for my giving some credence to p. I may well not give p the same credence as if the statement were in R; but veracity plus certain other personal qualities may justify accepting someone as an epistemic authority.

Generally, authors or publishers do not deliberately alter facts that are printed in a standard text or reference book. A general reference work or standard source has the added support that others in the field who would know if it contained errors have not so indicated. This is what it means for it to be generally accepted. On basic, straightforward material which requires little interpretation, it is reasonable to believe what such works contain. In general, we take this approach to the good dictionaries, to the better encyclopedias, to mathematical tables. But when it comes to interpretation of facts, the rationally justified approach to material that is contained even in standard texts and reference works varies. General agreement in a field is an indication that those who know must have independent ground for holding p. Such agreement provides a sounder basis for believing p than does disagreement. In cases of disagreement the word of any author should be taken with less confidence than is otherwise the case. The more disagreement, the more caution should be exercised and the more open to revision should be our belief.

It is obviously to everyone's advantage to have reliable sources of knowledge about some field. Since few people have access to experts in every field, people in literate societies rely extensively on the printed word. A variety of people, rather than just one person, may be involved in producing the printed word, and the authority of all of them, taken collectively, is more impressive than the authority of any of them individually. The review of a book before publication and its approval by a publication committee provide added reason for accepting the book as competent. Children learn to rely on their textbooks and reference works because they are assured by those whom they trust that the printed works are reliable. Children frequently transfer such reliance to all printed material.

Since not everything that is printed is to be believed, a basic problem is the question of who certifies the experts in a field. When there is general or fairly general agreement on the subject matter in question, there is little problem. Those members of a society who are not gullible, who are known for their care, toughness of mind, and trustworthiness, can satisfy themselves that some Xs know more than they themselves do in R, that there is or seems to be good reason for those Xs' holding what they do, and that the general agreement among those who are independent investigators in R reinforces the probability of the truth of the p's that those Xs assert. Such people can help ground the belief of others in the epistemic authority of those Xs. The situation becomes more difficult when there are restrictions placed on free inquiry in a field. For example, through governmental interference or fiat, some field may be closed to certain kinds of investigation. The agreement on what is to be published may not come about by agreement among the investigators who arrive independently at the same results. Rather, it may happen because all those who are involved belong to the same political or ideological camp.

When the interference is not political, the situation is sometimes even more complicated. Society wishes to know what to believe in a certain field. But freedom of publication may result in having unfounded works compete with well-founded ones, and in the general populace's not knowing which is which. In such situations the learned have frequently organized to establish their domination of the field. They form learned societies that are open only to those with certain credentials. They publish learned journals in which they debate their positions. They argue their cases in popular journals, relying not on their authority but on the strength of their arguments. In these ways they get social recognition of their knowledge and become the accepted authorities in the field. They are then invited to write articles for encyclopedias and textbooks in the field. Slowly they establish themselves as the authorities who are believed, and the basis for others' believing them becomes greater. Their authority is further enhanced as they succeed in applying the knowledge of their field to practical purposes.

Historically we have many instances of such developments. The rise of modern science spawned the growth of scientific associations whose aim was to establish their authority in society or to provide grounds for their being acknowledged as authorities by society. The chemists could thus battle the alchemists; and the physicists, the astrologers.

In the practical arts, society has followed suit by certifying those who are competent in certain areas. Doctors are licensed by the state; lawyers pass bar exams. In the United States we also have accrediting associations that impose standards on institutions of higher education. The degrees offered by such accredited institutions are generally considered to mean more than the degrees offered by institutions that are not accredited. The institutions in turn vouch for the knowledge or training of those to whom they give degrees. Thus, earning a certain degree is the basis for believing that a person has some knowledge of the field in which he holds the degree.

As I have mentioned, governments may impose restrictions on free investigation. At times, those who are entrenched in some disciplines also place limits on free investigation. We rightfully place less trust in the statements of anyone in a field that has open disagreement than in a field that has no disagreement. It is therefore sometimes in the self-interest of those who control a field to prevent internal disagreement. Those in control are sometimes successful in preventing research in certain domains or in preventing research using certain methods; they do this by restricting research funds and publishing possibilities. They may also use their epistemic authority to speak against their intellectual opponents, and they often carry the field by their authority rather than by their argument. The more original the doctoral dissertation, for instance, the more difficult it frequently is to gain approval from the professors of certain institutions in certain fields. In these and similar cases, the trustworthiness criterion is subtly violated, and epistemic authority is undermined.

The grounds for accepting an epistemic authority are often similar to the grounds for accepting other types of nonexecutive authority. There are some differences, however. We do not verify values in the same way that we verify knowledge claims, since values are not true or false, nor are they, properly speaking, believed. They are held. The exemplar of certain values can be more or less consistent, more or less inspiring. If he exemplifies a certain way of life, then his example may have relevance in many areas. This fact is exploited by advertisers, who hire athletes or successful actors or actresses to endorse their products. The implicit claim is not that the well-known personalities know more about the products than others do, but that they use them. If you want to be more like these persons, you also should use the products. If the claim were one of knowledge, then the canons of knowledge would apply. Where it is a claim of example, then the rational question to raise is the pertinence of what the exemplar prefers to the qualities that Y admires. If a famous baseball player endorses a certain cereal, is the simple fact that he says he likes it a good reason for others to eat it? If his liking it has nothing to do with his playing well, then one should not eat it thinking that it will help one play well. But if one has such admiration for the player that one wants to eat what the player eats, regardless of whether it helps one play better, the appeal is not to reason. Pertinent questions might be, however, whether the player in fact eats that cereal or only says he does; whether he eats it exclusively, or whether he eats other cereals as well; whether he only started eating it when he was asked to endorse it, or whether he has eaten it for all of his life; and whether he will probably go on eating it after he is no longer being paid for endorsing it. But if someone feels that it is enough simply to know that a model does something, then providing there are no stronger reasons for not doing it, there is no harm in following such an example. The limits to justifiable exemplary authority will further vary according to the different kinds of such authority at issue. The arguments involved in establishing such limits parallel the arguments establishing the grounds that justify such authority.

B. X Benefits at the Expense of Y

Authoritarianism represents an abuse of the exercise of authority in which the bearer of authority uses his authority for his own good at the expense of the subject of authority. There are degrees of authoritarianism, and it can be roughly quantified, as to extent, scope, or other factors, in a way that parallels the quantification of authority.

If Y accepts X as a nonexecutive authority when X does not satisfy the four criteria of knowledge, induction, relevance, and trustworthiness, Y accepts an ungrounded or only partially grounded authority. The defect is Y's, not X's, for Y turns X into an authority when Y has rationally insufficient ground for doing so. But if X abuses his authority, using it for his own good at the expense of Y, the defect is X's. X may, for instance, be a legitimate authority in one area but may be extending his claim to competence to another area in which X can get personal reward, even though X knows that X is not competent in the other area. X may trade on his acceptance as an authority and may tell half-truths from which he benefits. If X is paid for his knowledge, X may claim to have more than he possesses and may claim as true more than he knows to be true.

When Y's interest is violated by Y's acknowledging X as an authority, not only ought Y rationally not do so, but the social good may demand that X be prohibited from exercising his authority. Advertising can again provide a case in point. If some authority is paid to say only half the truth about a product, and the part of the truth that is not stated is injurious to the user of the product, then stating half the truth is in the interest of the seller and of the authority, but at the expense of the buyer. Authorities who prostitute their authority in such ways rightfully forfeit it, for they render suspect all of their statements.

We have seen that satisfying the veracity criterion is no easy matter, because it is sometimes very difficult to know whether any X has a reason for not telling the truth in R, as well as to determine his previous record of truth telling. X's interests may be served by speaking the truth, by speaking half-truths, or by preventing truths from being spoken . The greater the reason for suspecting self-interested motives, the greater should be Y's caution and skepticism.

If the basis for the reasonableness of Y's accepting X as an epistemic or other kind of nonexecutive authority is that Y finds that X satisfies the four criteria mentioned above, the general reason for Y's accepting X as an authority is Y's own good. By believing what X says, for instance, Y tends to gain knowledge. On an individual level, the justification for Y's accepting X as an authority is the good of Y; on a social level, it is the good of society in general. If Y's interest is not served by his acknowledging X as an epistemic authority for Y, Y ought not do so. Nor can Y be legitimately forced to do so. This latter claim may seem counterintuitive and so deserves some argument in support of it.

Epistemic authority involves belief. The appropriate means to change belief are rational persuasion, argument, and demonstration. The notion of forcing belief or of demanding belief involves a misconception of the nature of belief. If belief cannot be forced or demanded, then no Y can be forced or required to believe what any X says. Y may be expected and perhaps forced in various ways to pay attention to what X says and to remember what X says. Y may be forced to act as if Y believed what X says. But both Y's remembering *p* and Y's acting as if Y believed *p* are different from Y's believing *p*. Force is not only inappropriate because it cannot be effective. The attempt to force belief is rationally unjustifiable because it demands suspension of judgment with respect to *p* and therefore runs counter to the rational process. A teacher who demands that his students accept him as an epistemic authority misconstrues his position and function. Governments and other social organizations do the same thing. Compliant behavior may be demanded on the basis of executive authority but not on the basis of epistemic authority. The two types should be kept distinct, even when they are exercised by the same person or groups.

The authoritarian aspects of nonexecutive authority become more subtle when they are exercised by a group of socially recognized authorities so as to stifle competition in the marketplace of ideas. This is true when any group of experts gains control of a field and dominates the publication outlets, the learned societies, the allocation of grants, and the media, not for the good of society, but for their own good and for their own entrenched self-interest. Such violations of the limits of justifiable authority, whether in the realm of knowledge or in the realm of values, tend toward authoritarianism.

Society, for its protection, depends on the accrediting of the competent. But by making special groups the police of an area of knowledge or competence, it faces the problem: Who polices the policemen? The American Bar Association, the American Medical Association, and other similar organizations set up codes of professional competence as well as codes of professional performance. When these groups truly protect the common good and serve the people, they fulfill their proper function and are justifiable. When they protect the interests of the members of the profession at the expense of the public, they are unjustifiable. The price of self-policing must therefore be public accountability. The public is not expert in the fields of these associations; but the public can judge the validity of practices that condemn dissent without argument, that preclude open debate, or that disparage any ideas that counter the generally accepted views of the members of the association. The criteria for self-policing are not entirely matters of expertise of the profession. Nor are the social results of some of the practices that are adopted by professional organizations. Professionals should be allowed to regulate themselves and to become the accepted custodians of truth in their field, but only if their standards are high, their criteria are open and defended, and the good of the public is served.

C. Misconceiving Nonexecutive as Executive Authority

Nonexecutive authority also becomes authoritarian by aggregating to itself a right to command. It is not simply that by definition nonexecutive authority is not a right to command. Rather, nonexecutive authority is so called because it carries with it no right to command. This claim asserts that knowledge, virtue, competence, originality, or similar traits, which serve as a basis for nonexecutive authority, by themselves give no one the right to teach, to act for another, or to impose his views on others. Epistemic authority, which requires initial assent on the part of the subject, involves simply belief and not any commitment to obedience. It may be wise or prudent to utilize the knowledge of the learned persons in relevant ways. And knowledge may bring with it certain obligations. But knowledge gives the philosopher no right to be king, the scholar no right to teach, a brilliant city planner no right to impose his views on a city. Knowledge may be the basis for giving someone the operative or organizational authority to make decisions or to issue grades. But epistemic and operative authority have different sources, and for clarity's sake they should be kept distinct.

This does not mean that a teacher has no authority to make assignments or to establish requirements in the courses that he teaches; rather, it means that he does not have the right to do these things by virtue of his epistemic authority alone, but by virtue of some other kind of authority—operative, organizational, legal, or charismatic. If his epistemic authority is effective, what he says will be believed and will form the basis, if appropriate, of Y's actions. But since X has no right to demand that Y believe what X says, though Y may act on the basis of what X asserts, X has no right to demand this.

For this reason it is wrong to define epistemic authority as involving the *right* to speak or to be believed.[4] A general doctrine of rights may include in it the right of freedom of speech and of the press. But epistemic authority itself includes no rights. To smuggle them in is to confuse epistemic and other types of authority. Simply because someone knows something (or even knows a great deal), whether or not he is acknowledged as an authority, he has no *right* to be heard or to be listened to. Not to listen to someone who has appropriate knowledge may be foolish or imprudent; but no one has the right either to be heard or to be believed simply because of his real or purported knowledge.

Several reasons can be given for this claim. First of all, epistemic authority is justified by the benefit that accrues to those who are subject to it, not by benefit that accrues to the bearer of such authority. Those who are subject to it have the right to believe or not to believe what they hear. Such a right would conflict with any claimed right to be believed on the part of the authority. There is no obligation on the part of anyone to believe what another person says. It may be foolish not to believe what someone else says. Lack of belief

---

4. See R. S. Peters, "Authority," *Aristotelian Society,* supplementary vol. 32 (1958): 207–24, for a discussion of authority, including epistemic authority, in terms of rights.

may also be taken by some as a lack of trust. But belief cannot be forced, and a claim that X has a right to be believed seems to imply an obligation on the part of Y to believe *p* simply because X states it, an obligation that we have seen is not rationally founded. This leads to the second consideration. The conditions under which it is reasonable for Y to believe X do not include Y's knowing that X knows *p*, but they do include Y's having reason to believe that X does. If X had some right to be believed because X knew *p*, Y could not know that X had that right. Y would still rationally have to operate as if X had no such right. From a practical point of view the claim to a right to be believed would therefore be vacuous.

It might be objected that truth should have more rights than falsehood, that people have a right to hear the truth, that those who possess it have the obligation to make it known, and therefore that they have the *right* to make it known. This is compatible with the claim that epistemic authority carries with it no special right to be heard or to be believed and no right to command. In the first place, a society can protect truth by guaranteeing the free speech of all; it need make no special rules for epistemic authorities. Its citizenry or leaders may reasonably pay more attention to the utterances of the learned than to those of others. But freedom of speech, or the right to be heard, is a natural or a civil right; it is not a function of knowledge. Second, though truth, reason, or logic is a good for the rational man, it is the *demonstration* of truth that is rationally coercive. And when a truth is demonstrated, there is no need for authority. Third, the history of human thought has amply shown that attempts at authoritative imposition of belief have often precluded or hindered the development or discovery of other truths. The dangers that result from having a state or government claim that it has the truth and then imposing it are too well known to need recounting here. Consequently, since the acceptance of *p* on the basis of authority is often reasonable, this fact—and not any supposed special right of X—is the legitimate and rationally defensible basis for Y's acknowledging X as an epistemic authority. X can never legitimately command Y to believe X simply on the basis of X's knowledge, because it is always appropriate for Y to maintain a critical attitude towards what any X says, and it is always appropriate to give greater credence to demonstration and logical reasoning when these conflict with what is presented simply on the basis of authority.

Commanding obedience in the realm of belief or of acceptance of values is a form of authoritarianism which attempts to impose what cannot rightfully be imposed. Society may justly demand and impose or prohibit certain actions; but it cannot demand certain beliefs or the acknowledgment of certain values without doing violence to the nature of truth and value. Society gains a great deal through the rational acceptance of legitimate nonexecutive authority; but society should be conscious of the limitations of such authority, lest it suffer the tyranny of experts.

4

Executive Authority

Executive authority involves the right or the power to act in certain
ways. Schematically, executive authority in general is the right or the
power of someone (X) to do something (S) in some realm, field, or
domain (R). An executive authority is someone who has such
authority. We have seen that sometimes authority is a right, sometimes it is a power, sometimes it is both, and sometimes it is
ambiguously either of them. Power refers generally to an ability to do
something. One may have the right to do something but in fact may
not be able to do it; X may, in this case, be said to have the authority
to do S, but his authority is ineffective. If having the power to do
something means being able to do it and if authority is defined in
terms of power, then when one is not able to do that which he has the
authority to do, it would seem that he no longer has the authority to
do it. For one to have the power to do S and yet not be able to do it is
at least paradoxical. If a government has the power to raise taxes but
is unable to do so—for example, because of a lack of the means for
collecting it—then its power is more appropriately called a right. It
has the right to raise taxes but may be unable to do so. Not every right
is a power, and not every case of having power to do something
implies having the right to do it. The notion of authority straddles
both concepts. If authority is defined solely in terms of right, then one
builds legitimacy into the concept, and I have already discussed
reasons for not taking this approach when I discussed nonexecutive
authority. One can, however, capture the nuances of power and right
by using the distinctions I developed earlier: for example, legitimate
and illegitimate authority, effective and ineffective authority, de jure
and de facto authority. Not every instance of a right or of a power is
an instance of authority, although in every instance in which there is
executive authority, at least some claim is being made about a right or
a power.

To speak of authority as a power does not necessarily involve any notion of force or coercion. When we say that a justice of the peace has the power or the authority to perform a marriage ceremony, we are speaking of his legal right or ability to do so. We are not granting him any right to use force or coercion. Similarly, when the United States Constitution lists the "Powers of Congress," it lists those things that Congress is authorized to do, or those things that it and it alone has the right to do under the Constitution. The term 'power' sometimes means simply the ability to perform actions; at other times it means the ability to get others to act through force or coercion. The right to use force or coercion is a right or a power that is given to certain people: for example, to police in the enactment of their responsibilities. But authority itself is not the same as the use of force and coercion. The right to use coercion is granted to the police, the government, or the army through constitutions, laws, or other formal procedures. The granting of the right to use force or coercion is not in itself an instance of force or coercion. Whether or not it is justified is a separate issue. Such force and coercion, if properly circumscribed, is to be used against those over whom the state or government does not exercise authority or effective authority. The army is maintained, not to fight one's own citizens, but to fight outside enemies. The police enforce the laws against lawbreakers. For those who obey the law, those who recognize the authority of the law or the government, coercion is inappropriate. Executive authority, if it is effective, does not require force or coercion.

IMPERATIVE AND PERFORMATORY AUTHORITY

The right or the power that is at issue in executive authority is always the right or the power to perform some action. In this way it is distinguished from epistemic and other types of nonexecutive authority. Executive authority falls into two broad classes, which I shall call imperative and performatory. Imperative authority involves the right or the power of some bearer (X) to command someone who is subject to authority (Y) to act or to forbear from acting in certain ways. All other executive authority involves the right or the power to perform some action other than commanding: I term this 'performatory authority'. Performatory authority is the right or power of X to perform some action, sometimes on or for another person (Y). Thus a surgeon has the right or the authority under certain conditions to operate on his patient; the treasurer of an organization has the right or the authority to pay the bills for the organization; a justice of the peace has the legal power or authority to perform a marriage.

As with all authority, the field (R) to which either kind of executive authority is restricted depends on the kind of authority the bearer has, the source (if any) of that authority, the position he occupies, the circumstances, and other similar considerations. The range of the authority of a justice of the peace is more limited than is that of the governor of California, though the latter might have no right to do some of the things that the former is authorized to do. Executive authority, in the sense in which I am using it here, encompasses what is frequently referred to as executive, judicial, and legislative authority. A totalitarian government might claim unlimited authority, and so it might claim that in some sense its field is unlimited. Obviously, in the vast majority of cases the scope of authority that is claimed, recognized, and justifiable is limited.

To specify that it is in virtue of some context (C) that X has the right or power to do some action (a) is to tie the notion of executive authority to a system or a context. C might be a set of laws, a constitution, a tradition, a position, or a set of personal qualities that are appropriate to a set of circumstances. Any of these or several of them together form the context in which authority operates, and they are essential to an understanding of executive authority. Executive authority cannot be understood in abstraction from a context, for it is defined by the context. Why people either do or should obey commands, why people allow others to act for them, or why people accept an individual's signature as binding a group, for instance, can be made intelligible only in terms of given contexts. A justice of the peace has the right to perform a marriage ceremony within a framework of civil law; a business executive has the right to tell a secretary to take a letter in virtue of the structure of the business, their respective roles, and some agreement as to work and pay.

Since we have characterized executive authority as the right or power of X to do S in R in virtue of C, we have restricted X to being an agent, usually a person. Yet we do speak of the law or the rules of a game as being authorities, and we do refer to the law as commanding in some cases. Sometimes the law is considered as an executive authority; sometimes it is the source of the authority that people have.

As with epistemic authority, de facto executive authority is the weakest form of executive authority. We can use it to describe and discuss the phenomenon of executive authority, whether or not such authority is ever legitimate.

We can characterize de facto imperative authority by specifying the action of X within the above definition as being one of issuing a command and by describing the authority response of the recipient of the command, Y. X and Y are related as superior to inferior in the realm (R). X is a de facto imperative authority if when X issues some command *q* to Y, Y does *a* because it was commanded to do so, *q* being something in field R and in a context C which Y accepts as being plausibly legitimate (whether or not *q* is). To accept *q* as plausibly legitimate is to understand some rule or set of rules which define the context and the relation of X to Y, in terms of which the command is plausibly appropriate and appropriately obeyed.

When I give my wallet to a robber who tells me at gunpoint to do so, I do not consider my action to be an instance of an authority response, since it is clear that I am responding to the presence of the gun as well as to the command to hand over my wallet. The robber's gun makes him superior in the realm of force. But the context is clearly not one in which the gunman's command is plausibly legitimate. Though authority may be associated with coercion, coercive superiority is not equivalent even to de facto imperative authority.

The strength of the word 'command' may vary, and there are various ways to issue a command, some more formal and some less so. A command is an order from a superior to an inferior in the context and realm of the command. An inferior cannot appropriately command a superior, nor can an equal appropriately command an equal. A stranger who is ordered to do something may well take offense; he is being treated as an inferior in a context that does not justify it. Similarly a parent may be insulted if his child orders him to do something rather than asking him to do it. Although a command is appropriately issued by a superior to an inferior, it may be stated politely as a request or as a wish. In the context, Y understands the request or wish as being equivalent to a command or order. The command of an executive authority need not be joined with any threat of force; if it is, the threat must be plausibly legitimate. It would thus not be a case of executive authority if Y, a friend of X's, did *a*, which X had strongly requested, simply because Y wished to help his friend in the requested way. The reason Y does *a* is important in determining de facto imperative authority. Hence we have the stipulation that *q* be within field R and in a context governing that field and defining the relation of X and Y, such that Y is inferior to X and feels the command is legitimate as a command.

Motives are frequently complex. Fear might motivate Y's doing *a* (e.g., his fear of losing a job or his fear of being court-martialed), just as love or affection, a desire to please, or the hope of receiving special treatment, a raise, or a promotion might be part of the motive for doing *a*. Y might even anticipate what X will command and do *a* before being commanded to do so. In many specific cases it may be difficult to decide whether a given action by Y constitutes X as an authority, that is, whether Y's action is in compliance with a command of X that Y acknowledges as appropriate. The intensity of X's authority is a function of Y's acceptance of X as an authority, and the intensity may vary from little to complete acceptance.

Performatory authority is more difficult to circumscribe because it encompasses such a multitude of different kinds of actions. In every case, however, there must be some context in which the action is in accordance with some expressed or understood set of rules such that it conforms to them and is plausibly legitimate. A frequent case of performatory authority is one in which X has the authority to perform some actions for an organization because of the position X holds in the organized structure. Frequently, positions of authority, defined within a structure, carry with them both imperative and performatory authority. But the two are distinguishable.

A second frequent case of performatory authority consists of Y's authorizing X to act for him, as a client authorizes a lawyer to act for him. X receives from Y the authority to perform some action. If Y further agrees to obey X, then Y makes X an imperative authority for Y. Organizational structures serve as a mediator of executive authority and sometimes lead to role reversal. In the political realm, for instance, if the authority of a government comes from the people, they are the primary source of authority for the officials of the government who serve them. But through the network of the government the leaders are given the right or the power both to command and to act for those whom they serve. We shall examine this paradoxical situation in more detail when we discuss the legitimacy of political authority.

In the delegation of authority, X, who may be an imperative authority for Y, authorizes Y to perform actions for X which Y has the right or the authority to perform. If X authorizes Y to do *a*, Y may be an authority for someone else with respect to that *a* where this means that the other person recognizes X as being authorized to do that *a*. Recognition does not make a person subject to authority. The head of a firm, for example, may authorize a buyer to order goods for the firm. If I accept a purchase order from the buyer, I recognize his authority to make purchases for the firm; but I am not subject to his authority, nor is he made an authority by my recognizing him. The original bearer of authority retains ultimate responsibility for what he authorizes.

Clearly, people may be given executive authority because of their competence or knowledge, but this is not necessarily the case.

The authority of a position in some organizational structure may be defined by the structure and, in these cases, may not exist without it. When X has performatory authority without imperative authority, there may be no Y subject to X, or the notion of Y's being subject to X may not be entirely clear. The justice of the peace who marries a couple is, for them, a performatory authority, as is a notary public for someone who needs to have a document notarized. But the couple or the person with the document is not subject to the justice of the peace or to the notary public in the ordinary sense of Y's being subject to X. Rather, they are all subject to the rules or laws of the system which give performatory authority to some and require use of those authorities by others who wish to achieve certain ends that are attainable under the system. The relation of X and Y in the case of performatory authority is often complex, due to the mediating role of structures that break up and transmit function and authority in many ways.

In an organizational context, X has or is a de facto executive authority (either performatory or imperative) if, in virtue of X's occupying some position within a system, context, or organization, X is given the right or the power to perform some action, or if within it X is accorded by others the right or the power to command or perform in certain ways. The kind of executive authority that X has is a function of the organization. If the organization is a legal framework, X has legal executive authority; if it is a corporation, X has corporate executive authority (which may be legally protected). In some cases, X may be a de facto executive authority if X is implicitly accorded certain rights and powers by those who accept X's actions in those spheres as being legitimate, even though X does not actually occupy the office that would entitle X to those rights or powers. If X holds the proper office but if X's actions are not accepted by others, X's de jure authority is ineffective. If X's actions are accepted by others but if X does not hold the proper position (e.g., the leader of a revolution whose orders constitute laws, though they have not been passed by the legislature), X is not a de jure but a de facto authority, possibly an illegitimate one. An alternative description in the latter case would be to say that X has no authority until it is institutionally regularized. But this would restrict executive authority either to grounded (legitimate) authority or to de jure authority. By allowing illegitimate authority to be classified as de facto authority if it is exercised and recognized, it becomes possible to describe and handle these cases even if it turns out that there is no such thing as legitimate executive authority.

CONTEXTS OF EXECUTIVE AUTHORITY

Executive authority appears most commonly in three general contexts. The first is the family or the natural society; the second is free contractual-type organizations or societies; the third is the state or civil society. The family is the social unit into which one is born. A natural relation of dependence, and so of inferior to superior, exists between children and parents. The executive authority of parents can be called parental (or in an earlier period, paternalistic) authority. A child is usually born into a civil society as well. Most people have no choice but to belong to some such society, although in some instances they may leave a country and join another civil society in some other country. In addition one might join a great many organizations, clubs, societies, corporations, each of which is governed by certain rules. Some groups are also formed spontaneously; someone exercises leadership without there being any formal rules. In either case the executive authority, if any, is exercised within a free association of some sort. I shall term such authority 'operative authority'. The kind of executive authority that is found in the structures of the state I shall call politico-legal authority. Parental, operative, and politico-legal authority may overlap in certain instances; they are also found mixed with other kinds of authority.[1] Each kind may be either imperative or performatory.

There are ambiguous cases. When a doctor tells a patient, ''Take one of these pills three times a day for the next week, and then come

---

1. Other types of authority might be, e.g., the authority of a master over a slave, which may be neither an arrangement that is freely entered into nor one that is in any sense either familial or politico-legal authority; or religious authority, either imperative or performatory, which may be in a free but noncontractual society, with God as the source of its authority. On the latter type see chapter 9.

back and see me,'' is this an instance of imperative authority? Since no organization or established set of rules makes the doctor an imperative authority who is empowered to command his patients in the area of health, there is ambiguity. The informal patient-doctor relation assumes that both doctor and patient are interested in the patient's health and that the patient goes to the doctor for advice and instruction. The doctor is an epistemic authority, who has no right to command. I suggested earlier that what the doctor does when he tells the patient to take certain pills can be interpreted as a shortened form of saying, ''If you want to cure whatever it is you have, then take these pills.'' Most patients know that the doctor has no right to command them or to force them to follow his advice. If someone feels that his doctor is incompetent or that his advice is poor, that patient is free to go to another doctor or to ignore the doctor's advice or prescription. The right of a patient not to be operated on without his consent is usually protected in the United States by law. Yet patients frequently react to the prescriptions of a doctor as to someone who holds imperative authority; and in these cases we can say that the doctor is a de facto executive authority with respect to such patients.

The patient may consider the doctor's imperative authority legitimate, since the doctor has the same goal as the patient—namely, curing the patient's ills. By commanding the patient to act in certain ways, the doctor helps the patient to attain what the patient himself desires. The doctor has no right to force a patient to follow his advice, even though the doctor may threaten the patient with the natural consequences that will probably follow if the doctor is correct and the patient does not do as he is told. Neither formal structure nor the doctor's knowledge nor the good of the patient is sufficient by itself for the doctor legitimately to attempt to force the patient to obey. The doctor is not a de jure executive authority for his office patient, since their relation is not based on any formal organization. The doctor is a de facto executive authority for his patients, if his patients make him such; he has no right to demand that they treat him as such an authority, and he has no strict right to command them. The executive authority that he enjoys and wields over his patients, since it is not a right, depends on their free compliance with his prescriptions. His legitimate function is to issue hypothetical imperatives, to make his knowledge available, and to use his skill when it is desired by those on whom he uses it. The question of his authority in a hospital with respect to patients or to the other staff of that hospital is, of course, an entirely different matter; in that context he may, in virtue of the rules of the hospital and the laws of the state, enjoy a different kind of executive authority, which is de jure in terms of the rules and which may well be legitimate.

The doctor's orders to his office patient are completely compatible with the patient's autonomy. For the patient wills, not whatever the doctor orders, but his own health. His decision to act as the doctor prescribes is simply a decision to take the means appropriate to achieve his end. He owes the doctor no obedience, since he pays the doctor for his services or advice. The doctor who tells a heart patient to stop smoking has no way of enforcing that order and no right to enforce it, if his patient is a mature, competent outpatient. The doctor has no right to coerce such a patient to act in certain ways, even for the good of the patient, though the doctor may certainly reason with him and try to persuade him to act as is best for him.

The law gives doctors the authority to do certain things—for example, to prescribe drugs—thereby making available to patients what would not be available to them without a prescription. Such authority is not derived from knowledge, but from certification and licensing. In most countries these are now governed by law and constitute a particular type of authority which we shall examine later.

The authority of a lawyer is in some ways similar to that of a doctor. His client may go to him for advice and may take advantage of his knowledge, with no obligation to follow that advice, for which he usually pays. A client may also authorize his lawyer to represent him in court or elsewhere, similarly to the way in which he might authorize his doctor to operate on him. The patient or client can authorize others to act on or for him. This might be called a kind of permissive authority, for it does not constitute a command to the doctor to operate or to the lawyer to plead a case. The doctor and the lawyer receive performatory authority from the law: that is, they are given the right to operate and to plead in court by the laws and rules governing such activities. In normal cases the doctor or lawyer also requires the permission or authorization of the patient or client to act for or on him. The doctor and the lawyer are epistemic authorities, authorized by law to act in certain ways (i.e., they are given performatory authority), and are given permissive authority by their patients or clients to act on or for them.

The doctor and the lawyer are examples of ambiguous cases of de facto executive authority. There are numerous clear cases.

Parental, operative, and politico-legal authority are the major kinds of executive authority. But let us consider a fire in a crowded theater. Suddenly someone starts giving commands, telling people to move in certain directions and to take certain precautions. The people who are so directed act as they are commanded to do. This is an instance of a de facto executive who gives commands and is obeyed. The one who assumes authority in such a situation may have no official role and is not obeyed because of an official position. He is obeyed because in a time of panic or emergency he inspires those others to believe that their welfare will best be secured by doing as he directs. They are under no obligation to accept his direction.

A somewhat similar phenomenon may take place over a longer period of time when, for instance, the people of a country that is in a crisis respond to the lead of someone who places himself at the head of a group and leads the many who choose to follow him. Spartacus's assuming leadership of the slaves in their revolt against Rome is an example.

Closely related to such authority is what Max Weber called charismatic authority. Originally it described the authority of a religious leader over his followers, though it has come to refer as well to revolutionary leaders. In either case the leader exercises de facto executive authority over his followers through the force of his personality, the strength of his ideals, and his followers' belief in his special, privileged status.

The only general justification that can be given for spontaneous (including charismatic) authority is the right of people to act as they wish—a right that includes acting as others command. Sometimes it may be wise to follow the commands of someone who assumes the role of leader, if the alternative is chaos and panic. In other cases it may be unwise to follow such commands. While it is noteworthy that in crisis situations, some people do assume authority and are obeyed by others, such assumed authority carries with it no right to be obeyed. As Weber notes, if charismatic authority persists for any significant period of time, it tends to become routinized.[2] The same is true for other forms of spontaneous authority. Either they disappear with the end of the crisis, or they are transformed into operational or politico-legal authority.

2. See Max Weber, *The Theory of Social and Economic Organization*, ed. Talcott Parsons (New York: Free Press, 1964), pp. 363–73.

PARENTAL AUTHORITY

The many-faceted authority that parents have over their children is usually found intertwined with other ingredients—love, affection, respect, pride, even jealousy, shame, or dislike. Parents are usually epistemic authorities for their children, as well as being moral models. Laws of a country frequently both reinforce and circumscribe parental authority in various ways. It is more the exception than the rule that civil law must be invoked by parents, children, or some third party concerning the use of parental authority.

The ordinary sense in which parents are executive authorities for their children covers both performatory and imperative authority. Parents are responsible for their children, and they have the obligation to care for them. The obligation entails the right to do so, and they can be said to have the authority of moral obligation to care for their children. Societies vary as to how broadly or narrowly a family is construed and who has the obligation to care for children. In most Western societies the obligation falls on the mother and father. In an extended family the obligation may be shared by the grandparents or by uncles and aunts as well. In a commune the parents of a child might be construed as being all of the adult members of the commune. When the parents die or are unable to care for their children, other relatives may assume the parents' role, or foster parents may assume the role of the child's natural parents. We can speak in general of parental authority to cover the authority of any of the adults whose task it is to care for the nourishment, support, and upbringing of the children in any particular case.

The responsibility of parents towards infants is to care for them: to nourish, clothe, and clean them and to provide for any other needs. Parents have the authority to do what is necessary for the child and to the child. They have performatory authority over the child insofar as they do for the child whatever is required, and they represent him in various ways. Parents have the authority to authorize a doctor to treat the child or to operate on him if necessary. Parents represent the child and assume responsibility for the actions of the child, making reparation where necessary if the infant or small child does damage to the property of another.

The justification for parents' having such authority with respect to their children is threefold. The first is the need and good of the child. Parents represent children because the latter are unable to represent themselves. The performatory authority of parents has as its basis the good of the child and the inability of the child to perform required actions for himself. The second justification is the competence of the parents. This is assumed unless there is ground for thinking otherwise, in which case the state or others may intervene on behalf of the child. The third is the position of the parents as parents in our society, or the position of whatever parent type is appropriate in other societies. Those who are responsible for raising a child have the right to do what is necessary in raising him. Not all adults have authority over all children, despite the need of children and the competence of adults. Parental authority, at least in our society and in others like it, is restricted to parents, guardians, and those to whom the parents transfer their authority.

This general justification, however, does not justify each individual application of parental authority. Particular instances of parental authority can require particular justifications. In general, such instances are justified when appropriate reasons can be given for the rules the parents make, the commands they issue, or the actions they take with respect to the child. It is not necessary that the reasons be given; nor is it necessary that the child be able to understand the reasons or that he appreciate or accept them. But parental authority, like other kinds of authority, can turn into authoritarianism if the rules, commands, and actions of the parents are for the parent's good at the expense of the child's or if they are arbitrary or unreasonable.

As the infant develops into a child, he slowly grows into the family unit. He learns that his needs and wants must be balanced and harmonized with the needs and wants of others. He is slowly introduced to rules and ways of doing things within the family. For his own good and safety, as well as for the good and safety of others and their possessions, he is taught not to touch certain things—such as hot stoves—not to go certain places—such as into a busy street—and not to eat certain things—such as poisons or glass or gravel. Various techniques may be used in teaching him, such as physical restraints, verbal commands and reproaches, or praise and physical rewards for proper behavior.

Imperative parental authority includes the right to command one's children to do or not to do certain things and the right to reward and punish them according to their actions. It is one of the major ingredients in parental authority. By means of such commands the child learns what he may and may not do, both for his own good and for the good of others. The continuing underlying justification is that the child is the beneficiary of such authority. His physical safety is protected, his social life develops, and his ability to associate with others is promoted. By himself he is incapable of knowing how to do many things, what is safe and what is not, what rights others have, what hurts them or their feelings. He might learn some or all of these eventually by trial and error, but he might also kill or maim himself and others in the process. It is certainly to his benefit to learn from the expierience of others by being taught and trained. The good of the child, his need, and his lack of competence are the primary justifications for parental imperative authority; the good of other family members is also a concern, although the development of the ability to consider others and to get along with them is also a good for the child.

As a general statement and with respect to small children, this is not a very controversial thesis; it probably needs no more defense. The general defense, of course, leaves open such questions as what means might be legitimate to use for punishment or reward and, among those that might be legitimate, which are most fruitful in achieving their end. Whether corporal punishment, as long as it is not extreme and does no harm to the child other than the temporary sting of a slap on the bottom, is allowable and whether it is preferable to other kinds of punishment—for example, the denial of a candy or of a dessert, the administration of a verbal tongue lashing, or the withholding of affection—are in part empirical matters and cannot be settled simply by analyzing the notion of parental imperative authority. But if the general justification is the need and good of the child and, indirectly, the need and good of others in the family, then whatever reasonable means are necessary to procure that end are justified by it.

Parental authority is circumscribed by the general moral restraints that operate in regard to all executive authority. It is only justified to the extent that the good of the child in his social setting as a member of the family community requires it. Parents have the prime responsibility for the well-being of the family as a whole—that is, for themselves and their children in the nuclear family and for the broader group in the extended family where the responsibility is shared with other adults of the family. Parents must try to handle the needs and wants of all in the light of what is available to them all; they are primarily responsible for making the family a livable and, it is hoped, happy and mutually supportive unit. They have the responsibility not only because they (in most cases, at least) brought the children into the world but also because they can provide for their children physically, intellectually, morally, culturally, and spiritually in a way that the children are not able to provide for themselves or others.

As the children grow and develop, the parents gradually have less responsiblity for their children and less authority over them. The better the children have been taught to reason, to respect the rights of others, to act morally, the less they will have to be ordered to act in certain ways or to do certain things. When children become self-sufficient, so that they can care for themselves, and are no longer dependent on their parents, they are considered adults. The age at which this takes place varies from culture to culture and, within a given culture, from child to child, but the law may consider persons legally to be adults at a certain set age. When the need for the parents' authority is no longer present, the justification disappears, and their authority is no longer justifiable. Parents who refuse to give up their parental authority may attempt, sometimes successfully, to continue to exercise it after the child has become an adult and is no longer dependent on the parent; children may seek to be rid of parental authority even before they have become adults or even while, as adults, they are dependent on their parents in certain ways. But none of this affects the general principles of justification and limitation of parental authority. These instances simply provide an indication that it is not always easy to draw the line of where parental authority ends, since, as we have seen, it gradually diminishes.

I have linked parental authority to the need and good of the child and to the responsiblity of the parent. The parent does not have the authority over the children of others that he has over his own children. Parents, however, can delegate some of their authority to others to whom the children are entrusted: for example, to babysitters or to teachers. The amount of authority and the extent of that authority may vary; it should be sufficient to accomplish whatever end the parents wish with respect to the child, within the limits of what is good for him concurrent with the rights of others. Whether and to what extent such parent substitutes or those who stand *in loco parentis* can set rules and enforce obedience through punishment or reward cannot be determined a priori. Specific cases require specific discussion and consideration. Teachers of younger children may indeed exercise some parental authority over the children. They serve not only as epistemic authorities but also as parent substitutes. They take over the education of children, which is both the obligation and (some claim) the right of the parent, at the parent's explicit request.

The right of the child to education and to development of his powers within the available resources can be argued on the basis of the good of the child. In many communities the law that requires the education of children is passed for their good as well as for society's, and the community supplies the facilities for such education. If the parents have primary responsibility for the child's education, however, then in particular instances they may object to what a school teaches or to how it teaches; and they may claim the right to educate their children themselves. The various issues that arise in such cases can involve religious education, equality of education for all, or integration of schools. The present point is simply that parental authority may be delegated to others when certain parental tasks are delegated as well. The delegation of authority, however, does not involve the abrogation of authority. Ultimate responsibility is retained by those who delegate authority—in this case, the parents.

Ideally, parents make for the child the kind of enlightened decisions that the child would make for himself, were he capable of doing so, but that he is incapable of making because he lacks the knowledge, experience, strength, discipline, or resources necessary to make and carry through such decisions. Ideally, parental commands and rules do not constitute an alien will imposed on that of a child, but a loving help given for the child's good and in his best interest. Unfortunately, in some instances, such commands and rules may actually not be for the good of the child or for his best interest; and in even more cases the child may not perceive them as being for his good and for his best interest, especially when they thwart his immediate interests and desires. The general defense of parental authority is compatible with instances of mistakes in judgment on the parents' part. The impulse of the child to accept and obey his parents' commands may first be based on a simple conditioned response to reward and punishment. As he becomes older, it may also be based on trust and confidence in his parents, consideration for them even when they may be wrong, or a desire for harmony in the family at the expense of not promoting one's own good. At a certain point a child may feel that he knows better than his parents what is good for him, and he may assert his independence.

In discussing parental authority, I have spoken primarily of the good of the child over whom authority is exercised. As the child develops and grows, he may assume more responsibility for the family as a whole, he may be consulted on decisions that involve the family, and such decisions may be discussed and argued about.

Sometimes debate is not conclusive, or various equally good alternatives exist, and a decision must be made which commits all the members of the family in certain ways. One of the functions of executive authority is to make such decisions. It is proper for those who support and maintain a family to have a larger voice in such decisions. Children who depend on their parents for financial or other support, even when they might otherwise be considered adults and independent, are subject to the decisions of their parents in matters of support. How they are subject to their parents' authority is a matter for discussion, though it seems clear that their dependence makes them more subject to their parents than they would be if they were not dependent on their parents for financial or similar support. None of this implies that family relations either should or usually are regulated in terms of rights, responsibilities, regulations, orders, executive authority, dependence, or money, without also considering affection, respect, interest in the well-being of each other, and a willingness to sacrifice for the good of others.

Parental authority decreases as the child reaches adulthood and is able to take care of himself and to assume responsibility for himself and for his actions. When the child's development is impaired or when he cannot care for himself or when, because of physical or mental disability, he cannot assume responsibility for himself and his actions, the parents retain authority as long as they assume responsiblity.

Parents have de facto parental imperative authority to the extent that their children do as the parents require, ask, or demand. The more clear, consistent, and reasonable the parents are, the more their children will know what is expected of them, and the more effective will be their authority. As children become accustomed to acting in the expected ways, fewer explicit commands are needed. Parental authority then operates through understood and accepted modes of procedure within the family. Parents who command least may actually have the most authority, if they have in fact established operating guidelines which the children know and respect and within which they operate. Obviously the guidelines must be flexible and must change with the ages of the children. The range or scope of parental authority changes as circumstances change, and it diminishes as the children get older.

I have referred to parental authority as the authority of the parents, and have tended to consider it as a single authority exercised over as many children as there may be in the family. When the bearers of parental authority are both a mother and a father, their authority is a shared authority, just as their responsibility is shared responsibility. How their authority is shared—whether each has certain areas or whether both cover all areas or whether they speak with one voice or not—depends on the society in question, the traditions from which the parents come, their experiences as children, their observations and reflections, their temperaments, the kinds of people they are, the closeness or disparity of their ideas about raising children and about what constitutes the child's good, their relations to their children, and other similar factors. Though in some cultures the father's word constitutes law in the family, in other cultures the mother is the dominant figure and determines the rules by which the family is run. In still other cases there is consultation and agreement on all important issues. How parental authority is exercised, shared, or divided may vary. The parental authority of both parents tends to be enhanced when there is agreement concerning commands and rules vis-à-vis the child. When one parent's commands, requests, or decisions countermand the other's, the child sees no clear authority. He will probably learn to use the disagreements or indecision between his parents as a means to achieve what he perceives as his own advantage, even though this may actually be to his disadvantage. Or, caught between contradictory commands, he may be punished no matter how he acts. In this case he would very likely perceive the situation correctly as being unjust. In effect, parental authority is shared between the parents. There is no conceptual necessity why one or the other of them should be the final authority, though they may decide on, or tradition may dictate, some particular arrangement. Unless shared authority is coordinated and agreed upon, its exercise could lead either to the collapse of authority or to its ineffectiveness, or it could lead to injustice when both parents make contradictory demands that cannot be fulfilled by a child who is then punished for not fulfilling them. Conflicts between those who stand *in loco parentis* and the parents should be ironed out by those who are involved in the conflict. If parents simply delegate authority, they may rescind it. In the more complex case of schools, teachers not only act *in loco parentis* but also operate under rules established by the school and perhaps under laws passed locally or by higher authorities. The various strands of authority must be untangled, and the situation must be examined in the light of all of the existing and possibly conflicting demands.

Parental authority has served as a model of executive authority in a wide variety of cases that extend beyond the nuclear family. In some societies the respect of children for parents and the authority that parents have over children extend far beyond the time at which children become adults. In some such societies the elders of a society form a type of collective parent for all the younger members of the society, while the elders share their authority in a way that is perhaps analogous to the way in which a mother and father share it in a nuclear family. The whole clan, tribe, or society—however far the notion is extended—is treated as a family. The members, with their different needs and desires, live together; they share a mutual concern and perhaps blood relations. The elders perform the same kinds of activities as do parents: they set down rules of behavior, which they enforce; they settle arguments between the members of the group; they foster justice and mutual concern, reconciling the needs of each with the available goods. They claim that the justification for their authority is the same as that of parents—namely, the need and good of those who are entrusted to them but who are unable to handle such matters effectively for themselves. Executive authority falls to the elders because of their greater experience and their greater disinterestedness in administering justice. The members of the society, clan, or tribe accept their role as persons who are subject to the authority of the elders. The legitimacy of the elders' authority comes not only from their greater age and their actual or supposed greater knowledge but also from their acceptance by those who would normally be considered adults and therefore are not subject to parental authority. Whether such acceptance is itself legitimate is a question that we shall have to look at more closely later. The present point is that in an extended family situation the model of parental authority is sometimes invoked as the basis for a kind of authority that goes beyond the parent-child relationship.

Similar extensions of the parent-child model are made in order to justify not only the authority of the elders but also politico-legal authority, or the authority exercised by the head of a state over the members of that state.

A type of parentalism—more frequently referred to as paternalism—is also found in the exercise and sometimes in the justification of other types of executive authority, the claim being made that such authority is based on concern for the good of those who are subject to authority, a good that is perceived more clearly and known more fully by the bearer of authority than by those who are subject to it. We shall examine the legitimacy of such claims more fully once we have specified some of the other types of executive authority.

79

Parental authority applies properly only to the authority of parents or legal guardians over their children. It is sometimes said to be natural authority because it is exercised within the family, a natural unit based on biological ties. It is legitimate when exercised for the benefit of children who are incompetent in various ways and are dependent on their parents. It is unjustifiable when the commands are arbitrary, when the demands are unreasonably harsh, and when it is exercised for the benefit of the parents at the expense of the children. The latter type of case tends towards authoritarianism.

OPERATIVE AUTHORITY

A second major type of executive authority is operative authority. This is the executive authority that is exercised in freely formed groups, societies, or organizations. People belong to a family by nature—that is, by biological ties—as well as by social ties; they are, in most cases, born into such a unit and do not belong to it by choice. Similarly, one does not choose the state or political unit into which one is born. Some parents may exercise some choice about the country in which their children are born, and some adults may move from one country to another; but one usually does not have the option of belonging to no state at all.

Great differences exist among the many types of freely formed groups and organizations as well as in the freedom involved in the formation and memberships of the different groups. Some groups may include as members the children of members, and therefore the children may be said to be born into the group, whether they like it or not, just as they are born into a family or into a state. Some groups or organizations may refuse to allow members to leave once they have become members. Others may refuse or limit membership, so that though freely formed, the organization is not open to all. Some of these groups may also be circumscribed by law or legally formed, protected, or controlled by the state. For present purposes it is enough simply that they are not formally part of the state, in the way that a legislature, the judiciary, or the executive offices of a state are part of it. There are borderline cases. The army of a country might be considered part of the state apparatus even if all its members are volunteers. A state university can be—and frequently is—considered to be a free society in a way that an army is not. One might also question the extent to which members of a non-state-governed organization are free: consider for example, the case of workers in a one-factory town, who are forced by their circumstances to work in that factory if they wish to earn money or coupons to support themselves and their children. Or given a society in which all industry is state owned, one might question the sense in which these organizations or firms differ from so-called privately owned ones and the sense in which the authority is not state authority but operational authority. State authority may in fact be a form of operational authority, and it may sometimes be difficult to decide exactly which is in fact present. Yet in some cases the authority that is exercised derives not primarily or not at all from the state or from laws. I shall take these as the paradigms of operational authority.

A wide variety of freely organized groups comes to mind immediately. The groups form a continuum from very loose associations of individuals with almost no structure to very tightly organized groups. The groups may vary greatly in purpose and size, ranging from simple fellowships, such as bridge or poker clubs, to multinational business corporations. Despite their diversity, they can be considered together if they have some form of executive authority within them. And clearly, executive authority is present in most groups. Any principles we arrive at concerning such diverse groups will of necessity be broad and general. More specific principles may well be applicable to individual subclasses: for example, to universities, to business corporations, to trade unions, or to baseball teams, as we shall see in later chapters of the book.

What constitutes a group as opposed to a simple collection or set is first a common collective purpose or end that the members cannot achieve individually; they join together in order to achieve the goal collectively. A number of people may individually go to a theater to see a play, and though we can speak of the audience as a group, each member of which has the same end in view—namely, to see the production on the stage—they do not form a group with a single collective purpose. The members of the audience do not go so that other members of the audience can see the production, even though it might be the case that if a certain minimum did not show up, the production could not or would not be given. Within the audience, however, there may be a group of First-Nighters—that is, a certain number of people who have joined together formally or informally to see together this and other productions. They join together because they wish to see this production with others who have similar interests, and not simply because they want to see this production.

Perhaps they authorize someone to buy tickets for them *en bloc*, so that they will sit together. Perhaps they all get together before or after the production for a dinner or discussion. Their joining each other to achieve a common end together makes them a group. A second ingredient has already been introduced: namely, they coordinate their actions through some sort of organization, loose though it may be. A third is that their intention goes beyond seeing this one performance together. A fourth is that, loose as the organization may be, there is some organization, with someone perhaps being authorized to buy tickets or to make arrangements in the name of and for all members of the group. A fifth is a decision or an intention to join or organize as a group, together with follow-through on that decision.

Other than our First-Nighters group, we may find in the theater a group of four or five friends who have informally decided to attend this production together but who have no intention of forming or joining an organization, even though they may authorize one of their group to buy the tickets for them all *en bloc*, and they may decide that they will all go in one car. This group is very much looser than the First-Nighters, and although it contains some of the elements of the latter, it lacks others. It stands between the situation in which each member goes on his own to the same production and one in which a group is organized for this express purpose. From this intermediate stage, a more organized group might develop, become somewhat routinized and establish general rules about who might belong and under what conditions, who will buy the tickets each time, and who will drive.

We can distinguish at least three general kinds of groups: cooperative groups, managerial groups, and entrepreneurial groups. This classification depends, not on size or the end the group wishes to achieve, but on its origin and organization. A cooperative group is formed by a group of people with a common aim, end, or goal, in which the functions of the group, which are necessary for its operation, are shared by the members. A managerial group may be cooperatively founded, but the members of the group may turn over to inside or outside specialists the tasks that are complicated or time-consuming or that require expertise. The group appoints these specialists or managers who assume the managerial functions that are not routinely passed around. In a large organization the officers of the organization may serve as the managers, making decisions for the group, leading it, and governing it. An entrepreneurial group is established to achieve some end, and it then hires or otherwise gets others to work towards that end. The leaders of this group are the original organizers or their successors, and the others who belong to or join it work in or through an organization which is not of their choosing or creation, but one with which, for a variety of reasons, they affiliate.

The First-Nighters group might be any one of these three kinds. It might be a cooperative formed by a group of people who are interested in going to the first showing of each production of a season, who form a group with stated purposes and who elect or choose one of their number on a rotating basis to perform the tasks necessary to the group's operation, such as buying the tickets. The members may all decide whether new members may join, under what conditions, and what the maximum number will be. When the group gets large enough, the members may draw up a certain set of bylaws or a constitution. If they turn the running of the organization over either to some member or to a professional administrator who will handle all the details, they become a managerial group. If the theater manager had originated the idea of forming the First-Nighters as a way of assuring the sale of a certain number of seats, the group would be an entrepreneurial group. The theater manager would then handle the organization and try to recruit members to sign up and pay for the season's tickets in advance. In return the members would not only get to see the performances but would also have other specified privileges; they would at least have the benefit of associating with others of like interests. The members would have no say in the rules and would either join on the basis of the existing rules or would not join at all.

Authority in the three different types of groups or organizations operates differently. In the cooperative group, authority comes from all of the members of the group. What is done is the joint will of the group, since the members are members in order to achieve a certain end. Who has authority in such a group, and is it necessary? No one within the group may have imperative authority, but someone must have performatory authority, if a member is to act for other members in some capacity or other. The members of the theatergoers groups might decide that they will all go to the box office, they will all discuss the various possible seats available, and together they will all decide which seats to buy. Empowering or authorizing one person to make the purchase, however, would save the others time and energy, the same end result would be achieved more efficiently, and the time saved could be used advantageously to do other things. Eventually an elected treasurer could routinely purchase the tickets and collect the money for them; and the task might pass from member to member in turn after a certain period of time. The group might adopt rules. For instance, the group might decide that only unanimous decisions would be acted upon, thus ensuring that each person does only what he wants to do and that any action done by the group reflects the wishes of each one in the group. Operative authority would then simply allow one of them to do for the rest what each wants done. If unanimity is impossible or very difficult to obtain, the members of the group may decide that they will get to see fewer plays if unanimity is required. Since their aim is to see plays, they will get more enjoyment out of seeing a large number, even if now and then the procedure results in someone's seeing a play that he is not particularly interested in. They might decide, therefore, that only a two-thirds majority is necessary for a decision to carry, or perhaps even a simple majority, if they are convinced that this will assure more total enjoyment than would otherwise be the case. The members of the group subject themselves to the rules that they adopt. The rules embody the operative authority of the group, to which they are all subject. If someone finds himself too frequently in the minority position, he might ultimately decide to leave the group, since it would no longer fulfill the ends for which he joined in the first place. Constituting or granting operative authority in these instances requires little justification. For if people are free to act as they choose within social limits, they are free to act jointly or to have others act for them within similar limits. Operative performatory authority is justifiable to the extent that it is not coerced, that it does not violate the rights of others, and that it helps a person to achieve his legitimate ends.

A similar example can provide a rationale for operative imperative authority as well. Suppose that the group we are considering is no longer the First-Nighters group, but is the Little Theater group, which is composed of acting students who are making some money while learning and building up a background of experience. They all need a theater company to achieve their ends, so they form a cooperative one. They agree on how it should be run, how they will divide, distribute, and rotate the various chores from selling tickets to sweeping up, as well as how they will rotate the parts and pick the plays. Each of them in turn takes the part of the director for a given production. They decide on this course because they know that many interpretations of a play are possible, that only one interpretation can be staged at a time, and that they cannot continually argue about each detail. They agree that the director will have the final word. They agree that for efficiency and unity of effect, the director will have the authority to tell all the members of the group to do things a certain way, and they will follow his directions in playing their various parts or in designing sets. They accept the operative imperative authority of the director because someone must do that job if they are to achieve the final end that they all desire—namely, an effective unified production. One of them may be a particularly good director, and he may be constantly chosen to do the directing because of his talent in that area. The members of the group obey his orders because that is the best way to achieve the ends that those who subject themselves to his authority desire. The association is a free one, and therefore any member may leave it whenever he so desires. If he does, however, he may not be able to achieve the end that he can achieve only within a group, and he may be unable to assemble another group on his own. He must weigh what he gains from the group against the price he pays in doing what he might otherwise choose not to do.

The basic rationale that I have developed so far for granting either performatory or imperative operative authority to another person or group is that Y can thereby achieve what Y wants more efficiently and perhaps more easily than would otherwise be possible. Y transfers his will to X in the sense that Y lets X represent Y in certain actions and for certain reasons. Y subordinates his will and wishes to the will and wishes of others, at certain times and in certain ways, so that Y may achieve what Y wills and wishes in other and perhaps more important ways than would otherwise be the case.

The source of whatever operative authority exists in such groups derives from the members of the group who give the bearer of authority the right to act for them or to command them in appropriate ways. The authority that they give is always limited. It is limited in what they authorize the person to do for them, the area in which he is authorized to give commands, and the general nature of those commands. Those who are subject to authority may render the authority nonapplicable by leaving the group. Or if enough of those who are subject to it are dissatisfied with the way in which the authority is being used, they may take joint action to rescind it, change it, or limit it, and they could have made provision for such action before the need for it arose. In addition to the limits imposed by morality and possibly also by law, those who give the authority in the first place can determine its limits, because it is their organization, established to achieve their ends. They submit to authority because it helps them to achieve the ends they desire, either by making possible what would not otherwise be possible or by making it easier in some way to achieve their ends. All those who are involved act as free agents. They freely form or join the organization; they freely agree to accept someone in authority who acts for them or commands them in relevant ways. They are free to withdraw and possibly also to rescind the authority that they have previously given (thereby maintaining the group as the ultimate authority, although certain aspects of that authority are delegated to certain individuals). Those who exercise authority assume the burdens willingly. Under these conditions there can be no valid objection to the exercise of such authority.

Managerial groups or organizations are similar, although they may be more bureaucratized and therefore in some ways may be harder to change. The authority that is exercised comes from the members, who retain ultimate control. They empower certain persons to assume certain tasks in their name, which involves representing them, making certain decisions, or committing the group in certain ways. It is possible to make such authorities accountable to the membership. A constitution or a set of rules governing the organization may be adopted, with continuance not being dependent on the present members. Those who join after the initial organization has been established do not, of course, have as much say in setting up the society as did the original members. Even if there are provisions for amendment, such provisions do not usually allow changes at the request or desire of any individual member. A member who dislikes any of the provisions in the rules of the association must decide whether the advantages gained by joining and continuing to be a member are worth the cost of accepting what he dislikes. He may remain and work for change from within. Once a member, he would have as much right to initiate a movement for change as any founding member. The authority of the leaders, officers, or managers continues to come from the actual members, mediated through the rules, bylaws, or constitution. The leaders or managers may be less in touch or be less concerned than they should be about the desires of the members whom they represent. Conflicts may arise, and disputes may result. Authority may be abused. Yet the general argument in support of authority in a managerial group is similar to that in the cooperative group: namely, the free consent of those who are subject to authority. The danger of abuse increases as bureaucracy increases and as those in authority become less interested in or less responsive to the desires of the members.

To make the leadership more responsive, members may insist that more issues be brought to debate and vote by the members; they may attempt to break up the bureaucracy and increase the participation of the members; and they may move towards a more cooperative type of group with more participation by the members. Much depends on the interest and time of the members, the facility of communication, the propensity towards bureaucratization and abuse of authority, and the accountability of the managers to the members. In the cooperative and managerial groups that I have been describing, membership is voluntary, and the purpose of the groups is benefit to the members. The authority of any X within the group comes from the members, possibly mediated through rules or bylaws.

If the justification for accepting and submitting to organizational authority in the cooperative and managerial type of organization is the good of the members, then clearly the members should no longer submit when their good is not served by continued membership. If the organization is a free one, as I have assumed, the members are free to leave it. If many members are unhappy, they are free to change it. A manager or officer who exceeds the authority given to him or uses it for his own advantage violates the limits of his justifiable authority. Members may lose control of their own organization. They may find themselves alienated in their own group. They may not want to leave the organization because they feel it is theirs and that it does not belong to those who have taken it over. Whether authority has been abused in such cases is a matter for detailed investigation of the facts, not for a priori judgment.

Freely formed groups can become less-free groups. Some groups may be freely formed but may be difficult or impossible to leave. Some groups may be selective in their memberships. Some groups may be nominally free, but because membership in the group carries with it social benefits, membership may become a necessity for anyone who has social goals. The degree of freedom of the group— the freedom of entry, of exit, of participation in all its activities, the possibility of social and other advancement without being a member—is a clear factor in evaluating the legitimacy of the authority that is exercised within the group. If the group is free in a strong sense, then acceptance of and submission to executive authority can be justified within certain limits.

The entrepreneurial type of association is basically different from the cooperative or managerial type. It is started, not by the members, but by those who will exercise authority in the association and who then will recruit or assemble others into the organization or group in order to achieve some end. The end of those who are recruited may be different from the end of those who are in authority, even if their activities merge. We can distinguish two subordinate kinds of entrepreneurial associations: the service type and the production type. The first is exemplified by the First-Nighters when organized by the theater manager. He specifies the conditions of membership and its advantages. By attracting members to the group, he guarantees himself a certain number of sales. Theatergoers are free to join or not, but members join on his terms. The members get tickets to the productions, perhaps at reduced rates, gain the companionship of others who have similar interests, and whatever else the club offers. They have no say in how the club operates, though they may make suggestions. They have no authority to make changes, but they are free to leave the group. The authority to effect change rests with the organizer. Though the members give him no authority to command them, he may make hypothetical demands. If they wish him to do certain things (e.g., provide them with tickets), they must do certain other things (e.g., pay a certain fee or apply by a certain date). In general, the limits on his authority come from general moral demands: he must fulfill his promises and meet his obligations, he must not make false representations, and he must be honest in his dealings. The limits come also from any legal restraints that may apply to such groups and organizations and from the willingness of the members to agree to the conditions he sets. He has the authority to set unreasonable conditions; but if membership is truly voluntary, it is unlikely anyone would then find it advantageous to become a member.

If the association is free, then the members are not required to join, and they may leave it whenever they wish. Once the organizer has established the association, he may make certain commitments to members that preclude his abolishing the organization without due notice and without making appropriate arrangements with the members. If the organization is not free—that is, if the members in some way need what is provided or if some real need forces them to become members—then the situation is different. If only members of the electrical association could receive electricity or if only members of the telephone association could get a telephone, membership might be nominally free, but given the conditions of modern life, it would be a necessity. Membership would be forced or coerced by one's dependence on electricity or on telephone service. These conditions would make the operative authority of the manager different from the type I am considering here. The applicable principles would also be different. The region between these two kinds of groups may sometimes be cloudy, and members should be wary in cases in which membership is forced because of lack of options and because of need for the service. In an organization that is not truly free, the members have little control over authority because of the organization's structure. The bearer of authority will be greatly tempted to use his authority for his own good at the expense of those who are subject to his authority. He may use his authority responsibly. But if he does not, others may be asked to exercise the control that the members cannot exercise. Such control may be effected through other channels of authority: for example, through legal or state channels.

The production type of entrepreneurial association is also one in which the organizer establishes an organization that he controls for his benefit to achieve his ends. To do this he needs help. The obvious case is the businessman or entrepreneur. He starts up a business or corporation, and he hires other people to help him produce certain goods. His goal may be a high return on the money that he has invested. He hires people who are not interested in his end but who want to earn money to support themselves and their families. They may or may not be interested in producing the particular product they help make, just as the owner may or may not be interested in producing it, except insofar as it is a means to the end of making a profit. The authority of the manager and owner is in this case similar to the authority of the initiator of the service association. He sets up the rules of operation, he determines what is to be done and how, and he then attempts to get the cooperation of others by offering them something in return—for example, wages. As in the service organization, the workers in such a situation are (in theory and sometimes in practice) free to join or not, and they are free at any time to leave. The organizer has no obligation initially to set up the organization, though he may have to meet certain obligations before he can morally terminate it. As in the previous analysis, the organizer retains authority in the organization. However, his authority is not primarily performatory but is imperative. He pays those who work for him to perform certain specified tasks. He therefore pays them to do what he says. Limits to his authority are set by agreement, as well as by morality and possibly by law.

This is a description of a laissez-faire situation in which the owners make the conditions. The workers have no authority, and they agree to give up certain amounts of their autonomy in exchange for wages. In a free organization the owner exercises authority in virtue of his having set up the rules of operation. Those who serve under him accept the rules in return for certain compensation. The owner has authority over the workers, who give it to him in return for wages. They have no authority over the way in which things are done or over the rules; they have no authority to alter the rules or to effect changes in the operation of what is produced or of how it is produced. For such authority to be legitimate, the participation of all those who are concerned must be truly free. If those who work are not forced by their condition or status or by the economic system to work on terms that the employer sets, if they freely accept the terms, and if, when they find the terms unacceptable, they can realistically resign, then their submission to the executive authority of an employer can be legitimate. Whether such a situation actually exists for the vast majority of workers in any economic system, and in particular in a laissez-faire system, is doubtful. Whether it exists in any given society is a matter for investigation. The present point is simply that there is a theoretical defense for the use of and submission to executive authority of an entrepreneurial type, provided that all parties are truly free. Morality and justice, in particular, place limits on such imperative authority in organizations. But within these limits, such authority can in principle be legitimate. The good of those who are subject to authority can be achieved through acceptance of such authority, and for this reason they accept it. The good of the bearer of authority may also be served, but not at the expense of those who are subject to such authority. In the economic realm, to gain a good at the expense of the worker is to fail to give the worker what is due to him.

POLITICO-LEGAL AUTHORITY

Politico-legal authority is exercised by a state or a government, and it is exercised preeminently by the leaders of a state. It is exercised as well by all who work in or for governmental and official state agencies and by those who are legally authorized to perform certain official functions. Such authority stretches into almost all areas of public and less-public life; it enters our lives in innumerable ways. Politico-legal authority is varied and broad in scope. It reinforces and adds legal weight to some other types of authority. It also limits some other types and arbitrates conflicts between or among some of them.

Politico-legal authority differs from parental and operative authority in significant ways. Some of its distinctive aspects cause the most difficulty from the point of view of justification. Children are born into families and are subject to parental authority. But since parental authority is based on the need of the children and the competence of parents, it is temporary. Children eventually mature, and parental authority gradually diminishes and disappears. Children are also born into civil society and, as such, are subject to the politico-legal authority of the state in which they find themselves. Such authority, however, is not temporary but is permanent. Although one might escape a form of it by emigration, one is forced to submit to another form wherever one goes. We are free to join or not to join other groups or associations, and we can choose the operative authority to which we will be subject. But people are subject to politico-legal authority whether they wish to be or not. Since we have no effective choice with respect to politico-legal authority, can it be justified? If so, it must be a different kind of justification from that which is available in defense of parental or operative authority.

A second unique aspect of politico-legal authority is that it carries with it a claim to a monopoly of force within the area and over the people who are subject to it. It controls the coercive apparatus available within the society and can use it not only against the enemies of the society but also against members of the society. Its coercion must be limited if it is to be justifiable. But is it justifiable for any group of people to have exclusive control of the force in a society, and if they do have this control, how are the wielders of that force themselves to be policed? Politico-legal authority is enforced in a way that no other authority is enforced. And since those who are subject to it have not necessarily placed themselves willingly under such authority, the use of coercive force against them needs justification.

A third distinctive attribute of politico-legal authority is that it claims to be ultimate or supreme within the territory and over those who are subject to it. In the claim of nations to sovereignty, each nation claims to be the ultimate authority within its domain and acknowledges none higher. Whether any authority is by right supreme is at least a matter for discussion and debate, rather than an issue to be settled by definition or fiat. Yet when that claim is coupled with a monopoly of force within a society, the issue is most often settled by fiat.

Finally, although other forms of authority are restricted to a particular sphere, politico-legal authority appears to be all-pervasive.

It enters our lives from the moment of birth; it infuses all the important aspects of life from education to marriage, to family rearing, to business activities; it commits us to paying taxes and fighting wars; and it decides what constitutes death. Yet it is wielded by human individuals. By what right does any person or any group bear such coercively enforced authority over other competent, mature adults?

None of the answers that have been given to this question has satisfied everyone. Exactly what requires justification depends in part on how one conceives of the state and of politico-legal structures and frameworks. Different societies and the same society in different historical periods have viewed the authority of the state in different ways. The justification that has been offered in defense of politico-legal authority has varied accordingly. The complex arguments in its defense will be discussed in a separate chapter. Here we can note that a justification of the state in general is but the first step; the particular type or types of government must also be justified. Within such structures it is often necessary to justify individual laws as well as individual acts done by those with politico-legal authority.

Whatever the legitimacy of politico-legal authority, however, some forms of parental and of operative authority are legitimate. Their justification is primarily in terms of the good of the subject, and such authority is always limited. Both kinds of authority must be kept from becoming authoritarian. These conclusions are sufficient both to show that those who deny the legitimacy of all executive authority are mistaken and to serve as guides to our discussion of politico-legal authority.

5

Sources, Symbols, and Systems of Authority

Authority is frequently accepted for reasons other than those that justify acceptance; it is often clothed in trappings that have little to do with the rationale for authority; and it is commonly experienced as part of a larger system. The sources, symbols, and systems of authority flesh out the rationalistic model of authority that we have developed thus far.

SOURCES OF AUTHORITY

What is the source of authority? Where does it come from? Religious traditon gives the clearest and simplest answer: all authority comes from God. God is the source of all authority, the maker and master of all that there is, the author of the world and of its laws, both physical and moral. Since God rightly rules over all and since he works through human agents, the authority that these agents receive from God is delegated authority. God may delegate it for the benefit of those who exercise the authority, for the benefit of those over whom it is exercised, or for the benefit of all together. The authority of parents, of priests and kings, of teachers, and of executives comes from God. Each plays a role in the divine scheme of things, and God's delegation of authority justifies the exercise of authority that is thus received.

As a statement of the ultimate source of authority, this view may still hold some force for the believer. But even for him it is difficult to know who rightfully has authority from God and what the limits of that authority are. It is possible simply to believe that whoever is in a position of authority, or whoever is a de facto authority, receives that authority from God. Yet difficulties still arise in disputes over who is to hold a position and in decisions about which positions are to be created or eliminated. Holding that God is the ultimate source of authority, moreoever, does not preclude more proximate sources of authority. Nor does it render null any questions of legitimacy.

A second historically important claimed source of authority is nature. This view holds that nature gives parents authority over their children and that some people are born to be leaders and are endowed with the qualities that make them natural leaders in various fields. Those who recognize these qualities give positions of authority to those who have the qualities. But the source of authority is the qualities themselves, not the recognition of them. The ancients, including Plato and Aristotle, in believing that some men were born to be slaves and others to be masters, implicitly held that nature was the ultimate source of authority.

The view is at least partially correct. In the natural course of development, parents are both executive and nonexecutive authorities for their children. In this sense, nature is a source of parental authority. The knowledge, virtue, or ability of people often appropriately makes them de facto epistemic or exemplary authorities for others. But the relation of natural qualities to executive authority is tenuous at best. The less talented are frequently in positions of command over the more talented; the less virtuous, over the more virtuous; the less wise, over the more wise. Natural talents provide a basis for conferring authority on individuals, but the authority in most cases does not come from nature and is not simply a recognition of authority they have because of their qualities.

A third view holds that tradition is the source of authority. According to the defenders of this position, authority is accepted and considered legitimate because it has always been accepted. In a hereditary monarchy the king has authority, not because of special gifts, but because of special birth, reinforced by tradition. A society that reveres age and gives its elders authority puts tradition first. Yet as a final source of authority, tradition is not adequate. For sooner or later the question of where the long-accepted authority came from in the first place must logically be answered.

A fourth, a modern and democratic, view holds sway today in most Western societies. The movement towards recognizing the basic equality of all human beings challenged the view that authority came only from God, from nature, or from tradition. Authority is a social relation among human beings, and its source is ultimately human.

This view holds that no individual has the right to command another or to dominate another except insofar as he is given that right by the other. Doctrines of consent and contract have emerged from this view, together with an emphasis on the individual, his freedom, and his autonomy. Authority, in all of its variations, is seen as ultimately being a function of society and, at least in that sense, conventional. Since the authority present in different societies and the ways in which it is constituted, conferred, passed on, or legitimated vary greatly, there is no one natural way for authority to be constituted.

Democratic countries accept the view that human beings are the source of politico-legal authority. I argued earlier that human recognition could fruitfully define de facto authority of both the executive and the nonexecutive varieties. That model accommodates man as the source of legitimate and illegitimate, de facto and de jure, authority of all kinds. The views that held God, nature, or tradition to be the source of authority contained within them the quality of legitimacy. The view that man is the source of authority does not include this characteristic. To say that man is the source of authority states both that someone is constituted as an authority by receiving authority from others and that man can decide under what conditions authority is legitimate. The appropriate groups decide what is legitimate, though the quality of their decisions will depend on their knowledge, experience, moral sensitivity, and the like.

Inequalities of mind, body, talents, and drive give rise to authority, together with the needs of all individuals and the necessity of common action to achieve certain ends. Without denying that man is the source of authority, we can seek the reasons, justification, and explanation for why an individual or a group makes someone an authority and for institutionalized forms of granting and accepting authority. We have already seen that the benefit to the subject of authority provides a justification for some forms of authority. In this sense the need of individuals for help, guidance, and direction can be considered as a source of authority. This locates the source not simply in man but also in those specific human characteristics or qualities that lead to authority. The knowledge and competence of one person and the need and lack of knowledge of another provide a rational basis for a person's accepting as an authority someone who has greater knowledge and competence. But people do not always grant authority, and they probably rarely submit to it only for rational reasons. The psychological reasons for accepting authority are equally important and yield correlative psychological sources of authority.

Fear can be both a reason for accepting authority and a source of authority. Hobbes bases his justification for authority on fear at each stage of society's development. In the state of nature, life is nasty, brutish, and short. Fear impels men to form a society and to submit to a sovereign, whom they all fear sufficiently so that they obey the laws that he sets to govern their action. In return he protects them from conquest by foreign peoples. In this sense fear is a source of political authority. According to Hobbes, though we accept the sovereign and obey his laws through fear, we achieve more of what we want by doing so than we could if we were to remain in the state of nature. Fear is only one of the motivating forces; our desire to fulfill our needs and wants is another, a rationally justifying, reason. Fear may be both a motive and a reason for accepting illegitimate as well as legitimate authority. It may provide the reason a person has for accepting authority when forced; but by itself, it is not legitimating.

Need is a source of authority; it can provide both justification of authority and a motive for accepting it. People rely on epistemic authorities because they do not have the time, energy, opportunity, or competence to develop or discover for themselves the knowledge that they need and want. People rely on the competence of others for the goods and services that they need but cannot produce for themselves. Because of the need to act in concert with others in order to achieve certain ends, they submit to the coordinating direction or orders of an authority. Unequal natural endowments, unequal achievements, and the division of labor can all be called sources of authority. The weak feel the need to rely on and to submit their wills to authority for protection against the strong. Need serves both as a source for the development of structures of authority and as a psychological reason for accepting authority.

Habit also motivates the acceptance of authority. We are taught to live with the authority structures of the societies into which we are born. By habit we unquestioningly accept them, unless something upsets the established order or circumstances force us to reexamine what we accept. Inertia inclines us not to change things unless they become intolerable. We have neither the time nor the energy to question everything. The acceptance of established authority frees us to be creative in other areas. Habit does not justify accepting authority, for we can ask why the habit was established in the first place; but habit is a reason why many people automatically and without question do accept many kinds of authority.

The herd instinct is another reason why many people accept authority. If a group accepts X as an authority or if it submits to X, there is a strong tendency for each member of the group to do likewise. The acceptance of X by each person is reinforced by the acceptance by the others. The strength of each person's individual acceptance might be tested by the vocal appearance of dissidents within the group. By revealing to others in the group a lack of unanimous acceptance, the dissidents weaken the reinforcement of the group for each individual. If the herd instinct provides the major reason for accepting X, dissidents can trigger a reaction against X. But if those who accept X have reasons other than the herd instinct for submitting to X, they are likely to react against the dissidents. The herd instinct, by itself, provides no valid ground for accepting authority; but it provides an impetus for accepting as adequate those grounds that are accepted by others.

The psychological states of fear, felt need, habit, and the herd instinct provide motives for the de facto acceptance of authority. In this sense they may be considered sources of authority. Strictly speaking, however, human beings remain the source of authority. Psychological factors can explain the acceptance of authority, but they do not provide an adequate basis for justifying authority.

THE AUTHORITY OF POSITION

Although people bear authority and although people are authorities, people do not always receive authority directly. Authority is often first objectified and structured. It is attached to positions and is assumed successively by those who occupy the positions. The authority of a position or an office is not always the same as the authority of the person who occupies that position or office. One person who is invested with the authority of a position may exercise more or less authority than the next person who occupies the same position, even though no change in the authority officially attached to the position has taken place. At the time of the Watergate hearings, President Nixon was said to have lost his authority before he resigned from his office. As president, he still had all the powers entrusted to him by the Constitution, but he had obviously lost some other authority.

We can distinguish personal authority from the authority of a position. Some people are given positions of executive authority because of their knowledge, experience, or skill. In most instances those who are given positions of authority need certain personal qualities or qualifications in order to carry out the functions of the office effectively. When they fail to demonstrate those qualities, they rightfully lose the respect of those who are subject to them, even if they retain the formal authority of the position. The person must be appropriate to the position if others are willingly to accept his right to exercise the authority of the position that he occupies.

If it is reasonable to expect competence from someone who holds a position of authority, then it is reasonable to be uneasy and reluctant to obey someone who is incompetent. His position may oblige those who are subject to him to obey and to be bound by his decisions. But such a person certainly cannot be very effective in the exercise of his authority. We have seen this in the case of nonexecutive authority. The more an authority on molecular biology makes erroneous statements, the less he is believed. If he holds a teaching position in a university, he may retain the authority of the position while his students regard him as less and less of an authority in his field the more they learn of his errors. The executive authority of his position obliges his students to do the course work he assigns, but they are never bound to believe what he says. And if his epistemic authority is weakened, the students' faith in his ability to guide them through assignments in the subject may well also be undermined.

We expect positions of executive authority to be filled on the basis of competence. The required competence varies with the position: it can be knowledge of a certain kind, the ability to make certain kinds of decisions, or the ability to work with others or to get them to work together. Frequently, moral qualities are needed as well: trustworthiness, honesty, fairness, truthfulness, candor; sometimes courage, selflessness, self-control, or self-restraint. When those who occupy positions of government and public trust fail to exemplify the virtues expected of them, they lose support for their policies. They are no longer able to lead the people in the direction in which they believe the people should go. In these instances, such persons lose their moral authority, since this authority is based on their personal moral qualities. Some persons lose this authority when they fail to exhibit the qualities directly expected in their position—for example, truthfulness; sometimes moral failures in their personal lives can indicate their general moral fiber and therefore can undermine their moral authority in their official capacity. This happens frequently in cases of sexual scandals. Governments as well as individuals can lose their moral authority; some never have such authority to lose. Difficulties arise when those who should have certain qualities to fill a position turn out not to have them. Those who are subject to such an authority may see a justification for the position and for their own subordination to an appropriate person in that position, but they may feel no justification for being subject to the particular person in that position. When the position is a public office, a mechanism for removal or recall helps remedy the situation if the feeling is widespread. A competent but ineffective person, who holds a position only for a term, may be allowed to finish the term and then be replaced at the polls. This both provides greater stability and prevents constant short-term changes. Some governments call for new elections to test the confidence of the people after some crisis.

Armies sometimes use an inspector general to ferret out incompetent officers; some businesses use ombudsmen. In all of these cases, one can distinguish the justification for a particular office from the justification for a particular person's filling that office.

When incompetents fill high positions of leadership, circumstances sometimes tempt the competent persons to go outside the organized framework of authority and to lead those who are willing to follow him in overturning and reestablishing the authority structure. On a large scale this becomes a revolution. The leaders of a revolution may have no de jure authority within the structure. They are given authority by their followers because of their ideals and goals, their personal qualities, their magnetism, their intensity, their self-confidence and self-righteousness, their willingness to act and to lead. This may be Max Weber's authority of charisma, which is rarely de jure. Sometimes the goal of a revolution or a coup may be, not the overthrow of a system, but the replacement within the system of a tyrant or an incompetent ruler. As always, people endow the leaders with authority. In this case they do it directly rather than through established channels.

Justification of authority in an institutional setting involves two levels: both the office and the person who holds that office should be justified. Failure at the second level may indicate weaknesses at the first level and, in serious cases, may lead to disruption or overthrow of the system.

The gap between the position of authority and the person who occupies it is a positional gap. Another gap between authority and its justification can be called the justificatory gap. Justification for authority is always contingent in one way or another. We can specify rational conditions for believing someone's utterances, or conditions for obeying someone's commands. But there is always a gap between the conditions as outlined and specified and the particular instances of those conditions. In epistemic authority, the justification is given, for example, in terms of an induction on past verifications or on the basis of the creditability of past certifications. There is a necessary element of trust and faith ingredient in accepting someone as an epistemic authority. This is true in other cases of nonexecutive authority as well.

Executive authority also involves trust and faith on the part of the subjects of authority. There is no guarantee that submission to authority will help one to achieve more of what one wants than otherwise. Trust and faith do not preclude the fact that the bearer of authority may abuse it. He may use the power that accompanies his authority in unauthorized ways. Safeguards can be built into the assigning of authority, but some risk always remains, and some trust and faith is always required. For this reason, personal qualities are relevant in some instances of assigning authority. If those in authority lose the confidence of those who are subject to them, they become ineffective, or they may take recourse in force. If the bearer of executive authority can get people to act in the way he wishes, his authority is more effective the less he needs force or the threat of force. A leader cannot lead those who do not trust or believe in him; because of the power and force attached to his office, he can at best push them in the direction that he desires.

SIGNS AND SYMBOLS OF AUTHORITY

Because of the gap between the position and the person who is filling it, certain positions carry with them indications that the person has the authority of the office. The clearest instance of this is uniforms and insignia of rank in the armed forces. Members of royalty are distinguishable by their crowns, scepters, and clothing.

On the level of personal authority, children learn easily enough who their parents are; the charismatic figure is recognized by those who follow him. But in a great many instances, identifying someone as an authority is a problem. Society therefore identifies authorities in various ways. In the realm of knowledge, the conferring of a degree is certification that the named person has done a certain amount of academic work of a certain quality and presumably has the knowledge to which the prescribed work leads. When such knowledge and the discipline implied are necessary for effectively filling some position of authority, the certification serves to identify the appropriate people. Individual testing also measures the attainment of the appropriate knowledge for a position. We have seen that those who have knowledge in an area can appropriately certify others. Someone may be identified as an authority in a field on the basis of published works and peer review, as well as the awards and honors received. These imply some trust and reliance on the certification of others, on their ability to discriminate. In some instances such trust may not be well placed; but at least in many cases it is.

A teacher presumably has been screened for knowledge of the subject that he is to teach. Students trust the administrators to have chosen capable teachers who can be believed. Students are usually disposed towards such belief, even though that belief cannot be demanded.

In the moral realm, societies, groups, or religions have identified various models as being particularly worthy of emulation. The Christian saints, folk heroes, Christ, Buddha, Gandhi, Martin Luther King are all presented as role models. Society passes on to the young and to later generations the stories of their virtuous lives. The identification may be informal or formal, as in the elaborate Catholic rite of canonization.

Where private enterprise is allowed, people may informally identify themselves as experts by setting themselves up in business and by advertising their expertise. Lawyers, doctors, watchmakers, and plumbers can identify themselves through their shops, ads, or the yellow pages of the telephone book. The fact that someone has been in a business for a length of time is some indication of his ability and provides some reason to accept what he says or to entrust oneself or one's property to him. Word of mouth and the advice of friends also attest to the expertise of such people. Professional associations make known the names of people in good standing in their profession.

Positional authority may be indicated by a variety of means. Private corporations or governmental agencies may distribute tables of organization, listing the names of those who are in positions of authority. These people may have their names and positions on the door to their office, on a name plate, or on a business card. Only those in the organization or those who have dealings with the organization may know the positions and the authority they have, but individuals may carry their organizational prestige into their private lives. Those who represent or act for a constituency must be known to hold that position by that constituency.

Persons who carry on designated functions for the public and who must be identifiable by the public frequently wear distinctive uniforms or carry appropriate identification. Police are distinguishable by their uniforms and are known to carry certain kinds of authority. Within the police and the armed services, insignia and distinctive uniforms mark off different ranks. Those within the organization know what authority a specific rank carries, independently of particular assignments and special authority. If all officers had charisma, they might be distinguished from enlisted men without designations of rank. Since this is not the case, the designations are necessary. An insignia, except when used by unauthorized persons, indicates who is subordinate to whom within the organization.

Signs of authority do not only identify those in authority; they frequently help to bridge the gap between the office and the person. The king's magnificent clothes set him off physically as someone special. The crown and jewels indicate his special position and command respect, even if he personally, without his clothes, would not. A judge's robes add dignity to the court and mark him as special in the context. The symbols of authority come to be associated with positions of authority, and they make it easier psychologically for those who are in subordinate positions to accept the authority of whoever holds the position. The symbols of authority are tangible and physically present in a way that the office is not. The symbols do not indefinitely cover up incompetence; but they predispose many persons to accept the authority of the symbol bearers. The symbols develop a history and a tradition and bring to an office the importance that they symbolize. Investiture brings, in a visible manner to the particular holder of such a position, that authority with all its history.

The United States broke away from rule by a king and did away with many of the old symbols of authority. The president of the United States has no crown or scepter. Uniforms are not as prevalent in the United States as they are in some countries. Informally, different jobs and positions have different kinds of dress appropriate to them but do not constitute uniforms. A corporate executive, for instance, would not usually wear overalls to work, nor would a carpenter wear a suit and tie. The distinction between white-collar and blue-collar workers generalizes modes of dress as indications of certain types of positions.

Along with visual symbols of authority go verbal ones. Forms of address and titles not only identify persons as authorities; they also serve to place some distance between those who have the titles and those who do not. The use of a title such as "Doctor," or "Professor," or "Your Highness" may be a sign of respect, but may also be a means of bolstering one's authority. It may, of course, not be demanded by a given individual, but it may nonetheless be the expected form of address in certain contexts. It serves the same purpose whether it is demanded by an individual or is demanded by custom.

The language of epistemic authorities, even when obfuscating, sometimes gains them increased respect; and the language of executive authorities, when peremptory, decisive, and insistent, frequently wins them recognition, compliance, respect, and obedience. Language can be used in many ways to fill the gap between position and person, and it can yield significant differences in the effectiveness of one's authority. It can make one a de facto authority regardless of whether such an authority is either de jure or legitimate. Frequently language is both a symbol of authority and the most effective way by which it is maintained. Mastery of a vocabulary in an area of knowledge sets one apart as a member of an inner circle and confers authority on those who are capable of using the vocabulary with ease. Doctors, lawyers, and scientists all bear this out. The fluent language user has an advantage over the less-fluent speaker in many situations. The former's use of language is a symbol of expertise, education, or knowledge; and his linguistic dominance serves as the basis for his getting and keeping authority.

The gap between the office and the person is not logically bridged by uniforms, signs, or symbols of authority, since these make no logical difference to the competence of the person in the position. Their importance is psychological, but symbols alone cannot ease the positional and the justificatory gaps indefinitely in the face of overriding counterevidence.

Symbols of authority are also able to marshal allegiance to authority on a national scale. If a people have fought and sacrificed for their nation, they are attached to it and tend to defend their government and justify it. For if they do not, their sacrifice will have been wasted and will have lost its meaning. A flag that is displayed at the side of a country's president helps bring to him the acceptance that people bring to the government and to the nation.

The justificatory gap has to be bridged by trust and faith. Tradition and symbols help people to make the leap. The ideology of a system tries to combine the justificatory elements into a whole. But ideology always goes beyond what consitutes knowledge for any age or any system for which it plays a justificatory role. It combines goals, values, history, hopes, and anticipations. It is not self-critical, it cannot stand the rigors of close analysis, and it requires trust. Yet the leap of trust and faith that is necessary for the acceptance of any authority need not be irrational, though it depends at best on an inductive base. It may embody an ideal towards which those who are involved in the system wish to progress. Authority frequently involves action whose motivation goes beyond rational argument, for we are not only rational but also sentient, emotional beings. Executive authority enables groups to take action in the face of uncertainty, inadequate knowledge, or the lack of desired answers and assurances. To act under these conditions involves a certain amount of faith and trust. To allow others to decide for one involves a double amount of trust. The symbols of authority psychologically reassure us that we have placed our faith in competent people. These visible signs help people accept authority and make it effective.

In many areas of the world the growth of knowledge has undermined political authority rather than bolstered it. In a simpler age the leaders of a country were thought to know as much as was relevant in order to make informed decisions; today the ordinary person knows that no one can master all that should be known. Confidence in leaders is shaken when they make poor decisions that are easily criticized by others with access to the same information. The availability of information to the public makes it more difficult for leaders of a country to claim that because they are privy to information that is not available to their critics, they are in a privileged position to make informed judgments. People suspect the claims of leaders who are unable or unwilling to demonstrate the wisdom of their decisions by producing the privileged information.

Public accountability on the part of public officials tends to reinforce their authority. The more they can show the soundness of their decisions and the benefits that they bring to the governed and to society in general, the more the people will trust them to make other decisions. Incumbents use this tactic frequently in election campaigns.

The symbols of authority help people to bridge the justificatory and positional gaps. The symbols are sometimes obvious, sometimes subtle. They vary according to time, place, culture, and historical period. Their importance in every authority system is often underestimated.

SYSTEMS OF AUTHORITY

There are many systems of authority. Government forms one system, with the legal system being closely linked to it. Each independent corporation establishes its own authority system, as do religions. Some systems are formal and structured; others are informal. Systems of authority raise two major issues which deserve consideration. One concerns how authority is transferred, delegated, and exercised within a system. The other is the nature of the relation of authority systems to each other and to individuals.

First, there have been many detailed studies of authority structures within given institutions, organizations, and governments. My purpose is not to review this literature or to consider any particular organization or government. Rather, it is to consider in general the defensible parameters for the delegation of authority and the conditions that influence effectiveness of executive authority.

Nonexecutive authority cannot be delegated. The personal qualities of an epistemic or an exemplary authority make him an authority for others if they recognize those qualities and react to him appropriately because of those qualities. He cannot delegate his knowledge, virtue, or expertise. He may recommend, endorse, or certify others; but this is not delegation of authority. Such authority must be acquired, if acquired legitimately, on the basis of one's own merits. Delegation of nonexecutive authority is not justifiable, nor does it make much sense.

The delegation of executive authority, on the other hand, is a commonplace and occurs on several levels. I shall start with the political system. In the United States we hold that the government gets its authority from the people. They have the right to act freely and to join together to achieve common ends. Through the Constitution, they confer on the government the right to govern them as prescribed and within the limits set by the Constitution. Government receives its authority from outside the system to the extent that it receives it from the people and that the Constitution is accepted as the basic governing document. In accepting the Constitution the people accept the political system it establishes. The Constitution, then, designates the authority appropriate for various offices and the procedures for filling those offices. The people's delegation of authority to the government is mediated through the Constitution, which specifies the system of public authority. The Constitution spells out the limits of the delegation of authority to the system and within the system. Public officials are not allowed to delegate all of their authority, and only they are authorized to perform certain functions. We use the election process to choose our political representatives. It would violate the process for an elected representative to transfer all of his authority, as well as the rights and duties of the office, to anyone else. If we elect representatives who possess qualities appropriate to the office and who we believe are the best of the available candidates, we do not want someone else to do the job. It would be unreasonable for any officeholder to delegate all of his authority to someone else.

The Constitution spells out some clear limits to the delegation of authority. The president, for instance, has the authority to sign bills into law. He cannot delegate this authority to the vice-president or to a cabinet member. He can, however, authorize someone else to represent him at some official functions. He can delegate areas of authority to his staff so that he can more effectively accomplish what he alone can do. The delegation of authority is justifiable to the extent that it helps the holder of authority to achieve the ends towards which his authority is geared.

Systems vary in their ends, in their structures, and in the extent to which authority can be delegated. Authority can only be delegated within a system within certain limits. To the extent that authority is system dependent, it is authority only within the system. No one can delegate authority he does not have. Hence, no one can delegate authority outside of the system in which it is constituted. Each system sets the limits of legitimate delegation of authority within it. Most systems do not allow the total delegation of authority, because this amounts to the replacement of one person by another. Such replacement, if allowed, is usually distinguished from the delegation of authority.

The delegation of authority involves the delegation of responsiblity for the exercise of that authority. Since all authority is open to abuse, anyone who exercises it should be held responsible for its proper use. Authority to perform certain actions can be delegated totally in the sense that the delegatee has the same right to perform the action as the delegator; but delegated authority can also be revoked. If formally delegated, it must be formally revocable. Within a system, procedures may exist both for delegating and for revoking authority. The responsibility that goes with the delegated authority is delegated responsibility. Just as the authority remains ultimately with the delegator, so does the responsibility. The bearer of authority has the responsiblity to see that delegated authority is exercised appropriately.

Delegated authority can in turn be delegated further, but at each state of delegation, the same limits apply. At each level of delegation, less authority is delegated than is held. At lower levels, people typically have the authority to implement portions of policy that they do not have the authority to change, even if under certain unusual and unforeseen circumstances a modification of policy is reasonable. This is commonplace in dealing with the clerks and functionaries in corporations and governmental agencies. How much authority to delegate and how to maintain control of the actions of others for which one will be held responsible are practical problems. "Delegate enough authority to perform the function required" is a rough rule of thumb, but it does not supply explicit answers in specific cases.

Every case of delegation involves trust that the person to whom authority is delegated will use the authority appropriately. The greater the trust in the competence and integrity of the one to whom authority is delegated, the less supervision is required. Accountability, however, never appropriately disappears. Whoever exercises authority can and should be held accountable for what he does and what he fails to do with respect to the exercise of that authority. He should be accountable both to those who are subject to his authority and to those from whom he receives his authority.

A hierarchical model is implied in the delegation of authority. This distribution makes clear who has authority and responsibility at each level. It is not the only model, however; several models of authority may operate in a single system. Some systems may not clearly assign authority; it may be dispersed diffusely in the system. The United States government is a system of checks and balances in which the judiciary, the executive, and the legislature each has certain authority without any one of them being dominant or the source of authority for the others.

A system in which decisions are made by consensus might not structure authority hierarchically. Authority may also be held jointly or collegially and may be shifted by agreement but without delegation. No one person is always or exclusively in charge. A diffusion of authority tends to carry with it a diffusion of responsiblity and may result in a confusion of roles. A resulting sense of collegiality and a feeling of mutual respect among those within the system may compensate for lack of clear structure or lines of authority. In general, authority may be distributed and delegated in a variety of ways within a system. Specific problems of concomitant responsiblity and control will vary as the authority structures vary.

As authority filters through various levels, loss of effectiveness poses a problem within large systems. Hegel drew our attention to a paradox of authority in his discussion of the master and the slave. The master has authority over the slave and commands him to perform a desired act, which the slave learns how to do. In time the master is in fact dependent on the slave. For the slave knows how to do what the master wants done but cannot do himself.

When we either command or authorize others to act for us, although we have the authority, they perform the task in question. When faced with problems of how things are to be done, they make practical decisions that affect the outcome. Frequently we cannot control, supervise, or specify everything that they should do. Sometimes we do not have the competence to do so; sometimes we do not have the time or the foresight. Trust and accountability are again needed.

The exercise of imperative executive authority is a means by which a person executes his will through those who are subject to him. What he wills may differ considerably from what is actually done. An imperative executive authority depends on having those below him to accomplish an action. The more levels that the command must filter through, the more chance there is for delay, misinterpretation, or disagreement with what is commanded and for subtle changes or modifications.

A law that commands individuals to act in some specific way—for example, to pay income taxes—is likely to be followed more or less as prescribed. Through tax forms and instructions, the order is transmitted directly to the person who is to execute it. A presidential order, on the other hand, may filter down to various levels. It may end up by not being implemented at all or in a way different from what he intended. If the order is interpreted and further restricted at each level of authority, it may easily be distorted, or its implementation may be effectively precluded. The chances of distortion are proportional to the number of levels through which an order must go. The master/slave relation described by Hegel applies to authority within organizations and systems. Executive imperative authority enables the one who has the authority to achieve what he wills only if those below him carry out his will. Authority can be effective only if those below agree with what is commanded, are loyal, or are closely supervised.

The second issue concerning systems is the relation of systems of authority to each other and to individuals. Since authority is always limited to some field, no one person's authority extends rightfully to a person taken in his totality. To the extent that it can be effectively implemented, such subjugation would be slavery. But even slaves cannot be forced to assent to propositions, except nominally. A system that attempts to be entirely comprehensive in the subjugation of people is called totalitarian or totalistic. One might be subject to God in all domains; but even in this case, those religions which allow for free will, sin, or freely given belief limit the extent of God's authority or at least the effective appropriate use of his authority.

In ordinary life individuals take part in a large variety of systems of authority. Some of these are formal structures, such as governments and organizations; some are informal, such as systems of morality. If we speak of morality as a system to which people are subject in a sense analogous to their being subject to a system of positive laws, then morality forms an authority system that enters into all of one's activities and relations. One is authorized to do what is moral, and one is enjoined not to do what is immoral. The authority one claims for his actions in either case is the authority of morality or of the moral law.

If we want to speak of the authority of facts or of knowledge, then we have another pervasive system, since knowledge is part of all systems of authority. No system can make what is true false or what is false true, although some people within some political or religious systems sometimes try to do so.

Religion is a third system that in some cases claims pervasiveness. It affects all of the actions of individuals who adhere to it. The authority of religion might be an instance of the authority of God. Within organized religions, persons may claim to hold authority from God over other believers. Whether the authority of such persons is all-pervasive depends on the religion.

A fourth system that sometimes claims pervasiveness is the politico-legal system. In modern societies laws govern the interactions of people in business, education, social intercourse, marriage, child rearing. Even where government does not enter directly, law covers any dispute, no matter what the field. Although most modern politico-legal systems acknowledge areas of free choice for the members of their societies and areas of personal privacy where the law and the state should not intrude, they do not acknowledge any authority higher than that of the state.

109

In addition to these broad and encompassing systems other systems of authority include operative authority. An individual may have, exercise, or be an authority in one or more of these systems and may be subject to authority in many other systems. Systems of family, government, business, social organizations, and churches overlap, and the same people relate differently to authority in different systems at the same time. Large systems of authority may also include subsystems.

Difficulties obviously arise when there is a clash of authorities or a clash in the demands of different systems on the individual, or when different systems of authority clash over dominance of a field.

Within any field an authority is ultimate if there is none higher in the field. In the realm of politics each government that considers itself ultimate in the political field is said to be sovereign. Authority is absolute if there is none higher than it in any field. Is any authority absolute? Three plausible candidates for absolute authority are political authority, moral authority, and religious authority.

The possible claim of political authority to be absolute cannot at the present time be sustained. For political authority to be absolute, it would have legitimately to reign supreme in any clash of authorities. If spheres or systems of authority can conflict, then an authority is absolute only if by right it should always take precedence in a conflict. Since many sovereign states claim to be ultimate in the political realm within their territory, states can clash with one another. No single political authority can claim authority throughout the world. When two sovereign states clash, they are not bound by right to submit to any other political authority. If they were, they would not be sovereign or have ultimate political power. A world political system to which all individual governments were subordinated by right might plausibly be called the only ultimate political authority. Could it claim to be absolute? Defenders of both moral and religious authority could challenge such a claim.

Moral authority is said to be absolute because any kind of authority that comes up against morality must, from a moral point of view, give way. Whereas political authority might be morally justified, moral authority is not justified politically. It need not be justified at all. To speak of justifying morality is to fail to understand what it is. If what is commanded by any government is immoral, one may have the political obligation to do what is commanded, but one does not have the moral obligation to do so. And if one is faced with contradictory commands from politics and morality, then from a moral point of view, one must follow the dictates of morality. It will not do to counter that from a political point of view, one must follow the dictates of political authority; for if political authority is justified morally, then it is secondary to morality. A just political system respects the moral rights of its citizens and claims no right to demand of them what is immoral. A political system that enforces immoral demands may demonstrate its absolute force, but that is not the same as absolute authority. What is meant by moral commands are precisely those that are overriding in cases of conflict. In the realm of action, therefore, the claim that moral authority is ultimate is a plausible claim, and hence the claim that it is absolute. But if we attempt to translate these claims into practical terms, there are frequently difficulties. Even if the authority of morality is ultimate in the realm of action, we do not know in all cases what morality demands, nor does any individual or set of individuals know this. What are we to do when persons clash in the name of morality? Given the world-wide variety of moral views, the appeal on the part of each view to the authority of morality simply poses a clash of moralities. We have no access to a moral authority to settle the matter. We have only our ability to reason. On an individual level, moral obligation as one sees it takes precedence over legal obligation.

On a national level if the morality of an action is disputed, it is not clear what it means in practical terms to say morality socially takes precedence over legal obligation. If we have a political system that vests ultimate legal authority in a supreme court, then we have an identifiable body that can hand down ultimate judgments in its sphere. When people clash on what morality demands or on the morality of a government's action, one practical solution is to submit to the decision of the court. This does not imply that the court makes actions either moral or immoral by its decision. But in the absence of clear moral criteria, it can pass judgment on the legal status of an action. If an action that was held to be legally permissible is eventually seen to be morally impermissible and to violate the moral rights of persons, the court would have good reason to change its ruling, or the people would have good reason to change the law.

A person wishing to act morally must do what he believes to be moral. He may be mistaken in his belief, in which case he may do what is objectively immoral. But this moral risk does not allow him to do what he believes is immoral, just in case he is mistaken. This constitutes a moral dilemma, but this dilemma is a moral fact of life. Subjectively, a person may hold that morality is the absolute authority governing his action, in the sense that if any other authority commands him to do something that he believes is immoral, he should not do it. From an objective point of view, there is no moral authority that can be practically appealed to in a serious clash of moral views. If a decision must be made, society may hold that the legal authority has the final public word, at least until the issue is clearer.

Abortion is such an issue. If the fetus is a human being with the right to life, it should be defended and protected. Its life should not be given up without serious reason. If abortion is murder, it should not be legal. But the morality of abortion is a disputed issue. Although each individual's view of morality should determine his action, as far as public policy goes, courts and legislatures should properly determine public policy with respect to it. In the practical realm, morality sometimes leads law; law sometimes leads morality.

The other plausible candidate for absolute authority is religion. Historically the claim to the absolute authority of the Church in the Middle Ages pitted popes against emperors. The pope crowned the emperor and made him legitimate. But could the pope depose the king and overrule him because papal authority was absolute? The situation with respect to religious authority is in many ways similar to that of moral authority. It is also different in that some religions have a temporal representative of the deity who holds and wields religious authority.

Religions clash with other religions, and religious authorities clash with political authorities. The conflict of religious authorities cannot be settled by recourse to authority, since that is precisely what is in dispute. Just as each country is sovereign, so each religion can claim sovereignty. If religious authority claims to be absolute, it must do so by following either the model of moral authority or the model of some hypothetical world religious temporal authority.

Sören Kierkegaard's knight of faith holds that he goes beyond the ethical into the religious realm. The leap of faith takes one beyond the rationality and universality of morality into a realm in which one is directly subject to God's commands. If both religion and morality were held to be rational, there would be no clash, though religion might be more comprehensive and therefore on a higher level. A consistent God who determines morality can also surpass it.

In some parts of the world, religion and politics are still intertwined to such an extent that they cannot be easily separated; and unless separated, they cannot clearly clash. In other parts of the world, religion is clearly subordinate to the state, and state orders are taken legitimately to override religious authority. In other countries there is a division between church and state, with different spheres of authority being appropriate to each area; although each may claim superiority, sometimes one wins a conflict, and sometimes the other one does.

Even if we admit that moral authority, religious authority, or political authority is in some abstract sense absolute, there is no clear way of rendering an effective verdict in specific clashes. On the practical level whenever a clash occurs between church and state, some societies decide the church will always dominate, and other societies decide the state will. It is less plausible to say that in a clash between morality and political authority, a morally grounded political authority will always dominate. But it is not implausible to say that for public purposes political authority will decide disputes between proponents of different moral views.

From a personal point of view, one may make morality absolute in any clash of commands, and one may alternatively make religion absolute. The difference between the authority of morality and any one person's or any society's view of morality, however, is one source of difficulty; another source is the difficulty of knowing what God commands when different claims are made.

Each person, if he wishes to be moral, must do what he believes to be moral despite contrary commands from any kind of authority (with the plausible exception of religious beliefs that override moral ones for those who can live with the paradox that the right thing to do, if commanded to do so by God, may be the immoral thing). Any other system of authority may clash with morality. If and when it does, it must, from a moral point of view, take a subsidiary role. This poses serious problems for any individual who may have to suffer political, economic, or social consequences for acting contrary to the authority in some system. A political system that claims to be morally justified should provide a means by which those who are subject to its authority can effectively express the view that what it commands is immoral and can get a fair hearing. The same is true of other systems as well.

Within a system, clashes of authority may occur between two smaller systems or between one of these and the government. In the latter case, the authority of government dominates to the extent that it is sovereign in the sphere of civil and political life and to the extent

113

that the dispute is settled ultimately through the courts. Similarly, serious disputes between other systems in a society are usually settled by recourse to the political system and its courts. No general rule decides in advance that corporate authority, for example, takes precedence over the authority of some other organization unless both are parts of a system in which one is subordinate to another.

In general, higher authorities dominate when authorities are hierarchically ordered in the same sphere. When they are not hierarchically ordered and they clash, they must have recourse to something other than to authority in that realm. Two epistemic authorities on the same topic must settle differences, not on the basis of authority, but on the basis of facts and reasoning. Two corporations with no corporate authority above them most frequently have recourse to the authority of the courts. Two systems in different spheres cannot solve differences by recourse to authority unless they are both subject to the same higher authority.

Sovereign authorities cannot appeal to a higher authority except possibly to morality, reason, or religion. Two countries may agree to be bound by the World Court or a United Nations body. If they do not, the usual alternative is for a solution to be sought through force.

Systems of authority not only clash; they can also reinforce one another. Morality and religion can support political authority, and vice versa. All of these systems can reinforce parental authority, various kinds of operative authority, and even epistemic authority. Societies in which authority systems reinforce one another are in general more stable societies than those whose systems are constantly at odds. The coordination of authority systems strengthens the trust that is undermined by clashes.

This discussion of the sources, symbols, and systems of authority, together with the nature of authority, completes my formal and general analysis of authority. Authority is a complex and multifaceted phenomenon. No one kind of authority is privileged. At least certain types of authority are justifiable. Justification is a crucial aspect of authority, especially in a time of change. A society's relation to authority is central to the way in which it identifies itself; each generation must clarify this relation. The models I have presented and the distinctions I have drawn provide the necessary tools for studying the status of authority in the public and the private realms and to determine both the appropriateness and the limits of authority in many of its contemporary forms.

PART 2

*The Justification
of Public Authority*

6

Freedom, Anarchism, and Authority

Historically, political theorists have thought that political authority needs justification. Whereas the absence of authority and restraints on authority have not had to be justified, restraints on freedom have had to be, because freedom and human liberty have been seen as good in themselves. While anarchists have attacked authority in the name of freedom, traditional political theorists have defended politico-legal authority as being necessary for the general enjoyment of freedom. Both sides value and champion freedom. Both sides raise and answer differently the question of whether political authority can be justified. Since both the attack on and the defense of political authority most frequently is couched in terms of freedom, we should initially sort out several different meanings of that term and relate them to some of the different kinds of authority we have already distinguished.

Anarchist positions are often thought to attack all forms of authority. This is true of some anarchist views—that of Max Stirner, for instance—but it is not true of all anarchist positions. The anarchist who has done away with the established government and wishes to form a community or a miniature society without government is logically forced to accept some kinds of authority as justifiable. A number of prominent anarchists, despite their attacks on government, hoped to establish organized societies. Pierre Proudhon sought to bring about a decentralized democracy. In an unpublished letter, Mikhail Bakunin mentions the need for an "invisible dictatorship," and the anarcho-syndicalists wished to give all power to union leaders or to municipal governments. All such organized societies require some forms of authority. But the relation of freedom and authority in them, as well as in traditional societies, is not a simple one.

116

FOUR KINDS OF FREEDOM

Freedom and authority are frequently considered to be antithetical. More precisely, the claim is that freedom and imperative executive authority are antithetical, since if anyone is bound by the commands of another, his own freedom of action is to that extent limited. Paradoxically, however, it can as plausibly be maintained that freedom and imperative executive authority are complementary. Even more strongly, freedom is a prerequisite for authority. But 'freedom' is different from what those who claim freedom and authority to be antithetical mean by the term. I shall distinguish four kinds of freedom: rational, relational, teleological, and negative.

Rational freedom, which is a prerequisite for executive authority, is the ability to conceive of and to understand rules. It is the ability to act in accordance with rules, as well as the ability to refuse to act in accordance with them, and the ability to act contrary to them. Such freedom is a prerequisite not only for executive authority but also for society to the extent that society is the organization of human beings who do not simply act in determinate ways but who act according to understood rules. Such rules make possible the organization of society as human society; they are forms of authority to the extent that they normatively regulate human conduct. They also provide the framework for other kinds of authority. Authority, seen in this way, is necessary for human society. The state, government, and laws are forms of authority; but as we have seen, it is a mistake to *equate* authority with them. It is also a mistake to maintain that *they* are necessary—either conceptually or in fact—to human society.

Rational freedom is a descriptive term, and every human institution presupposes it. Even in the institution of slavery, both the master and the slave must be free in the descriptive sense of understanding and having the ability to act in accordance with a set of rules (obviously, not moral rules) if the institution of slavery can be properly said to exist.

The slave is free in one sense, despite the fact that he is a slave. Many people, from the stoics to Hegel and from Thoreau to Sartre, have seen this. In another sense of the word the slave is not free. Freedom is here understood in terms of an interpersonal relation. It is the absence of its opposite—slavery, domination, or submission. One who is free is not a slave or dominated or submissive. Full freedom consists of complete independence (individually or collectively) from others, although it is doubtful that such a high degree of freedom is

117

ever achieved. This relational sense of freedom is descriptive; it describes whether, in fact, one person is owned by another within some social framework, is bound to him, is subject to him in certain ways, and is used by him for his (the master's) own purposes. One is free to the extent he is not so bound. Relational freedom has two evaluative poles. The positive pole is a desirable state of affairs—it consists of complete independence; the negative, undesirable pole is complete bondage or slavery. The extent of the domination and subservience involved in the relation varies. The sociological and psychological gradations between the two poles are often subtle and interrelated. Socially, we can see the difference between a slave and a serf, between a serf and those who work for wages, and between wage earners and employers. Psychologically, independence involves risk and maturity and is not always actively sought. The relation between the persons or groups is mediated in a variety of ways: for example, through obedience, coercion, work, or property. The obedience that is involved need not be servile, demeaning, or coerced, though it frequently is; some even speak of a slave of love. Hegel and Marx perceptively remarked that the master is bound to the slave on whose work and service he depends as much as the slave is bound to the master.

A third sense of freedom I shall call teleological freedom of action. Human beings who can see themselves as ends have interests; they can both envision ends and sometimes take the necessary actions to attain them. 'Freedom' here does not refer to a relationship between two human beings but between a human being and the ends that he wishes to attain. Because he can reason, a human being can envisage and present to himself any ends that he chooses. By 'teleological freedom of action' I mean not only the ability to present ends but also the possibility of attaining them. This possibility depends positively on one's own abilities and enabling circumstances and negatively on the lack of restraint by circumstances and by others. A human being's teleological freedom of action is effective in a weak sense when he has the ability to attain his end and there are no impediments or restraints placed in his way. When, in addition, he actually has the necessary means to attain his end, his freedom is effective in a strong sense (even though he still may fail in his attempt). Like relational freedom, teleological freedom of action can be either descriptive or evaluative. By characterizing various kinds of actions, we can speak of different kinds of teleological freedom, such as the freedom of the press. The freedom to print what we want to print without interference from others is effective in a strong sense only for those who actually have the means to publish. Teleological freedom of action admits of degrees in a way that the first and even the second cannot. Those who claim that relational freedom is desirable do not usually claim that people should be free to do anything that they are capable of doing. Similarly, not all forms of teleological freedom are desirable in themselves.

Fourth, we can speak of negative freedom, or freedom *from* something. Negative freedom, which is value laden, describes a condition in which such things as fear, want, or starvation—which one sees as a harm or threat—do not dominate him. It would be odd to say that one is free from health, knowledge, or happiness; but it is perfectly natural and correct to say that one is free from sickness, ignorance, pain, or suffering. Such freedom often amounts to security against misfortune. It frequently involves the intervention of authority, restraints on teleological freedom, and the preservation of people from suffering the natural effects of their actions.

The four kinds of freedom are frequently confused because they are interrelated, they overlap, and they sometimes merge. Rational freedom is the basis for relational freedom and for the teleological freedoms. The master's relational freedom leads him to allow the slave to exercise the teleological freedoms that will benefit the master. These make the master dependent on the slave and sometimes benefit the slave by aiding in his own self-development. The cry of subjugated persons for freedom is sometimes for the positive pole of relational freedom (either on an individual or on a collective level), sometimes for teleological freedom to act to achieve their own ends, sometimes for negative freedom. But a slave may find that relational freedom is not enough if as a free man he has less effective teleological freedom of action and less negative freedom than he had as a slave. The four types of freedom are dynamically interrelated and may sometimes conflict. The relationship is not strictly hierarchical.

FREEDOM AND AUTHORITY

The relation between freedom and authority is a function of the mix of the various kinds of each; it is therefore multifaceted and complex.

With respect to rational freedom we might say that human beings, when free, are subject to the authority of reason or to the rules of logic; but in one sense this is false. Rational freedom does not depend on one's always choosing in the most rational or logical way but simply on the ability to do so, on the ability to understand rules, and therefore the ability to break them as well as to keep them (if the rules are constitutive of the activity, to violate them might be to choose not to engage in that activity).

Authority plays an obvious and central role in relational freedom. The slave is subject to the authority of the master; the master is an executive authority for the slave. By virtue of the master's coercive power, the slave must obey his commands or else risk punishment or death. The Hegelian dialectical description of the master's dependence on the slave shows how, at times, the slave may tend to limit or undermine the master's authority. The same dialectic is true for the less-extreme instances of the dominance that is present in relational freedom.

Teleological freedom of action requires that one learn the laws of nature so as to be able to act effectively. In this sense, freedom involves, as the Marxist claims, insight into necessity. Frequently in social life such freedom is limited, not by nature, but by the restraints that social, cultural, and political authority place on action. The justifiability and the proper limits of such restraints are central questions in which freedom and authority mix most interestingly and sometimes clash.

Not all authority involves restraint of freedom. Epistemic authority, for instance, involves none. To the extent that epistemic authority is justifiable, X has no right either to force Y to believe X or to force Y to act on the basis of whatever X says.

Executive authority presupposes relational freedom. But the domination and subjection, found in the master/slave relation, is clearly not necessarily found in every instance of executive authority.

In cases of teleological freedom of action, executive authority may limit one's actions, but it may also increase one's effective freedom of action. The members of an orchestra follow the lead of the conductor: they start at his command; they play at the tempo he sets; they listen to his criticisms; they submit to his correction. Coercion is not necessary, despite the fact that coercion may sometimes be present. Each musician accepts limits on his freedom to play as he wishes in order that all may play effectively together.

The authority of a state or civil government may prohibit slavery and other forms of relational freedom. If the state provides the conditions for each member of a society to achieve his goals, then the argument in defense of its authority is that it fosters and protects the effective teleological freedom of its citizens. A person who wishes to develop in the field of science or the arts must submit to the discipline of the field. He may work under authorities in the field and may be bound by the authority of the field. The goal and justification of such submission is mastery of the field and the freedom to act competently within it. The tradition of any field of science or the arts provides guidelines for development and accepted restraints for the channeling of creative energy. When these become excessively restraining, someone within the field may no longer feel bound by them and may break with the tradition and the authorities. If successful, he may establish a new approach, method, or paradigm, which in its turn may become authoritative. The interaction of freedom and authority can operate on many levels, with authority on one level protecting freedom on another, and with authority in one area promoting freedom in another. The opposite may also be the case, with authority limiting, prohibiting, or crushing free expression and effective freedom of action.

POLITICAL FREEDOM AND THE ANARCHIST

Authority is not necessarily antithetical to freedom; but although coercion is not necessary to authority, coercion accompanies executive authority in many instances. In these cases, despite the fact that authority presupposes some kinds of freedom, it is plausibly seen as antithetical to other kinds. The outstanding instance of authority that is joined to coercion is political authority. The anarchist has made this the focus of his fiercest attack.

On its positive side, anarchism is a theory of society without a ruler. It refers popularly to any theory about a society that has no government, no state, and hence no laws, courts, police, armies, politics, and bureaucracy. By extension, it is often considered to be a theory about society without any established authority on any levels: that is, not only without government, but also without established authority in business, industry, commerce, education, religion, and the family. Some theories of anarchism want the total abolition of established authority, ranging from the smallest units of society to the largest; others are more restrictive and piecemeal. Theories of anarchism range from the radical individualism of Max Stirner to the anarchist communism of Peter Kropotkin; Proudhon, Bakunin, and the anarcho-syndicalists fall in between. There are also anarchists of the right, such as Murray Rothbard, who defends private property and free enterprise. There is no single statement of anarchism to which all recognized or self-proclaimed anarchists would adhere. Anarchists are more easily identifiable by what they are against than by what they are for.

The anarchist agrees with the traditional political theorist that if the state, government, and law can be justified, they must be justified in terms of promoting freedom, justice, or human well-being. The traditional political theorist starts out by accepting the state, government, and law; he sees his task as articulating the justification for this acceptance. The anarchist, who is a skeptic in the political arena, insists on complete justification of any political or legal system prior to accepting it. Hence the anarchist serves the same function in political philosophy as the skeptic does in theory of knowledge. He shakes us from our dogmatic slumbers.

The traditional political theorist usually defends something like the status quo of the society in which he finds himself, on the grounds that it is the best available system under the given conditions and times. He may hold up some ideal towards which a society should strive; he may even at times outline conditions under which radical change or revolution would be justified. But even then his aim is to replace one government by another, one state by another, one system of law by another, arguing that the new versions will be better than the old, though of course not perfect. If a revolution is successful, he will then justify the new society as others may have justified the previous one.

The anarchist, however, refuses any justification of government that is based on the claim that it represents the best situation under existing conditions. He sees clearly the existing injustices and restraints on freedom, and he denies that the present social order is the best possible under the circumstances. He envisages something better. He believes that the sources of many social evils are embedded in the structure of the state, its laws, and its government and that tinkering with them will not solve the difficulty.

The traditional political theorist provides an internal justification of the state, government, and laws. An internal justification of authority shows that it is de jure. Within a given system of law, for instance, a particular law may be internally justified (in the sense of being formally valid) by showing that it has been passed by the appropriate bodies, which are authorized to pass laws, in the specified way, and that it conforms to the constitution of the state in which it has been passed. An internal justification of law-in-general within a state is similar to the justification of the rules for a game: they are to some extent constitutive of it. The state, government, and law are all internally related in the sense that they form a system and that their definitions form a conceptual network. Similarly, political obligation and political freedom make sense only within a political framework. They are systematically defined within it and are internally justified when they are shown to be systematically necessary or when they help the system to achieve its end.

The anarchist does not deny that such rationales or internal justifications can be given either for law, the state, or government in general, or for particular instances of them, or for political obligation or limited political freedom. He denies that any justification in a strong sense—that is, any external justification, for instance, on moral grounds—can be provided for political systems as such. And in the absence of such justification, he sees no reason for accepting any political system and therefore claims that he cannot justly be forced to belong to one. Governmental authority may be de jure, but he insists it cannot be legitimate.

The anarchist argues, first, that no satisfactory external justification of the state, law, and government has ever been given (hence they have not been justified) and, second, that they cannot be justified and so are unjustifiable. The first is an empirical claim; the second, a conceptual one.

The first argument challenges those who defend established authority to produce a valid external justification of the state, law, or government. The anarchist examines and shows the deficiencies of such theories as divine right, social contract, and consent; and he confidently awaits any other suggested justificatory theory. He willingly adopts the utilitarian critique of contract theories and the contract theorists' critique of utilitarianism. That no justification is generally accepted by political philosophers and legal theorists does not prove that there is no such justification. But it does raise the interesting questions of why people, who have no such explicit justification for doing so, submit to demands and commands of governments and whether they should. Various justifications have in the past been presented and accepted for a time, only to be cast aside

123

later as being flawed. This reinforces the anarchist's belief that all such attempts at justification are conscious or unconscious ideological rationalizations of the status quo.

The anarchist then uses either of two arguments to show that the state, government, and law are unjustifiable in principle. Each of the arguments is successful only if one accepts the anarchist's definitions; but he claims that his definitions are appropriate to the facts of the case. In the first argument, the anarchist defines the state as the instrument that one class uses to oppress another; he defines law as a tool that is used by the ruling class to protect itself and its property and to foster its aims; and he describes government, together with its armies and police forces, as the handmaiden of this ruling class and the means whereby it dominates the ruled and enforces its will.[1] If the state, law, and government are defined in this way, they have injustice built into them. They are then unjustifiable. The traditionalist replies that these definitions do not accurately capture existing institutions. He claims that justice is achieved through laws and that society is governed by just rules which are known and agreed to. The people together achieve their joint projects through government. People together in a certain territory form a state, and it is through the state that they carry on intercourse with other large units of people in different geographical areas. The anarchist counters (and many nonanarchists would agree) that these statements do not accurately describe the actual conditions under which men live, even if they describe some ideal situation.

Fact, not theory, divides the anarchist and the defender of the state, law, and government at this point. Is more justice achieved or is more harm done by the existing laws? Is more freedom developed by government than would otherwise be the case, or does it in fact unduly restrict freedom? Is there more crime and violence in a society that has police than there is or would be in a society that has no police? The anarchist points to governmental abuse, to unjust imprisonment, to war between states, to police brutality, to domination of the poor by the rich. He then claims that because of the evil that they do, government, law, police, and other oppressive instruments

---

1. The definitions, held for instance by Bakunin (*Bakunin on Anarchy*, ed. Sam Dolgoff [New York: Vintage Books, 1972], passim) and other anarchists, were also held by Marx and his followers.

124

of the state are unjustifiable in fact.[2] Some of the anarchists' facts, if taken in isolation, tend to support their claims. But critics assert that the anarchists are selective and do not weigh all of the appropriate facts: no society—for instance the Wild West in the United States—has had more justice or effective freedom before the arrival ·of law than afterwards. Although the anarchist makes claims about how a society without authority should or will work, these unsubstantiated claims have no facts or experience to support them.

In the second argument, some anarchists define freedom (or autonomy) and then define authority in such a way as to make them incompatible. For instance, Robert Paul Wolff uses this line of attack in his book *In Defense of Anarchism*.[3] It is possible to deny that these definitions are appropriate (because they do not apply to actual societies); it is also possible to deny the claims made for them.[4] The anarchist, therefore, does not actually prove that the state, government, and law cannot be justified. He may show that moral autonomy and political obligation, as he defines them, are incompatible; but he does not show that alternative defensible definitions are not valid.

The anarchist moves quickly and with little argument from the claimed unjustifiability of state, government, and law to the assertion that they should be done away with. Everything that cannot be justified should not necessarily be done away with. But the anarchist argues that the existing structures are in large part the cause of injustice, the restraint of freedom, and the exploitation of the masses. He believes that they can be done away with because he believes

2. For example, see William Godwin's *Enquiry Concerning Political Justice,* Benjamin Tucker's *Instead of a Book,* Max Stirner's *The Ego and His Own,* and Emma Goldman's *Anarchism and Other Essays.* Two readily available anthologies that contain extracts from the anarchists are Leonard I. Krimerman and Lewis Perry, eds. *Patterns of Anarchy* (New York: Anchor Books, 1966), and Marshall Shatz, ed., *The Essential Works of Anarchism* (New York: Bantam, 1971).

3. Robert Paul Wolff, *In Defense of Anarchism* (New York: Harper Torchbooks, 1970). For a reply to this book see Jeffrey H. Reiman, *In Defense of Political Philosophy* (New York: Harper Torchbooks, 1972).

4. Thus Richard Taylor (*Freedom, Anarchy and the Law* [Englewood Cliffs, N.J.: Prentice-Hall, 1973], pp. 46–54) denies the absolute status that Wolff imputes to moral autonomy; Lisa H. Perkins ("On Reconciling Autonomy and Authority," *Ethics* 82 [1972]: 114–23) claims that the two concepts are not compatible and that autonomy requires authority; and Rex Martin ("Wolff's Defense of Philosophical Anarchism," *Philosophical Quarterly* 24 [1974]: 140–49) argues that Wolff really describes the incompatibility of moral autonomy with moral obligation to obey laws or with the government's right, through legislation, to decree what is or is not moral.

there are viable alternatives to these structures. It is not unreasonable to claim that the source of injustice should be removed, providing it can be done without causing more harm as a result.

The means by which the state, government, and law should be eliminated and the speed with which this should take place not only are matters of disagreement among anarchists; they are also areas of special theoretical weakness in anarchistic writings. The anarchists usually see the workers or the masses of the oppressed as the movers of change in opposition to the status quo; but how these masses are to be moved to do something about their situation is not usually clear. Education as a method is a slow process, especially since the schools are controlled by those who defend the status quo. Anarcho-communists fall back on a Marxian type of analysis, though their views are repudiated by Marxists, just as they were repudiated by Marx and Engels.[5] Those who resort to terrorism and bombings have not only shown that such actions are usually counterproductive; they also act in violation of the claimed freedom, autonomy, and valued well-being of others. In a more gradual approach, the workers take over control of their factories and businesses either through unions or on their own, and then they demolish the instruments of the state and government. This is the most plausible alternative. Contemporary anarchists, such as Daniel Guerin, emphasize workers' self-management on the Yugoslav model; and Paul Goodman called for reform and change in education and in neighborhoods and civic groups which can seize the initiative from government.[6] The means they advocate for achieving change are frequently defective, but their negative critique of conditions is as frequently salutory.

Detailing how the new society is to function after the revolution is both a matter of dispute and, in general, another weak portion of the anarchist position. The anarchist can hardly spell out what the society after the revolution will be like if he maintains that those who live in the society must enjoy the freedom to do what they wish. The most that he can do is negatively to rule out the existence of the state, law, and government as previously defined, affirm certain very

5. The relevant texts of Marx, Engels, and Lenin on anarchism have been collected in *Anarchism and Anarcho-Syndycalism* (New York: International Publishers, 1972).

6. Daniel Guerin, *Anarchism* (New York: Monthly Review Press, 1970). For samples of Goodman's views see *Patterns of Anarchy*, pp. 449–72.

general conditions which will prevail, and answer certain objections that are proposed by his critics.[7]

The anarchist insists on high standards of justification for the state, law, and government. But he does not insist on such high standards for all forms of social organization. When consistent, he is realistic enough to know that any social organization involves some limitation on some aspects of freedom, and possibly of autonomy, and that imperfect men cannot achieve a completely just society. Whereas the state, law, and government, as the anarchist defines them, are inherently unjust, not all social organizations are. Most anarchists at this point move towards a less-rigid statement of the criteria necessary in order to justify social structures. Like other political theorists, they are willing to distinguish several meanings and types of freedom or to restrict complete freedom by certain principles. Without constant fear of attack or harm from others, people can actually achieve more of their desires and so can actualize more of their freedom than would otherwise be possible. This usually leads the traditional political theorist to a justification of the state, government, and law; but the anarchist has already blocked the traditionalist's move by ruling that the state, government, and law are illegitimate.

FREEDOM, ANARCHISM, AND SOCIAL ORGANIZATION

The most consistent anarchist position is not that of the radical individualistic anarchists but is that of communitarian anarchists in the tradition of Proudhon and Bakunin, resulting in an amalgam of the positions of the anarcho-syndicalists and the anarcho-commu-

---

7. For instance, to the charge that a society without a government and without any army would be easy prey to the armed forces of another country, the anarchist replies, first, that he expects anarchism to spread so that there will be no nation states; and second, even if anarchism were to succeed initially in only one country, no foreign power would gain much by using arms against it. Without a centralized government to take over, any invader would find no seat of authority to capture and replace. It would find a multitude of independent overlapping organizations, together with a people who individually would not readily submit to losing their freedom. Under these conditions, no army could keep a large population in subjugation, nor could any foreign power control such people through the ordinary means of manipulation—law, police, government—since these will have been done away with and could not easily be restored.

nists.[8] Such anarchists do not wish to return to an earlier, simpler agrarian or industrial society. They seek a form of social communitarianism. Unlike the Marxist-Leninists for whom the withering away of the state is a far-off event, these anarchists deny the present necessity of centralism in society, of statism, of the dictatorship of the proletariat, and of the leadership and domination of a party—Communist or other.[9]

Communitarian anarchists are not opposed to social organization. If they wish to be self-consistent (they are not always), then logically they cannot oppose those forms or structures of authority which are necessary for such organization. In fact, they seem to oppose, not authority, but authoritarianism, the coercive imposition of authority from above, which they empirically equate with political authority. They reject present forms of government and law as being oppressive because government and law protect the vested interests of some members of society at the expense of others. But communitarian anarchists cannot consistently reject those aspects of the state, government, law, or authority which promote freedom, well-being, and justice.

The communitarian anarchist must accept those conditions that are necessary for any society. These include the moral norms common to all societies, as well as the public conditions necessary in order for people to meet and act together. In addition, the anarchist accepts only as much of existing structures as is justified in order to increase freedom, well-being, and justice.

What if people do not want freedom, well-being, and justice? By what right does a minority impose these goods on a complacent majority? Can and should anyone be forced to desire, to choose, or to work for these goods? The anarchist cannot consistently force people to want what they do not want; nor does he wish to. But he believes that most people do in fact want freedom, well-being, and justice and would choose to live in a society that maximized these if they could be brought to see this as a real possibility. The difficulty of providing the necessary education along these lines is practical, not theoretical. The anarchist hopes that the attainment of one such society would influence all societies.

8. Daniel Guerin is the best example.
9. History has vindicated Bakunin's critique of Marxism with respect to the dictatorship of the proletariat. The descriptions in Alexander Solzhenitsyn's *Gulag Archipelago* go far beyond Bakunin's worst fears.

The communitarian anarchist does not equate freedom with license. He accepts the principle of freedom that establishes the right of each person to act as he wishes insofar as this is consistent with the right of every other person to do likewise. His view is completely compatible with his being subject to the moral law. Communitarian anarchism is also compatible with the Kantian view that though each person is autonomous, he should give himself laws that are rational and universally applicable. Hence, if respect for human life is morally right and murder is morally wrong, no one can make them otherwise by legislating differently for himself. The moral law therefore, although legislated individually, is the same for all rational creatures. Not only are autonomy and moral law mutually compatible, but autonomy requires the moral law. Thus, if the rules governing a society are moral rules, they in no way impinge on the freedom of any individual. Moral laws are not coercive in the sense that they are imposed on an individual forcibly by an alien will. Moral laws are coercive in the sense that they impose obligations; but these obligations are self-imposed. If a society adopts such rules, then all of its members should adopt the rules. Difficulties arise, of course, when some member either fails to adopt the rules or violates them in practice while accepting them in theory. The anarchist is not at a complete loss here, because anarchists have the right to defend themselves. Someone who does not wish to adopt the rules is free not to belong to the society that wishes to adopt rules. If he attacks the society or one of its members, however, he may be repulsed with as much force as necessary. The same is true for those who violate the law while remaining members of the society.

The consistent communitarian anarchist must admit that society is more than the coexisting of single individuals. The relations among individuals must be structured so as to permit joint activities. Since some of the things a person wishes to achieve cannot be achieved by his individual effort alone, individuals in an anarchist society should be free to establish groups to help achieve their ends. The groups should enjoy freedom comparable to that enjoyed by the individual members and should be subject to comparable restrictions. Groups may, in turn, also affiliate or join with other groups in order to achieve common ends. Such groups typically require operative authority, whether it is shared or held in common. Such authority can be rejected by the communitarian anarchist only at the cost of precluding much joint action and efficiency and of denying the right of an individual to allow others to act on or for him or to obey their orders.

Besides *individual* moral autonomy and freedom, it is also possible to speak of the freedom and autonomy of groups, such as the autonomy of a university or the autonomy of a people. This autonomy is not directly tied to any moral notions, but it can be defined in terms of a set of social concepts. In this sense a group or organization is autonomous when it has the right to govern itself, free from outside interference in its internal policies. A university claims to be autonomous in questions of curriculum or of hiring and promoting members of the faculty, when in these areas it acts independently. Any attempt by someone outside of the institution to change its decision, overrule the decisions, or force the university to act in a certain way is a violation of its autonomy. The autonomy of groups, institutions, or organizations is compatible not only with the autonomy of individuals but also with the existence of rules (or laws), in general, and with a broad range of specific rules (or laws).

As the size and level of organizations grow, we may eventually approach a social organization on the scale of present-day national or international levels. Size does not bother the anarchist. An anarchist can accept operative authority on any scale, if it is necessary, freely accepted, and of benefit to those who are subject to it. However, the step from freely accepted operative authority to politico-legal authority is a large one, which the anarchist refuses to take. Because politico-legal authority is imposed on those who are not willing to accept it, it involves a monopoly of force, and it cannot be kept from becoming authoritarian.

The anarchist further objects to the state's claimed right to interfere with the autonomy of individuals or of subordinate units, to impose its will on them, or to usurp their functions. The anarchist therefore can be construed as holding two further principles. The first, the principle of authority from below, asserts that justifiable authority comes ultimately from below, not from above. Each higher group should respect the autonomy of each individual and of each lower group. The higher groups are formed so as to achieve the will of the lower groups; the higher groups are responsible to the lower groups and are responsive to their will. In general, anything that can be done by the lower groups is to be done by them and is not to be usurped by the higher groups. The function of higher groups is simply to achieve those ends which the lower groups desire but cannot achieve on their own. The principle of authority from below precludes the coercive imposition of authority from above and hence precludes authoritarianism. Second, the principle of decentralization abolishes the concept of a sovereign nation state. Nation states are arbitrary divisions; with their traditional sovereignty, they both dominate those who are under them and exist either to defend themselves from attack by other nation states or to attack them in return.[10] Both aspects of the nation state are condemned by the anarchist. No nation state is needed in order to dominate the people of a land. A large territorial group may perform a variety of functions that smaller units cannot, but there is no reason to assume that the same units will always carry out all the functions on that level. The existence of some national states is frequently arbitrary, reflecting historical events rather than natural groupings of either language, culture, geography, or interest. The rise of world-wide trade and commerce has made many regions of the world interdependent; international corporations, for instance, operate beyond national boundaries. If there were no national boundaries, there would be no fear of invasion by a foreign nation. Fear of violence may necessitate a security force, but those below should control it so as to serve their interests.

Together with the abolition of the state, most communitarian anarchists call for the abolition of classes. They also frequently want to abolish private ownership of the means of production, which leads to classes, exploitation, and the need for laws that protect private interests. Freedom and autonomy do not involve the right of exploitation; freedom is to be tempered by justice—equality of treatment and opportunity—concern for the welfare of all individuals, and the promotion of such welfare.

In the economic realm, private ownership would be discarded. Industry would be run according to the self-management concept, in which those who are involved make the decisions and operate the industry, not for the benefit of stockholders, but jointly for the benefit of themselves and of society. Competition would be allowed where it makes sense but would be spontaneously and voluntarily discarded where it does not. Since there would be no state, state ownership is precluded, as well as private ownership of the means of production. In fact, the notion of ownership would be superseded; ownership of land, as well as of everything beyond personal possessions, would be

---

10. Many who defend the state and its sovereignty against anarchists promote anarchy in its negative sense on the international level by refusing to give up any sovereignty.

kept within reasonable limits, since prestige would not be based on what one had.

Conflicts between justice, freedom, and well-being would have to be settled. Although some individuals will disrupt social harmony, it does not follow that a state and its apparatus are necessary. To ensure justice, certain recognized unabridgeable and inalienable rights must be recognized, as well as justifiable procedures for protecting the innocent and for settling disputes. Those who choose not to accept these procedures should be free to leave. Protective force can be used against attacks from without and within. Those who freely choose to remain freely accept necessary restraints and sanctions for illicit behavior. Minor offenses could be handled locally by neighborhood groups, which could sit as an informal court, dispense reasonable sanctions, and enforce them. More-serious crimes could be handled differently; such cases should also be heard quickly and need not involve penal institutions, where crime is taught to those who were not hardened criminals. The point is to avoid coercive imposition from above of rules that are not acceptable to those below.

This broad-brush sketch leaves many of the details open. But it is typical of most anarchists to refrain from filling in all the details of how society should be organized. They find it sufficient to point out the defects of the present systems and the basis of the future system; and then, in the spirit of freedom, they let people evolve the kinds of organizations necessary to fulfill their own purposes. To draw up a complete blueprint would be to assume that there is one best organization and that everyone should or must adopt it. But there is no one best organization, at least not one that any individual or small group can hope to develop; nor should any particular kind be imposed. The anarchists expect a great deal of the ordinary person in the way of self-regulation and self-government; but they do not assume that everyone will want to take part in everything or to have a voice in everything that concerns him—since no one has the time or energy to do so. Some will take more active part than others; some will choose to spend their time and energy on local matters, others on matters at a higher level.

Although many anarchists attack all authority, this cannot be what they really intend, if they are to be consistent. With the possible exception of extreme individualists such as Max Stirner, anarchists speak of the good of society after the revolution. The syndicalists spoke of trade unions and organizations of labor managing the affairs of a people. Bakunin envisaged small groups which would organize themselves and carry on their affairs. The anarchist communists envisaged the stateless society in which each would give according to his ability and would receive according to his needs; they realized that production and distribution would continue in such a society. They decried, not authority as such, but authoritarianism. They refused to submit to an alien will, to be dominated, to be ordered and used for the good of a ruler. Such domination is found in some forms of authority; but it is not a necessary part of all authority.

The root problem is to provide organization without authoritarianism. Certain forms of authority should be abolished, just as certain institutions should be abolished; but other forms of authority and other institutions might legitimately replace them. Anarchists attack the authoritarian type of authority that starts at the top and coercively directs those below for the benefit of those above. The authority that is compatible with anarchism comes from below, is constantly responsive to its source, and is used noncoercively for the benefit of the people who are subject to it. Anarchists frequently do not see the necessity and the possibility of this type of authority and of the institutions that flow from it, nor do their attackers. But to the extent that operative authority is necessary to any organization, it must be implicitly accepted by the consistent, rational anarchist.

CONSISTENT ANARCHISM AND AUTHORITY

My purpose has not been to defend anarchism but to show that a consistent communitarian anarchism demands the recognition and acceptance of some kinds of authority as legitimate. Whether there have been such anarchists is beside the point, which is a logical, not a historical or exegetical, one. A productive, prosperous society without classes, without a state, without the classical instruments of oppression, and without private ownership of the means of production may or may not be possible. However, the concept of such a society, as desired by communitarian anarchists, is not even theoretically possible without some forms of authority. There is constant danger that executive authority will become joined with coercive power in the hands of some for the domination of others or that it will become an objectified constraining force oppressing all—as the authority of tradition sometimes does. Nonetheless, some authority is not coercive and not authoritarian.

133

If the state, law, and government are done away with or if a society in which they do not exist is achieved, anarchy does not preclude such a society from having associations, rules, or leaders of a certain type. By pushing this analysis further than the anarchist does, by rendering the logic of his position consistent, and by paying closer attention than he does to the phenomenon of authority, we can show that even on his grounds, some forms of authority are necessary and justifiable.

An essential part of the anarchist's argument involves an alternative type of social organization. Since all organizations involve some type of authority (though it may be called by other names), the anarchist is not forced to choose either a state that has coercive authority or a society that has no authority. The anarchist can explain which kinds of authority he finds acceptable and within what limits authority is to be exercised.

It would be absurd for an anarchist to deny epistemic authority or to deny that some people know things which others could learn from them. An anarchist like Bakunin admits the legitimacy of epistemic authority while rightly noting that X does not have any right to command Y in any way.[11] Nor need an anarchist deny that some people are more competent than others. When he requires brain surgery, an anarchist need not, because of his principles, be as willing to let just anyone operate on him as to let a brain surgeon do the job. There is no reason to think that in a society without government, someone would not bring his car to a mechanic to be fixed and his shoes to a shoemaker to be repaired. Authority based on competence will exist no matter how society is organized; but the anarchist insists that whereas brain surgery, car repairing, and shoemaking require special skills and knowledge, this is not obviously the case in running a government, where the most-necessary talent has been the ability to get elected or the good fortune to be born into the right family. Part of what government does is set the ends that a society will pursue; but no special group knows better than the people themselves what the people want. Historical facts do not support the belief that those who govern are somehow able to see more clearly what has to be done and what it is good to do. The people should decide for themselves how they will spend their

---

11. *Bakunin on Anarchy,* pp. 229–33.

money, how much they want to be taxed for what they want, when and if they will go to war. The authority of competence remains in an anarchist society; but it does not extend to the governing of people. Industry, as well as areas of self-government that are presently presided over by state power, need epistemic authorities. However, they should not have any special right to decide what should be done; they should simply convey pertinent knowledge.

Parental authority of the type that I have previously described is also compatible with the anarchist position, since it is based on parental competence and the need of the child. Anarchists need not deny the justifiability of parental authority with respect to children, although some argue that much that is done in the name of the good of the child has more to do with the good of the parent. The anarchist correctly denies that government can be justified by claiming that it exercises some sort of parental authority over its citizens. Adults may vary in intelligence, education, or strength. But unless seriously impaired mentally or physically, each adult should freely take responsibility for his actions, and each one should know his wants and needs better than a supposedly benevolent parent figure.

In both epistemic and parental authority, I spoke of a justification based on the end, desire, or good of the one who is subject to authority. We can distinguish the proximate good and a more ultimate good of the subject, as well as of the bearer of authority. If both the proximate and ultimate good of the subject are attained, then, other things being equal, the authority in question is justifiable. An authority may induce or command one who is subject to his authority to act in a way that satisfies the subject's proximate good, though the authority knows it will be opposed to the person's ultimate good. If such an action is to the advantage of the bearer of authority, we can speak of the manipulative use of authority. If the bearer of authority acts for or commands those who are subject to authority for the benefit of the bearer alone, this constitutes tyranny, and possibly slavery. If the bearer of authority uses his authority only for the benefit of those who are subject to him and at the cost of some harm to himself, he is usually selfless, or he loves those who are subject to him. The general principle at which we arrive is that authority is justifiable if it is in the ultimate, but not in the proximate, interest of those who are subject to it, providing that the subject, if a competent adult, obeys the authority willingly. It is not justifiable if compliance is coerced or if the exercise of authority is not in the interest of the subject but is only in the interest of the bearer of authority.[12]

Neither organizational rules nor the existence of officers of an organization in any way violates any of the principles of anarchism, as long as the members are free to belong to the organization or not, the members make the rules, and the members give authority to the officers in order that the officers may carry out the will of the members. This type of authority exists for the good of the subjects and is thereby justified. Those who have authority have had it delegated to them by those who are subject to it, who can also revoke it. This stands in direct opposition to imposed authority, or authoritarianism, which is coercively initiated from above and which is therefore not revocable by those who are subject to it. As long as authority and its acceptance are initially generated from below and those to whom the authority is delegated are held accountable, and are subject to review and removal, authoritarianism can usually be avoided, even if those who are in authority in turn delegate that authority downward.

Operative authority may be substitutional in that the authorities act for those whom they represent; or it may be substantive, either in the sense that the members of a group agree that those who are placed in authority may make decisions for them or in the sense that those in authority have the right to command members in matters relating to their common end. The very nature of an enterprise often demands this: an orchestra needs a conductor, and a ship needs a captain. Neither the conductor nor the captain may issue commands arbitrarily, however; each can be held accountable, and his position is revocable. Operative authority, to be justifiable, does not require unanimous agreement on decisions made for the group. Anarchism need not require more.

We have argued that a consistent communitarian anarchist should accept nonexecutive authority and some kinds of executive authority—at least parental and operative. What of politico-legal authority?

---

12. This leaves open the possibility that the exercise of authority is in the interest neither of those subject to authority nor of the bearer, but of someone else (e.g., the subject's children, or the next generation); this can be reduced to the interest of those who are subject to authority, if it is to be justifiable, even though their interest will be in someone else's good.

ANARCHISM AND POLITICO-LEGAL AUTHORITY

As a special type of imposed executive authority, politico-legal authority is unacceptable to the anarchist; but we can go quite far in substituting freely accepted operational authority for various aspects of traditional politico-legal authority.

Universal direct democracy is not a strict logical requirement for most anarchists. Nor is majority rule anathema to an anarchist if he thereby gets what he wants more often than he otherwise could, even though he does not always get what he wants. In an anarchist society there must be agreement on the protection of certain basic rights of all members of society; there must be basic rules for the regulation of the actions of individuals and groups in accordance with the principles of justice. These will not only be necessary, but since they are just and reasonable, they will, in a rational society, be acceptable to all. Only in this way can the minority benefit from continued association in society at large and also be assured of protection from the majority.

No one openly defends a government because it protects the wealthy or because it keeps workers subservient or because it lines the pockets of politicians or because it passes legislation with tax loopholes to help the well-to-do or because it promotes unjust treatment or because it provokes wars for the benefit of the munitions makers or because it corrupts minor offenders in its penal institutions. However, the fact that all of these things go on in society underscores the claim of the anarchists that authority is frequently abused, that presently existing systems are bureaucratic and frequently unjust, that nation states that are armed with nuclear warheads threaten all men, and that there is a better way for men to live.

If laws are the instrument by which the rulers of a state dominate those who are under their control, there will be no law in this sense in an anarchist society; yet there will be certain rules of society, publicly stated and considered binding. Since the anarchist's insistence on human freedom and moral autonomy is completely compatible with the moral law, the basic rules of society will turn out to be the basic moral rules that are common to almost all societies, which outlaw such things as murder, violence against another member of the society, dishonesty, and injustice and which promote respect for the freedom of each member of society and respect for him as an end in himself. What in general is outlawed by both the moral law and present-day criminal law would continue to be outlawed. Those aspects of civil law that specify and facilitate certain kinds of activities could also be continued.

Furthermore, though moral autonomy precludes the possibility of an action's being made right or wrong simply by the fiat of another, and hence, through it, precludes the possibility of an authority's making something right or wrong by legislation, it does not preclude the possibility of there being indirect moral obligations to act in certain ways as the result of social rules or arbitrary conventions. If, for instance, a society were to decide that all cars, under normal circumstances, should drive on the right side of the road, then to drive on the left would be to endanger one's own life and the lives of others. If endangering one's own life or that of others is immoral, then driving on the wrong side of the road is immoral, not directly because of an admittedly arbitrary rule, but indirectly so. If, however, a social rule were to command something that is forbidden by the moral law, then there can be no moral obligation to obey it. The point is that moral autonomy is not *necessarily* incompatible with publicly proclaimed rules governing a society.

If the state is an instrument of oppression, there will be no state in this sense in an anarchist society. But there can still be organization, administration, and delegated authority. Governments will be replaced by a variety of self-governing units, from very small to world-wide. The highest social organs that enforce the general rules governing society, so as to provide protection of individual rights and the fair adjudication of disputes and breaches of the rules, need not be large or have a broad charge. Their charge should be as narrow as possible, and their members should be recallable. Nor need the present functions of government all be centered under single control. Society without government in fact means that the various organs that are necessary for running society will not be centrally controlled, and a variety of different groups of varying size will operate at any number of levels and will replace the monolithic organization of modern states.

The anarchist is stingy in the delegation of authority, which always remains ultimately with the people as its source. He need not wait for a change in human nature; he can work with human nature as it presently is—which makes him all the more wary in the power that he relinquishes to authorities. Finally, if anarchist principles provide the basis for something like government, it is the basis for a minimal government, closely controlled from below and responsive to those below; it is antibureaucratic and is dedicated to the principle that lower autonomous units will do as much as possible before any task is taken on by units above.

The anarchists have frequently overstated their theses, which have as frequently been dismissed without an adequate hearing. Many advocates of anarchism desired and still desire the overthrow of existing states and systems; this revolution will not take place in the foreseeable future. The nineteenth-century anarchists frequently cited the Paris Commune as their model; today the model of self-management socialism in Yugoslavia is the favorite one. The Yugoslav model suffers from many defects, and it operates within a state system that is not entirely hospitable to it. Nevertheless, self-management in industry is an idea that is finding more and more favor in Scandinavia and even in some industries in the United States. The dangers of unlimited power are more clearly seen nowadays in the United States than was previously the case; the need for reforms and for a means of guaranteeing a decent standard of living for all people indicate the need for rethinking the structures of government and for developing social models of the future.

The anarchist leaves many practical questions unanswered. He leaves some unanswered purposely, since the people who are involved in decisions must be free to make them and since there is no predesigned system that he wishes to force on the people. The problem of the control of violence on the part of certain groups—be they outlaws or big business—and the counters to them are among his major problems. In part he hopes that these problems will lessen with time and with the eradication of armies. In part he hopes that unfair marketing practices and the desire for profit will diminish when workers control industry and when they come to see their interdependence.

As presented with its internal logic made explicit and its consequences drawn out, the anarchist's position is not very different from that of most political theorists who seek a justification for social organization in terms of justice, freedom, and human well-being. His position does not involve a rejection of all authority; it is perfectly compatible with many kinds of authority. Yet the anarchist's threshold of acceptance is so high, his faith in the rationality and morality of the ordinary person is so little in accord with what many people experience in their dealings with their fellow men, and his scheme for

139

bringing about his desired anarchist society is so vague that he is not a political realist but is an idealistic utopian.

Anarchism is not a serious alternative to political states at the present time. It is a timely antidote to political and moral complacency. The anarchist attack on political authority forces us to evaluate seriously and to examine afresh those forms of political authority that we consider legitimate.

7

The Justification
of Political Authority

People are neither born free, nor are they born in chains. They are born into societies that are structured and organized, which they find already constituted. As children grow up, they slowly learn about these structures and their place within them. Children find adult figures who wield authority over them and whom, they learn, they are expected to obey. The obedience required of them as children dissolves as they become mature adults. The adult still finds that the social structures surrounding him involve authority and require obedience of various kinds, wih penalties for disobedience. These are givens with which he is faced. The reflective adult may wonder why things are the way they are; the critically reflective adult may seek justifications for the way things are. But the structures do not await his individual consent; they operate with or without his individual consent or agreement; they require neither his approval nor his permission, even though the structures themselves may specify certain areas in which his consent, agreement, approval, or permission are necessary for certain actions.

JUSTIFICATION AND LEGITIMACY

Theories that range from divine right to general will, from social contract to consent, attempt to formulate the reasoned ground that justifies the acceptance of government and law. Each has its defects; some are still being debated; and none forms the reason why ordinary citizens of a state accept or accede to the laws and government of that state. But when the political theorist fails to find compelling grounds to justify government in general, he does not usually advocate revolt. He continues to have the same faith as the ordinary citizen has in the justifiability of his government.

Americans, for the most part, accept their system of government; the British accept theirs; and the French, theirs. Each is accepted, not because it can be shown to be better than others, but because it is the system into which the respective peoples have been born or in which they have been reared. People in other societies similarly accept or acquiesce in their governments. Even after a coup or revolution, the successful government is soon tolerated and eventually, if not immediately, accepted. Among established governments, tradition tends to induce acceptance of what seems to have existed and to have been accepted for a long time, despite the fact that what tradition justifies may be radically different from what was accepted originally or shortly before. The United States government is vastly larger, more complex, more bureaucratic, possibly more secretive, and more authoritarian than it was at the time of its inception. To claim that "it was good enough for Washington, so it's good enough for me," fails to take into account how "it" has changed.

Carl J. Friedrich suggests that legitimate political authority involves a "capacity for reasoned elaboration."[1] If he is correct, acceptance of political authority as legitimate implies the belief that there is such a capacity. However, such belief does not imply that a valid, reasoned elaboration can actually be produced. The anarchist refuses to accept any government as legitimate until such a reasoned elaboration *is* produced; but he is the exception, not the rule.

'Legitimate' (as I originally defined it) means grounded, in the sense that what is legitimate has a rational foundation justifying it, whether or not this is made explicit or elaborated. But people may accept a government as legitimate because they believe that it is well grounded and justifiable, when in fact it is not. There are then two ways to go. First, we can consider a government legitimate if it is accepted as justifiable by those who live under it, whether or not their reasoned elaboration to justify the government is correct. If people believed that their king held his office by divine right and accepted him because of this, he would be a legitimate ruler, even if there were no divinity to give him any right. Hence, acceptance by a people, together with some belief that there is a grounding and justification, would suffice for legitimacy. The second route maintains that a

---

1. Carl J. Friedrich, *Tradition and Authority* (London: Macmillan, 1972), p.52.

government is not legitimate if the reasoned elaboration of its justification cannot be given, regardless of what the people who are subject to the government believe. Government may be de facto because of popular acceptance, but it cannot be legitimate on that basis alone. It may also be de facto without popular acceptance, if a government controls state power without having the support of the people whom it dominates. If legitimacy demands only reasoned elaboration and not concomitant popular acceptance, then a government might be legitimate and de facto in the sense of holding power but not in the sense of being accepted.

Admitting legitimacy if some plausible but not actual solid ground is produced can justify any government that has ever existed. This, of course, is the anarchist's point. If we say that maybe government is justified but that we simply have not yet discovered the justification, then any government can make this claim. There is then no way to distinguish between legitimate and illegitimate governments. Legitimacy must be defined in such a way as to allow us to discriminate among different cases, if it is to perform some function.

The anarchist's position, on the other hand, is too strong because it denies legitimacy to any past or present government, contrary to what many people have felt and presently feel about the legitimacy of their governments. A government may have the full support of all of its people, who believe that it is legitimate and that it is grounded on a sound moral basis. Suppose that their general belief is founded on the theory of divine right. If some later generation correctly discards this as a poor foundation for defending the legitimacy of a government, then it was always a poor foundation, despite the belief of the earlier people. If a strong requirement for legitimacy is demanded, then the government was always illegitimate. Since what a people believes to be a sound foundation may later be found not to be a good one because of some false belief, we may never be able to know that a government is well founded.

The best that we can do is to be satisfied with our reasoned beliefs, always leaving open the possibility that we may be wrong. We can judge past governments to have been legitimate if the people accepted them and thought there was good reason for doing so.

With respect to present governments we can take a similar line. An existing government is legitimate if it is accepted by the vast majority of people who are subject to it and if these people think that the government is in some way justifiable. These criteria are admittedly loose. Weak acquiescence may constitute adequate acceptance, but may not constitute acquiescence to force or acceptance based only on force. Acceptance requires that those who are subject to government consider it justified and act accordingly, which implies that they do not act as the government prescribes simply from fear. A people may come to think that their government is not and perhaps never was justifiable; they may overthrow it and replace it with another. At one time the American colonists considered British rule to be legitimate and acceptable. After a period of grievances without redress they thought the government was no longer legitimate; so they revolted and established their own government. When Washington was elected president, he was both the de facto head of the government and the de jure head. Presumably, most Americans felt the government was legitimate. Some may have considered the British government the legitimate, though not the de facto government, and the British king the legitimate head of the country, though he was, under the new American system, neither the de facto nor the de jure head of state.

For those who accept their governments as legitimate, a wide range of degrees of acceptance is possible. Acceptance of government does not preclude complaining about particular laws or about the actions of particular officials, any more than complaining about the heat or the rain precludes the acceptance of the seasons and the weather. Some people indeed seem to consider government and law as natural as the presence of seasons and changes in the weather, and they think that they can complain about both but are unable to do anything about either. A small portion of those who complain feel strongly about injustice in law and corruption in government. Even when they are not personally or directly affected, they are willing to protest. When the object of active protest is some particular law or some particular act of government, we speak of dissent; when particular laws are broken, we may speak of civil disobedience. The militant activist does not simply protest a particular law or governmental action; he tries to achieve significant changes within a governmental system. Attacks on the system of law or government itself constitute revolt; the revolutionist attempts to change the system radically, replacing it by another. All, however, implicitly accept the legitimacy either of the government under which and within which they find themselves or of the one that they wish to put in its place.

INTERNAL AND EXTERNAL JUSTIFICATION

Those who operate within a system and who dissent or question particular laws or practices may do so either from an external or from an internal point of view. To criticize a political system from an external point of view means to criticize it from the point of view of some other system. The most frequent external point of view from which to criticize a government is the moral point of view. But one might also do so from the point of view of another governmental system or of an ideal governmental system. To criticize a political system from an internal point of view involves accepting the values, structures, and producers of the system. One then faults particular laws or practices as violating the values, structures, or procedures of the system. The two are not always clear-cut. If someone believes, for example, that the United States Constitution is basically moral but that if it is immoral in some detail it should be amended, he may challenge a particular law on internal—for example, constitutional, grounds—while presenting moral arguments. For he may claim that morality is built into the system with the Constitution. Yet one should distinguish internal justifications from external ones where possible, even if they are sometimes mixed.

In a system like that of the United States, the Constitution is the highest law of the land. It creates the positions of president, of Congress, and of the judiciary, and it spells out the authority that they have and its limits. Their authority is justified internally by the Constitution, and claims that they have exceeded their authority are argued in terms of the Constitution. Legal and political obligations are internal to the system. Those who are bound by the laws of the country are subject to certain penalties if they fail to act in accordance with the law. Who is bound and who has the political and legal obligations in question are separate issues. However, those who are part of the system incur certain obligations which go together with citizenship.

The Constitution and the laws that are passed under it provide procedures for elections and for passing other laws. The constitutionality of a statute is an internal question to be decided by the courts. The justification for this, as well as for the president's performing those actions which are prescribed or allowed by the Constitution, is the Constitution. Internally no other justification is needed. The Constitution cannot justify acting contrary to it, and this imposes limits on those who derive their authority from it.

The system internally defines the authority to levy an income tax, as well as the legal obligation to pay the tax when levied and the penalty for failure to comply. The system requires interpretation, and amendment is possible. Arguments for interpretation and amendment may be internal, for instance, in terms of consistency. Moral considerations that are external may also sometimes be appropriate. Federal authority is defined internally as being supreme. The Supreme Court is the final arbiter of legal disputes and constitutional interpretations, although the possibility of amendment is present as well.

The internal justification of authority, of legislation, and of particular acts is frequently complex. Yet once one accepts the basic system, one also accepts the internal definition of authority and the procedures for allocating, transferring, exercising, and limiting it.

Political liberty, political authority, and political obligation are all internal concepts. Different systems define, interrelate, and justify these concepts in different ways. But however political authority is defined and justified internally, it cannot be justified externally in terms of authority unless that authority is externally justified. Political authority may be de jure (i.e., internally justified) but illegitimate. If the question of legitimacy rests on acceptance by a people for reasons, other than force, which they think valid, then the legitimacy of any system involves not an internal but an external justification. The reason for accepting the system must ultimately be external to the particular system under consideration. If tradition is the reason, it must be considered as the tradition of accepting a government and, therefore, as a tradition external to the government. It is not the tradition of or within the government that ultimately counts. Similarly, if the system is accepted for moral reasons, these must be external to the government, not a function of a government-dependent or prescribed morality. Otherwise the justification would be viciously circular. Since it would remain internal, it could yield only de jure status, not legitimacy.

If we ask why anyone should accept, respect, or submit to the constitutional system of the United States and the obligations that it imposes, we raise an external question. Can the system be externally justified? What reasons justify or make reasonable the acceptance of the system? The simple affirmation of tradition or acceptance is not enough. Why is tradition a valid reason for accepting a particular government, and why were those who originally accepted the system justified in doing so?

Since most people accept the system that they are born into and since even those who seek justification for the system in which they find themselves do not revolt if they fail to find completely defensible justifications, a search for justification, though of theoretical interest, is not of compelling practical concern. People do not revolt unless they feel seriously oppressed by their government or unless they feel that a revolution will make available something better. Most people believe that those who are subject to political authority are in some way better off in accepting government and its controls, limitations, and obligations than they would otherwise be.

We have already considered the positions of the anarchist and the counterarguments put forth by the traditional defender of political authority. A defense of authority is compatible with the assertion that all men should be free in the sense that none should be subject to another as slave to master. Moral autonomy is compatible with executive authority as long as one is never obliged to obey a command to do what is immoral (one can never have a moral obligation to do so; one should never have a political obligation to do so, though difficulties arise in procedures governing cases in which the morality of what is commanded is disputed). But political authority does not necessarily promote freedom or human well-being; nor is all government, however constituted, justifiable.

Political authority has traditionally been justified externally in two different ways. The first can be called the hierarchical method of justification; the second, the method of consent.

In the hierarchical view, the established order is seen as natural and proper, and the hierarchy present in society is justified as such. The justification may take any of several not mutually exclusive forms. The doctrine of natural authority, or the natural superiority of some members of society over others, may be considered a moral justification; but it need not be. Since experience, intelligence, competence, strength, charisma, wisdom, age, or lineage makes some people suitable to govern, to rule, and to lead others, the justification might be simply pragmatic. Such a view may be joined with a paternalistic justification of authority and obedience, according to which those who are governed are governed for their own good, as parents govern and command their children for the good of the children. This, too, may either be morally justified or be based on expediency. Another hierarchical justification holds that all authority comes from God to and through those, both religious and secular, whom he has chosen for positions of authority. Their imperative executive authority carries with it the right or the power to command and the concomitant obligation, on the part of those who are subject to authority, to obey. Obedience is built into the system and is justified on religious rather than moral grounds.

The hierarchical view of political authority was challenged by the rise of individualism, the breakdown of the traditional hierarchy in society, and the growth of the idea of basic human equality. The consent theories of government that came into prominence during the modern period were morally based. The doctrines of equality before the law, of one man one vote, of guaranteed rights for all, and of democratic procedures are built on a view of individual moral autonomy, on a moral defense of individual freedom, and on the dignity of the individual. Except in the case of children and incompetents, authority, according to this view, is not natural and, if justifiable, is justified by consent. Although this external justification is usually stated in moral terms, it can also be defended on religious or on pragmatic (nonmoral) grounds.

Consensual methods of justifying political authority and obedience have not been immune from serious attack. The theory of consent accompanies an ideological form of individualism which does not correspond very closely to social reality. It sometimes fails to recognize the extent of human interdependence and the fact that human beings are truly human only in and because of society. The myth of the state of nature prior to the formation of organized society, which since Hobbes first formulated it has been so frequently invoked, fails to recognize that prior to organized society there were no truly *human* beings. The myth assumes the intelligibility of radical individuals outside of society: independent, rational, and somehow giving their consent to being governed. Consent is not independent of social structures. Notions of original contract and of individual consent being given in a state of nature to government fail as basic explanations. Such justifications attempt to do what cannot be done. They are based on a false view of what it means to be human, and they float in quasi-logical space but have no resting place in history or political reality. They miss the logical point that consent is itself a social action and that *political* consent is an internal, not an external, concept.

External consent to a political system (which can be called social consent) can be given either from a condition of civil society or from within some other political system. It is not made from the state of nature. Those who vote for a new constitution or a new form of government give social consent to the political system they thereby adopt. Most people do not have the opportunity to express such social consent, because they are born into a system. They can ask themselves whether, if they had the opportunity, they would give their social consent to the political system within which they find themselves. If they can give good reasons for consenting, they have grounds for considering the system legitimate. Such vicarious consent does not constitute a justification for the system; it is a search for the reasons for consent.

Political consent as an internal concept is defined and is meaningful only within a system. What political consent involves and how it internally justifies political organizations can only be answered within a given political framework. Consent within the framework, however, is different from consent to the framework.

Consent does not justify government-in-general, as opposed to particular governments, on the part of a previously ungoverned people. The notion of government-in-general is an abstraction. People do not consent to government-in-general, and no one is governed by government-in-general. The understanding of the historical development of particular governments and of the similarities in their development might provide some understanding of government-in-general. No particular government can be justified by arguments about government-in-general, and no people can consent to government-in-general.

A particular government might be justified because it provides protection to its citizens from external attack and domination, because it enlarges their sphere of effective teleological freedom, or because it promotes some common good. The grounds provide a reason why people form governments and why they agree to be governed by them. The reasons for the consent make the consent rational. As in other areas, however, consent cannot make morally permissible what is immoral. If slavery is inherently immoral, consenting to any enslavement does not make it right. If submission to political authority were inherently immoral, consent to political authority would not provide moral grounds for justification.

The argument for legitimacy varies from case to case. Consent itself is not a legitimating reason, since the doctrine of consent claims that a government is legitimate only if people freely accept it for some good reason. By the logic of consent and morality, consent theory precludes legitimacy to any system that is immoral, because it cannot be morally consented to. Second, the system that is accepted must be such that all persons within it enjoy positive relational freedom. Any legitimate political arrangement must be an arrangement among free persons who are recognized as equals in their original rational freedom, as ends-for-themselves. Third, there must be good practical or vicarious reasons for accepting the political authority.

FREEDOM AS A GROUND FOR CONSENT

A good reason for people to accept a particular system of political authority is that it will enhance the effective teleological freedom of action for all within the society, both individually and collectively. Thus political authority is legitimate to the exent that it is necessary in order to enhance or increase such freedom.

The satisfaction of the condition of positive relational freedom and of the enhancement of effective teleological freedom of action constitutes what I previously referred to as the principle of freedom. Even for the anarchist, this principle does not preclude, but clearly allows, social organizations that are freely entered into. Since an individual may only be able to attain some things with the help of others, he would clearly be free to join them to achieve their common ends. In doing so, he subordinates his freedom to the necessities of the end. If achieving his ends requires cooperation, then he justifiably limits his freedom to the extent justified by the necessary cooperation. Groups enjoy freedom comparable to that of individuals and suffer similar restrictions if they unite to fulfill larger goals. People can choose political authority to regulate everyone's actions so that all can act effectively in relative safety, secure from arbitrary interference.

The principle of freedom contains limits on what government may do. Within a political system, specific political freedoms, such as the freedom to choose representatives or to recall them, are frequently termed rights. These freedoms are both created and circumscribed internally by a set of rules or procedures that presuppose the authority of such rules. Other freedoms, such as freedom of the press or freedom of religion, express restraints on the government and circumscribe political authority. Although such restraints may be considered external restraints, they are most effective when they are contained within the system.

Freedom from want and fear may be achieved by structuring what is available for the use of all or for the protection of all. This may require constraint and the limitation of some practices by rules or laws and therefore by the exercise of authority. In these cases, politico-legal authority is necessary for the existence of some freedoms and for the effectiveness of others.

Political authority that is justified by the principle of freedom is clearly distinguishable from authoritarianism. The former is justified in terms of the good of those who are subject to authority and, for this reason, is accepted by them. Authoritarianism starts from above, benefits the bearer of authority at the expense of those who are subject to authority, and if necessary, uses force against those who are subject to it. Instead of increasing or protecting the teleological freedom of action of those who are subject to it, it lessens and circumscribes that freedom.

Effective teleological freedom in a society can to some extent be measured; in this sense we can speak of some societies as being freer than others. In such calculations, not preventing someone from doing something or simply allowing him to do it without his having the necessary means to do so may be a vacuous freedom. We can, nonetheless, roughly measure the effective freedom of the society as a whole to achieve its ends; the effective freedom of individuals to achieve their ends; and the amount of governmental interference as individuals attempt to achieve their ends. We can use the principle internally to evaluate particular laws, procedures, or actions of government.

The principle is open to two interpretations: one emphasizes equal freedom, and the other emphasizes maximal freedom. The principle of equal freedom is based on the nature of each person as an end in himself, a rational being who can perceive himself as an end and who has an interest in himself as an end. Maximal freedom refers to the greatest amount of effective freedom that each person can attain and use, consistent with what each other person can attain and use, while allowing the attainments of different people to be unequal. Maximal freedom may permit one person to have effective teleological freedom at the expense of another, providing that the freedom overall is greater than if each had an equal amount. The decision between the two interpretations cannot be based on an analysis of freedom alone; it requires the introduction of a principle of justice.

The principle of freedom does not specify which teleological freedoms a society must have if it is not able to achieve—as no society can—either equal or maximal effective freedom of all kinds for all persons. Each society must choose which mix it prefers. Do we want the freedom to act if it entails the freedom to fail disastrously and ruinously? Or do we prefer to be restrained from attempting more than we can reasonably achieve? Some teleological freedoms may clash not only with authority but also with security, equality, or justice. In such clashes we cannot determine a priori whether freedom, or which freedom, is to take precedence. For the freedom at issue is not the rational freedom which all values presuppose but is a variety of teleological freedoms which are themselves values, some of which may be preferable to others, and some of which should be sacrificed for other values.

The various assessments on the proper mix of freedom, security, individual happiness, and social welfare supply the grist for rational differences and disputes among citizens and nations, as well as for much discussion in political philosophy. However, an analysis of freedom and authority can take us only so far and is insufficient by itself to spell out what this mix should be in a good society.

Justifications in terms of justice, morality, or general welfare are similar to those based on freedom. The general argument holds that these are enhanced by accepting a particular government. Some people value freedom more than welfare, and some people value justice more than freedom. Since people prefer different mixes, it is possible for people justifiably to choose different kinds of government. The individuals who make up a country may have different reasons, one from another, for justifying the same government. In all cases the justification is based on the belief that accepting the restraints of government allows them to achieve more of what they want on the whole than would be possible either without the particular government that they accept, or without a real possible alternative. The justification must be applied to particular governments. Whether the stated criteria justify any particular government is an empirical matter, though not easily open to empirical test. If someone believes that the criterion is met by his government, this is enough to supply rational ground for his consent to the government. Unless they find their condition intolerable, most people implicitly hold this belief and accept the system under which they find themselves. They are unwilling to accept the risks of revolution to achieve unknown, even if promised, results.

JUSTIFICATION AND ENFORCED OBEDIENCE

Although this argument is strong enough to justify acceptance of government by those who are willing to do so, it is not strong enough to justify the imposition of a government on those who do not accept it. Although a person may be morally justified in belonging to such a society with such a government, he is not morally required to join such a society. If the overwhelming majority of a society, however, accepts a government that it feels is justified, then those who do not wish to accept it may have little choice if they cannot go to another country whose government they feel is justified. For governments have authority over all persons in the territory that they govern. Some persons are recognized as citizens with certain rights and duties; others are recognized as visitors. There is usually no way to accommodate individuals who do not accept a government as legitimate, who claim immunity from its laws, and yet live within its boundaries. So long as a government allows free emigration, its failure to accommodate small numbers of those who do not accept it is in itself not an adequate basis for criticism of the government, even if the dissenters have nowhere else that they prefer to go. To require acceptance by all without exception is in practical terms to preclude legitimate government unreasonably. Consensual theories cannot consistently force consent to a government; but from a practical point of view, they cannot require that a government is legitimate only if everyone who is subject to it consents to it.

From the point of view of the government, all those within its territory are subject to its authority. Those who form or adopt a government initially do so for the whole territory. In the American experience the Constitution was democratically adopted, and the thirteen original states entered the Union on the basis of majority vote in each state. The minority had to either abide by the government so constituted or leave. The same is true of those who are born under the system: for the most part they remain. Those who remain but do not consent to the system are still bound by the laws and are subject to penalties for violating them. Their obligation to obey the law, however, may be only political, not moral.

It is important to distinguish between political and moral obligations in a society. If one takes a Kantian approach to morality, morality cannot be imposed from without. The moral law is self-imposed. One cannot therefore agree in advance to follow the majority's decisions, for they may be immoral. This does not preclude general obedience to law. Nonetheless, for morally competent adults the political obligation to obey a law can never override the moral obligation to refrain from doing what is immoral. The terms legal and political obedience are defined within the legal and political systems.

153

The systems, as well as what they command, can be evaluated from a moral point of view. This applies to both those who consent to a government and those who do not.

From a moral point of view adult obedience can never justifiably be blind. If I follow someone's command to murder, what I have done is morally bad; if I obey someone's command to respect my neighbor, what I do is morally good. In each case I have done something in addition to being obedient. The murder is morally bad, and the respect for my neighbor, not the obedience, is morally good. Any discussion of obedience should consider not only the act of obedience but also the act that is done as a result of being obedient. An act of obedience is in this sense a double action; for any action of obedience is also another action as well, namely, the action that we are told to do.

Some adults choose obedience because it is the route for their self-development in a given field. Others avoid obedience by resigning from a job, church, or organization that demands it; but one cannot escape the political obligation of obeying the laws of a country except by leaving that country. The burden of obedience to law is somewhat ambiguous, however, and falls more heavily on some than on others. Not all laws command, and therefore not all laws require obedience. Some laws facilitate private arrangements, some have as their aim the settling of disputes, others aim at supplying and redistributing goods.[2]

When the law commands that individuals in a designated class perform certain actions—for example, that they pay income taxes—then active obedience to law is required. When the law forbids certain actions, such as murder or theft, the ordinary citizen may well feel no inclination to act to the contrary. His actions normally fall within the law. Whether at each instant that someone abstains from these legally forbidden acts he is obeying the law depends on how we wish to characterize obedience. But such laws require only that persons not commit the specified acts. No additional act called "obedience to law" is required. One who does not break such laws is said to be law-abiding, though he might also be characterized as one who obeys the law. In these cases, obedience to law is passive. No particular motive is required, nor is it even necessary for one to know of the existence of

---

2. See J. Raz, "On the Functions of Law," *Oxford Essays in Jurisprudence* (2d ser.), ed. A. W. B. Simpson (Oxford: Clarendon Press, 1973).

the laws with which he is in compliance. Obedience to law in these cases is different from the construal of moral obedience that requires action not only in accordance with what is right and what is commanded but also because it is right and commanded—that is, action from the proper motive. The legal obligation to obey the law consists of the legal obligation not to do those acts which are forbidden by law and to do those acts which are prescribed by law if, when, and as they apply to us and our activities. Since, from a moral point of view, moral obligations override political obligations, it is not immoral to obey just laws even if one has not consented to them. Nor is it immoral for governments to enforce laws that have been passed for the common good and to demand compliance with laws that are not immoral on the part even of those within its jurisdiction who do not consent to the laws or to the government.

Those who consent to a government and to its laws have no problem: in obeying government, they are doing what they choose to do. Those who do not consent may be forced to do what they would rather not do—for example, pay taxes—but they can never legitimately be forced to do what is immoral. This negative moral restraint, when placed on government, limits what it can legitimately do. A government, if it abides by this restraint, if it is accepted by a large majority of the people it rules, and if it helps them to achieve more of what they want than they could achieve without it, legitimately enforces its laws on all within its territory.

GOVERNMENT AND CONSENT

In the American system the authority of government is said to come from the people. A government of, by, and for the people is not a government separated from the people, opposed to them, or oppressive of them. Citizens are participating makers of society. The citizens are not subject to a sovereign, but all are citizens under law.[3] The government is not identical with the members of the executive, judicial, and legislative branches, since each of those people only fills

---

3. The justification of the authority of law should be distinguished from justification in law. In the United States, the Constitution is the basic document establishing the government and the system of law. Checks and balances operate within the system. In judicial decisions not only black-letter law but also precedent and common law carry great authority.

a position; nor is the government equatable with those who work for it in any other capacity. The government does not belong to any small group of individuals. All members of the society are subject to laws which, in a broad sense, are made by the people. Everyone from the president down is subject to them. The people who consent to this government consent, not to domination by government or by its leaders, but to regulation by law.

The doctrine of consent, however, has been made to carry too much weight with respect to the justification of governmental authority. Universal consent is not necessary for a government to be justified. Nor need consent be construed as consisting of a positive action. The notion of consent is basically symbolic of the freedom and autonomy of the human person in a democratic society. It shares with freedom and democracy the strain of overuse and ambiguity.

Given the many forms of government, the claim that one of them is best or most rational or that, if given the choice, rational men would choose one of them in preference to all the others, simply does not fit the facts. The British, the Germans, the Americans, and the Russians all seem to accept and, in some sense, to consent to their governments. None of those governments was established by some original consent on the part of all its present, or even of all its past, members. Such consent is neither expected nor required for the justification or legitimation of government. Nor is it clear what such consent would consist of.

If some formal consent to a government were expected or required for it to be justified, it would be easy to institute a rite of political initiation. Upon reaching one's eighteenth birthday, for instance, a person who had been born in the United States could take an oath of allegiance to the government and to the Constitution, similar to that taken by naturalized citizens, thereby expressing consent to them. A person who chose not to do so would be treated as an alien. The process could be renewed every four years as citizens voted. But what would be the point of such a procedure?

Such a rite would offer the choice of formally accepting what is already established or of being treated as an outsider. It would not offer the choice of establishing one's own government or society, because one person does not constitute a society. If each individual really had to consent formally in the indicated way, the assumption would be that one had to work with what was already established. Since this would in fact be the case, the rite would add nothing new. So long as groups of nonconsenting aliens remain in the minority, they are not likely to form a government opposed to the ruling one.

What would be the point of giving one's consent once in a lifetime or once every four years? Would such a formal ceremony significantly change what we have at the present time? "Consent of the governed" does not mean a once-in-a-lifetime act. Such consent could not bind one to unquestioning acceptance of whatever the government does or obedience to whatever the laws command.

Since Locke's day the doctrine of tacit consent has caused much debate and uneasiness. But if the doctrine of consent were really supposed to serve as a foundation for and a justification of government, it would be easy to move from tacit consent to explicit consent by using the above model or something comparable. The fact that we feel no inclination to do this suggests that the doctrine of consent is not expected to function in this way.[4]

Consent does not justify government-in-general, and though related to freedom, equality, participation, and autonomy, consent does not justify particular governments if it is interpreted on a radically individualistic level. As an internal method to discriminate legitimate governments, consent is circular. Either as a means of

---

4. Alan Gewirth in "Political Justice," in *Social Justice,* ed. Richard B. Brandt (Englewood Cliffs, N.J.: Prentice-Hall, Inc., 1962), p. 137, both rejects the radical individualistic approach to consent and offers a plausible substitute. Gewirth interprets consent, not on the level of individual consent, but on the level of democratic election processes. He claims that "it is this method which, according to the liberal democratic tradition, legitimates political authority and political obligation." He also believes that this interpretation is what "we mean when we say that the United States and Great Britain have, and the Soviet Union and Communist China do not have, governments that rest on the consent of the governed." He believes that the doctrine of consent of the governed has, as one of its functions, the provision of the means by which to distinguish some governments from others—presumably those that are legitimate from those that are not. The difficulty is that he has defined consent in terms of a process that he wishes to defend, and then he uses consent to defend it. He is correct in seeing that the doctrine of consent, as he defines it, is an internal doctrine which is accurately described by him as in the "liberal democratic tradition." But his notion of consent would certainly be rejected by the Soviets and the Chinese, who would claim that the process he describes and defends, insofar as he claims that it exists in the United States and Great Britain, does not really express the consent of any but the ruling class. In the United States the ruled are allowed to choose every four years between two members of the ruling class who is to govern and dominate them. The Soviet and Chinese systems, on the other hand, they claim, allow for real representation of the interests of the people as a whole, not of different members of the ruling class, and in that sense and for that reason, they can truly claim to have the consent of the governed. Consent is systematically defined in both cases. Each can claim its own version as being a discriminator of legitimate government within its own tradition.

distinguishing legitimate from illegitimate governments in a comparative, international sense or as a means of justifying particular governments in any strong sense, consent is defective.

My purpose is not to decide which governments are legitimate and which are not. In its external function, consent theory sets the conditions for legitimacy. It can also serve two internal functions: first, within a given system that holds freedom, equality, and autonomy to be important, it shifts the initial presumption in favor of freedom to that in favor of obedience to authority; second, through this shifting, it is possible to justify disobedience at various levels and thus to question internally the legitimacy of authority.

People are born into established societies and find themselves subject to governments. They are forced to obey governmental authority and to do so without the government's first proving to them that it is legitimate. If the people in this society think they are being dominated unjustly and against their will, that government does not enjoy the consent of the governed. This is clearly the case in countries that are occupied and governed by a foreign conqueror. People who do not openly and violently dissent, who respect their government, who are not forced to do what they consider to be immoral, and who feel respected by government as free ends in themselves are part of a country whose political authority enjoys the consent of most of the governed. In such circumstances it is not obedience to politico-legal authority that requires defense; rather, *disobedience* to such authority requires defense. This is to experience and look at the system from inside. The process of initial acceptance of the government by those who established it is finished. If one looks for justification in the process that I called vicarious consent and finds no such justification, then he has grounds for arguing that the system is not legitimate. If he is convinced of this, he may feel obliged to leave if possible, to obey only when forced to do so, or to foment revolution; but within the country, if there is general acceptance of the system, the claim that it is *unjustified* will require strong defense and argument. In the eyes of those who accept the system, disobedience to it is what must be justified.

I began by noting that it is freedom, not government, which is initially assumed and needs no defense. Hence, prior to the establishment of government, the presumption is in favor of freedom, and restraints on it require justification. Once a government has been established and accepted, however, the presumption is in favor of government. Then obedience to government requires no defense or excuse, and dissent or disobedience to government requires defense. Since the presumption is that the governmental forms and procedures are legitimate and that the people are bound by the results, active consent is not needed. Passive consent, or even acquiescence, is enough. This shift from the presumption in favor of freedom to the presumption in favor of government and law places the onus of proof on those who would challenge the government or its laws. Thus, an accepted government need not continuously engage in justifying its authority. If original and continuing consent serves to shift the onus of proof, however, it also provides the necessary means for challenging particular forms of government, particular acts of government, and particular laws.

This is clearest in a society in which the theoretical basis for switching the presumption from freedom to obedience is the belief that government and law will enhance the effective teleological freedom of those who are subject to them. Since the presumption is in favor of the government, the government need not justify every law that it passes by showing how the law enhances the effective teleological freedom of its citizens. However, those who do believe that a particular law restricts instead of enhances freedom can challenge the law. Once the law sets out and protects a certain area of freedom for its citizens, the presumption again shifts at this level in favor of freedom. The effective freedom of action by citizens in this area cannot be encroached upon by government, organizations, or individuals without justification. The individual, for personal reasons, or the society, for common reasons, can expressly consent to give up some freedom or to be bound by a contract. Then, breach of the contract requires justification. The presumption is not that one is free to act but that one is bound to act as the contract specifies. The limiting case in the transfer of the presumption is the case in which consent is not acceptable as a means of the transfer, and this constitutes the limit of effective consent.

In liberal theory the shifting presumption and the shifting burden of proof can be traced in the opposite direction as well, and doing so may help to clarify the interrelation of authority, consent, and obedience at each level of shift.

Let us start from the initial presumption in favor of freedom on the individual level. If we assume that each individual rationally seeks his own good when he weighs the reasons for his choosing among alternatives, then it is rational for him to limit his initial unrestricted freedom if he gains effective freedom by so doing.

Initially, no one is by nature an executive authority for anyone else. Anyone who is an authority for another person is constituted such by the other, though he may be so constituted for good reason. For some good reason, Y may constitute X an imperative authority for Y in a given domain. Y may agree not only to do certain actions for X, but Y may agree to do, within certain limits, what X tells Y to do in that domain. In this case, Y consents to being bound by X's orders and thus consents to being obedient to X. The obligation of obedience results from the commitment of a competent adult to do what another person commands within a certain domain. The initial presumption in favor of Y's right to act as Y wishes is, by Y's commitment, switched in the given domain to a presumption in favor of obedience. Whereas before Y could legitimately ask why Y should obey X, now X need supply no reason for Y's doing as X says, and Y must give a reason if Y disobeys X. By Y's commitment, Y switches the burden of proof.

The same argument applies on the organizational level. If people are free, they are free to develop organizations. They are free to structure those organizations and to authorize certain offices to do certain things. They can give the occupants of superior offices the right to command the occupants of the inferior offices, and they can require obedience on the part of the inferior with respect to legitimate (as organizationally defined and within the restraints supplied by morality) orders of those who are in appropriate superior positions. The obedience is organizational obedience, just as the authority is organizational authority.

In agreeing to occupy an inferior office, one incurs the obligations to obey that go with that office. In general, therefore, rational free consent can justify organizational authority and obedience. As long as the consent is not forced, the presumption in favor of the legitimacy of the obligations that are assumed is reasonable.

When we move beyond freely joined organizations and freely assumed tasks, agreement is no longer explicit. For instance, we are born into and inherit our economic structures. We do not explicitly consent to the structures; yet the structures constrain our freedom within that realm and effectively force compliance. Only at great cost to ourselves can we choose not to comply. The presumption is that the economic system is justifiable. If we believe it is not, the onus is on the dissenter to show it is not justifiable. Because the overwhelming number of those who take part in the economic system implicitly accept it, the onus of proof is on those who challenge it. The implicit acceptance rests on some justifying belief about the system: for example, that it provides those who take part in it with more and better goods than would competing systems. Aspects of the system that result in fewer or poorer goods can successfully be challenged internally by showing that those aspects violate the basis for the favorable presumption. Because individuals are unequal vis-à-vis large corporations, they have been able to argue successfully for unions and for governmental regulation of business. Initially the presumption in favor of freedom made it necessary for unions and governmental regulations to be defended. Once established, the presumption is that they are legitimate, and the onus of showing that they or their particular actions are illegitimate falls on those who made such claims.

The final level is the level of government and law. The legitimacy of the established government is presumed, and the dissenter must justify his dissent.

THE FUNCTION OF CONSENT

If this account is correct, consent by itself does not *justify* government. The doctrine of consent, however, justifies the switch from the presumption in favor of freedom to the presumption in favor of obedience to political authority if people accept their government as legitimate. However, it is plausible to accept the presumption of obedience to government and law only if disobedience can be justified. If disobedience were not allowable under any condition, there would be no legitimate way to show that consent did in fact exist with respect to government, its activities, and its laws.

Although the doctrine of consent provides an internal presumption in favor of obedience, it also provides a foundation for justifying disobedience. Through disobedience we are able to falsify a government's claim to our acceptance. The possibility of disobedience is necessary in order to make the presumption of obedience acceptable. The Declaration of Independence uses the doctrine of consent so as to justify disobedience. The Declaration notes that "Governments long established should not be changed for light and transient Causes." It thus acknowledges the presumption in favor of obedience to the established government and accepts the onus of justifying disobedience. But the signers of the Declaration used the doctrine of the "consent of the governed" not to justify their new government—which they had not yet formed—but to justify their rebellion.

The doctrine of consent supplies the basis for internal justification of rebellion, as in the case of the American colonies. It is the basis for civil disobedience when the object of complaint is not the government or the system as a whole but particular acts of the government or particular laws. It is also the basis for certain cases of individual abrogation of agreements, contracts, or obedience. The more the consent is tacit rather than explicit, the greater the grounds that the doctrine gives for justifying disobedience. It has been most effectively used, not by those who defend particular governments or laws, but by those who challenge them.

Although obedience to law may be justified, it cannot be justified *simply* by consent. Both consent and obedience have the common characteristic of suffering from the problem of the "wild card." If I consent to X's doing a range of actions or to X's doing them in accordance with certain procedures, I authorize X to do specific actions without my having prior knowledge of the exact content of those actions. (Those actions are equivalent to "wild cards" because they are unspecified.) Similarly, if I have an obligation to obey X, I am bound to X's orders, even though I do not know in advance exactly what particular actions X will command. However, a moral agent who is obedient to authority and who is bound by procedures to which he has consented cannot be morally blind either in what he does or in what he allows to be done; nor can he authorize another to do what he has no right to do himself. He cannot legitimately consent, for instance, to his own murder or maiming; nor can he validly consent to giving up all or even the greater part of his freedom. Although people may implicitly consent to tyranny and to obey the tyrant, their consent neither justifies the obedience nor the tyrant. Beyond certain limits, consent is null. The limits to consent preclude the possibility of using the doctrine to justify any and every government.

The presumption in favor of freedom operates at the lowest end of the scale within the system. At this level it precludes our consenting validly to what would essentially deprive us of our freedom. To do so would render the doctrines of consent and of freedom contradictory within the system. The limits to consent form a part of the necessary guarantee of freedom. It is only with such limits that consent can validly shift the initial presumption from freedom to obedience.

Since we find ourselves in an already constituted society, the doctrine of consent, if interpreted as I have suggested, supplies us with an adequate basis for assessing the presumption in favor of the legitimacy of our government and of our obedience to its laws, as well as for protesting its actions and laws when necessary. To ask that consent theory justify any government in a positive rather than in a presumptive sense is to ask for more than it is capable of giving. It is also more than we should reasonably expect of it.

Consent cannot oblige anyone to obey an unjust regime or an unjust law. Nor is consent necessary to ground a citizen's political obligation to follow the legitimate rules of a just regime. The justice of a regime is not a function of consent, though within a just framework, consent may be necessary in order to justify certain restrictions on liberty. Some of the duties of justice are independent of obligations that are assumed in a contract or incurred by the acceptance of certain benefits. Although consent is not enough to justify a government, consent is a necessary component of a democratic government that claims to protect the freedom and autonomy of its members. The extent to which it successfully does so, as well as the extent to which it provides protection and promotes the general good, determines the extent to which acceptance by the people is justifiable. This provides the framework and mechanism for defending the claim that a particular government is or is not justified, though the particular argument in each case requires the empirical data. The conclusion is that particular governments can be justified, not necessarily that a particular government is justified.

To say that a government is justified is not to say that it is perfect, that it is the best one possible, or that it cannot be improved. The notion of the best possible society is an abstraction. Any supposedly best society, when described in any detail, can be made better, if only by increasing the happiness that it contains. A society in which everyone is completely happy; all the human and subhuman inhabitants live in perfect harmony; no pain or sadness exists; death is gentle, timely, accepted, and appreciated; no parting causes sorrow, and no presence causes impatience; and wants and desires are satisfied at the optimal time in the optimal way may be a description of heaven, but not of any earthly society. Nor is it clear that such a society would be better than one in which an unfulfilled desire makes the fulfillment of other desires more precious or one in which labor and sweat make achievement more satisfying.

Present societies have governments that, if sufficiently justified in the ways I have described, may be found acceptable to the people who are subject to or are participating in them. An anarchist may

163

consider such an approach inadequate. Others may claim that this view justifies the status quo and fails to consider better available alternatives. They might argue that even a society that is accepted by the people is not justifiable if some better alternative is available which the leaders keep hidden from the people or whose implementation they fight. From the external point of view a government that was at one time justifiable may no longer be justifiable because of changes either in the government or in the society. Those who claim that the authority for government comes from the people must let the people decide when and how they wish collectively to change their government. Those who believe that a better alternative is possible should make that alternative known. They appropriately criticize a government that prevents them from presenting better alternatives to the existing system. But those who take democracy, autonomy, freedom, and consent seriously cannot also hold that the better alternative must, should, or could rightly be forced on a people. The existence of a better alternative is not in itself sufficient to show that a given government is not justified or is illegitimate.

People who are the source of the authority of a government retain the right to revolt and to change in a fundamental way a society's system of government. A system that claims to rest on consent should systematically include the right to express dissent. And someone who feels that there are moral grounds for refusing to accept a government or to obey its laws, though subject to the sanctions of the government if he is caught, has no moral obligation to accept it or to obey. This does not preclude the justification of government to the extent that I have outlined. And this much justification is all that can reasonably be required.

The doctrine of consent does not deny that particular governments should be continuously appraised and assessed in terms of what they do, in terms of what they could do and are not doing, and in terms of what, if they changed, would enable a society to achieve its ends more fully. But it places the onus on those who advocate change and implies the prima facie legitimacy of accepted, established politico-legal authority.

8

Operative Authority and the Marketplace

Although the justification of political authority has been a matter of concern to theoreticians for a long time, relatively little attention has been paid to the justification of authority in the economic realm. The principles that govern operative authority in freely formed groups apply as well to business firms. Just as people are born into societies that have political systems and just as they are subject to political authority, so people are born into societies that have economic systems about which they have no choice. Insofar as large corporations form an integral part of an economic system, is the authority that they exercise over workers simply operative authority, or does the system exercise authority through such firms—authority that is not freely agreed to by those who are subject to it?

Economics is sometimes considered simply as the study of money or production, of relations between supply and demand, or of other similar abstractions. But economics also involves those human relations that are mediated by money, commodities, goods, and services. Different structures form different economic systems. A bartering system is a structure of relations among equals. Most systems are not built on relations among equals. A system of slavery, for instance, involves an unequal relation between master and slave. Feudalism is more complex; it involves a number of different relations, including, for instance, the unequal one of lord and serf. In each of these systems the lower member of the pair is subject to the higher member. The subjugation can be described in terms of the authority of the higher over the lower.

In these cases the authority relation is based on an economic relation. It is also protected and in part defined by the political framework in which the economic relation is found; at times the two

165

may be so merged that it is difficult to separate them. It is also difficult to decide theoretically whether the political arrangement and the authority of the leaders of a society—for example, of the slaveholders and of the lords—exist as a result of the economic relations and are formed to protect the property rights of the leaders, or whether the political formation makes possible the economic relations. The former view holds that the stronger, more powerful, or more intelligent persons seize economic control and then form political structures to protect their interests. The latter view holds that only if political authority keeps certain people subordinate can those in authority enslave, enserf, or otherwise economically dominate their fellow human beings. Whatever the causal relation between the two, economic and political relations exist simultaneously, and each accommodates to changes in the other.

Some people see government as simply the handmaiden of the rich and economically powerful. According to this view elected officials may nominally hold political authority, but those who control the economy choose the candidates. Their authority may be hidden, but their power is real. An opposite view maintains that government in a democratic society limits economic relations and is the only force that is powerful enough to restrain those who control society's wealth. Legislation limits the authority of the rich as well as their power. In a society such as that of the United States, government plays both roles.

AUTHORITY AND THE DUAL LEVEL OF ECONOMIC AUTHORITY

Authority in the economic realm operates on two different primary levels. The first is the level of the system as a whole; the second is the level of particular firms or enterprises. How a society chooses to develop and utilize its resources results in certain economic and political relations and systems. Just as political arrangements and the exercise of political authority must be justified, so must the economic system that is found with it. In choosing an economic system, a society determines who will have the authority to decide how its resources will be utilized and what kinds of authority relations it desires. Justifying the system involves justifying the distribution of such authority within the system. No matter how the system is justified, the authority exercised within a given firm, company, or enterprise must also be justified. The two levels of authority are related, but their justifications may vary. Within both a free-enterprise economy and a centralized socialist economy, individual enterprises may run on an authoritarian, a hierarchical, a democratic, a cooperative, or a collegial model. The justification for each model may vary depending on the justification for the economy as a whole. The possible justification of authority in a firm that is part of an unjustifiable system is an example of the problems that are raised by the interrelation of levels of authority.

Adam Smith and others have pointed out the link between economic and political independence. During the Middle Ages, independent merchants, traders, and artisans were not as politically subject to the nobility as were those who depended on the nobility for their livelihood. Economic dependence binds and subordinates Y to X. It subjects Y to X's executive authority by putting Y in a dependent position. Economic dependence makes Y subject to X and disposes Y to follow X's orders. This is true whether the kind of executive authority is political, parental, or operational.

Wealth yields power. A wealthy man can achieve results that he could not attain without wealth. He can buy the products he wants and the resources on which others are dependent; he can hire others to do his will and to obey his commands; he can influence those who have political power and authority; he can make funds available for campaigns, control the press and media, hire lobbyists and lawyers, and even offer bribes. But can wealth yield authority, and if so, of what kind of authority is it the source? Is economic authority a specific kind of authority, a disguised form of political authority, or simply operative authority in the economic realm?

The right to dispose of goods or property can be considered the authority to do so. This may be either political or operative. Every society has at its collective disposal certain resources that it can develop. In that society whoever by right disposes of the resources or determines how they will be used and whether they will be wasted, developed, or conserved has authority over them. This constitutes the field of his authority: he has authority with respect to the resources vis-à-vis others. This authority is sometimes stated in terms of property or ownership rights; sometimes, in terms of agency authority. We can consider not only raw materials and productive capacities but also human abilities as being part of a society's resources. In a slaveholding society, the slaveholder has de facto and frequently de jure (though not legitimate) authority over the slave as a productive resource. At the other end of the scale, in a society of autonomous, equal, self-governing individuals, all might nominally have equal control over the resources of the society. How such a society would allocate its resources is not easy to imagine, and no society has yet been so organized on any large scale.

In a society such as that in the United States, how is authority over the disposition and use of resources derived, who holds it, and how is it justified? Starting from a simplified model, we can divide the resources of the country into three kinds. The first is human resources; the second is privately owned natural and productive resources; the third is governmentally owned natural and productive resources. With respect to human resources, we start from freedom as the fundamental assumption of the political system. In the economic realm this means that each competent adult owns himself and has authority over himself. Slavery is prohibited by law and does not form part of the present economic system. For productive activity, however, a person needs not only his own labor power but also materials on which to work and, in an industrial society, the means by which to transform the materials into usable goods.

Those who do not own or control the means of production must depend on those who do for the possibility of productive work. Such dependence leads to subservience and submission to the authority of others in the economic realm. Thus the crucial question is: who has authority over the means of production? Such authority may or may not be equivalent to ownership of the means of production. Though ownership may confer authority to use or dispose of the means of production, this need not be the case. Effective authority may be exercised by persons other than the owners, if, for instance, the authority has been delegated by the owners to the managers or even to the workers.

Given our simple model, the means of production are either under the authority of individuals or groups of individuals, or under the control or authority of the government. If the government has authority over the resources and the means of production, our general analysis of governmental authority applies. The economic activity of the government is justified in the same way that its other activities are justified, if in fact they are. Even under a free-enterprise system the government not only owns and has authority over certain resources; it also has authority over many areas of the economy. Although it may not itself produce goods, it does buy them, and it spends large sums on defense, highways, and other public works. It employs millions of people. The funds it uses to pay for these activities come for the most part from taxes. It also engages in the redistribution of wealth through taxation, welfare, and a variety of social programs. The government has the authority to engage in these economic activities through legislation. Its authority in the economic realm is thus legal and political.

The United States government allocates and uses some of the nation's resources. The authority to use the remainder, which constitutes the largest portion of its resources, is not given directly to anyone or to any group. The political system is structured to safeguard the freedom of individuals and groups from excessive governmental interference. Economic activity is considered one of the realms of protected activity. Society allows private ownership and private allocation of the means of production. The authority to use or to conserve the resources of the country is given to the people in general and effectively to those who are able to secure ownership and control. The assumption is that if the people all seek their own ends, more of them will achieve what they want than if a centralized group were to try to direct the activity of all. The arrangements of society allow certain individuals and groups to gain ownership and control of resources. One of government's functions is to see that the rules by which ownership and control are secured are in certain ways fair.

The fact that authority to allocate resources in the case of individuals and groups is not directly given by a constitution or by any other document approved by the people, as it is in the case of government, obscures the fact that society does grant certain individuals and groups the authority to use the nation's resources as they wish. The concept of political authority is a familiar one, because it is explicitly given, whereas the concept of economic authority seems strange. Although Americans have traditionally feared the power of government and have restricted its authority, they have tended to ignore the power of those who own the means of production and who control the allocation of natural resources.

By what right do certain persons allocate the resources of a nation? In our system an answer to this question amounts to a call for a justification of the private ownership of the means of production or of private property. In a society of abundance it seems plausible to argue that whoever can use the natural resources that he takes has the right to the goods he produces. John Locke claims that each person has the right to take what he can use, provided he leaves ''as much and as good'' for others. Each of us has the right to the air we breathe, assuming that there is enough and that it is as good for everyone else. Before we had the problems of mass pollution, there was a clear and convincing example of a situation of plenty. It would have made no sense for anyone to try to obtain more air than he could use. There was so much air in comparison to the amount that is required by individuals that even if someone did try to get more than he could use, it would have made no difference. No one could seize or control enough to prevent others from having what they needed.

The Founding Fathers were men of property; they established government in part to protect their property and the right to own and use that property as they saw fit. They did not question whether those who had property had acquired it justly, or whether propertied people had a right to use the resources of the nation as they, rather than as all the individuals in the society jointly, saw fit. The existence of private property and private ownership of the means of production, as well as the freedom to use one's property in one's own interests, was to be respected and protected. In terms of our earlier discussion of political authority, the presumption was in favor of the legitimacy of private property, and the burden of proof was on anyone who chose to attack it. Tradition and theories, such as those of John Locke and Adam Smith, helped establish its legitimacy. The point is not whether private ownership of the means of production or private property are justifiable but that such ownership carries with it certain authority. Although wealth and economic position are the proximate source of this authority, the ultimate source is the society as a whole. The members of the society have the right, if not always the ability, to change how we allocate resources. For instance, after a revolution, some societies change the kinds of ownership allowed, prohibit private ownership of the means of production, and centralize the use and allocation of a society's resources.

In a democratic society the economic system, like the political system, should be the result of a social decision. If we acknowledge that all people have a right to a voice in whatever affects them seriously, then they have a right to a voice in the way in which the society's resources are to be used and allocated. To call the resources the society's resources is already to imply that they are not necessarily individual resources, even if individually owned. Private, as well as social, ownership is a social relation, socially authorized.

Just as the political system can be justified either internally or externally, so can an economic system. The system is internally justified if all of the rules for transactions within the system are followed and if the rules that govern the transactions are equitable as defined by the system. As long as all of the transactions are individually justifiable, then whatever the results, they are justifiable. Mercantilism defines the rights and duties of colonies within a system. It does not question the legitimacy of colonies.

The justification required from an external, moral point of view looks not only at the equity and justice of the internal transactions but also at the justice and equity of the starting point and of the end result. As in the political realm the tendency is to accept the given state of affairs into which one is born and reared as being somehow justifiable. It is justified by tradition if by nothing else; but the ideology that accompanies any given system tends to justify it from an internal point of view. The burden of proof does not rest on those who defend the system, since its existence is taken as an argument in its defense; the burden is on those who would attack the system. This may be done from an internal point of view if the justice, equity, and other values that the system claims to exemplify are in fact not exemplified by it or are not exemplified to the extent that the critics think they can or should be. It can also be evaluated from an external point of view.

The justification of the original starting position was never really considered by those who adopted the Constitution. They did not consider whether those with property had come by it justly or whether those who lived in poverty deserved to be there. The fact that some people had wealth and others did not was the accepted state of affairs. The free-enterprise system of the time was simply incorporated and protected by the new Constitution and legislation.

The classic model of the free-enterprise system envisaged small businesses competing with one another. Competition would provide for the success of the most efficient producer, who would sell his goods at the cheapest price. The workers would competitively sell their labor at the highest price to the manufacturers. The freedom of all those who are associated in any transaction to secure the best terms for themselves would provide the greatest advantage to all. For the system to work, adequate information about opportunities had to be available to ensure that both capital and labor would flow to the most advantageous places. The market, in terms of supply and demand, would determine what would be produced. The entrepreneur would move into an area in which demand exceeded supply, since he could receive a higher return there on his capital. Labor would likewise flow to the area of greatest demand.

171

This system was attractive and received the support and indirect authorization of the American people. The open frontiers, the possibility of social mobility, the hope of personal success through initiative, hard work, and sacrifice—all gave the system general support and appeal. Some abuses were tolerated, but government was eventually called upon to remedy the more flagrant ones.

A number of changes occurred as the United States developed, however, and it is no longer clear that the authority given by society to the free-enterprise system carried with it the authority to do all that businesses have found themselves in a position to do. The closing of the frontiers and the realization that natural resources are limited have awakened the general consciousness of the people. Who has the authority to decide which of our natural resources shall be used and which shall be preserved? Who has the authority to determine at what rate the natural resources will be used up? These social matters require social decisions. Yet the authority to decide has not been given directly to the government; it has been given, by default, to business, especially to large corporations. It is not clear that the original authorization of corporate activity included the allocation of society's resources as corporations see fit. Nor did it foresee that the actions of corporations in producing certain goods and services can adversely affect the community. Pollution and waste disposal are only two of many undesirable side effects of production. The initial authority for individuals or groups to carry on their business affairs did not and does not carry with it the authority to affect other people's lives in serious, deleterious, and unforeseen ways.

For many years the mandate that American society gave to business was to grow, to increase profits, to produce consumer goods at the lowest possible price, and to provide jobs, thus raising the American standard of living. Business responded to the mandate. The mandate was relatively simple, and no one could complain if business responded simplistically. For a while it seemed almost true that what was good for General Motors was good for America. But as society became more complicated, as all of the pieces of the social complex became more interdependent, the freedom of business to pursue its own ends as it saw best was slowly curtailed. Such things as air and water, which were thought to be free, are now seen as damageable and limited.

There are increasing signs that the old American mandate to business has changed. The change has come gradually and has not been sufficiently articulated. But the change is now significant enough to constitute a revised mandate. It can be found not only in movements such as consumerism and in public outcries over bribes and windfall profits but also in legislation dealing with such things as environmental protection, worker safety, consumer protection, social welfare, affirmative action, truth in lending, fair packaging and labeling, truth in advertising, workmen's compensation, and pension reform. The public now demands more social accounting as well as financial accounting. The right of corporations to use, save, or allocate scarce resources as they see fit and for their own benefit, rather than for that of society, is being questioned. The authority of corporations in this regard is ultimately derived from the people, in accordance with the principles of democracy and authority from below. When such authority is not used for the benefit of society and its members but is used for the benefit of those who hold authority at the expense of other members of society, then it is legitimately forfeited, or it is no longer legitimate. Whether the United States has reached that point is a question that requires detailed empirical investigation. The principle is clear, however. Those businessmen who argue that social accounting is not part of their job, that they are responsible only for the limited ends for which their corporations were formed, and that social accounting is the province of government are frequently those who also complain about the increasing governmental regulation of business. They fail to see that unless business gives a social accounting, it will lose its legitimacy. Otherwise, government will do the accounting and will enter more and more intimately into the control of business, possibly to the demise of free enterprise as we have known it.

AUTHORITY AND THE ECONOMIC SYSTEM

Evaluating the economic system externally involves an overall moral evaluation not only of its origin and development but also of the resulting state of affairs at any given time. Though each individual transaction considered separately might be justifiable, the aggregate may not be. If the principle of freedom involves the right of each person to hire whomever he wishes, no individual can claim injustice if any particular firm chooses not to hire him. But if all the firms refuse to hire him and if he starves to death as a result, the system can be faulted. Similarly, if someone is discriminated against because of his race by all employers or if each employer, acting in his own interests, presses the wage scale to subsistence level or below, the system can be faulted, even if each employer, considered independently, might be defended on the grounds of freedom. The sum of individual actions might produce results that none of those who were involved in the individual actions foresaw. These results can be considered to be the results of the system, and they can legitimately be evaluated. Through the mediation of economic structures the legitimate authority of individuals can lead to the illegitimate authority of certain groups over others. Individual freedom of action may lead to tyranny. In these cases the system as such and as a whole can be faulted. If remedies cannot be taken, then the system as a whole can appropriately be condemned as being illegitimate.

What kind of authority is involved in an economic system? Although operative authority operates within the system and although political authority may interact with the system, the kind of authority that the economic system has is not clearly any of those that we have already distinguished. To speak of the authority of systems suggests another kind of authority, which I shall call systemic authority. Systemic authority is a form of executive authority; politico-legal authority is one of its types. Much of the analysis that is appropriate to that type can be carried over to other types, including systemic economic authority.

Systemic authority is the executive authority a system has in virtue of which it determines the actions of those who are subject to it. It does so through its structures and through the procedures it mandates. The structures are patterns of action that are implemented by human beings, who, because of the authority that has been transferred to them by the system, are empowered to act on and for others.

Politico-legal authority is a form of systemic authority by virtue of which political and legal structures transfer authority to certain individuals who are thereby empowered to act in the political realm. The establishing structure in the United States is the Constitution. Through ratification of that document, the thirteen original states established it as legitimate and transferred their authority to the new structures. The Constitution in turn transfers executive political authority to individual officeholders. Once accepted, the legitimacy of the political structures limits the freedom of action of the individuals who are subject to it, and it transfers the onus of defense from those who support to those who attack the system.

In the United States, free enterprise constitutes another related system, carrying with it systemic authority. By virtue of the system, those operating within it have the right or the authority to act in certain ways. The political system limits but does not directly form the economic system. Authority within the economic system is not transferred only through the political or legal process. Even with respect to such legal entities as corporations, for instance, it is plausible to claim that the state simply recognizes such joint efforts by individuals rather than that it creates them. The procedure is similar to the state's recognizing the birth of children; it is not responsible for their birth simply because it registers them.

The authority of those who act within the system comes from the system. The American economic system is not justified in the way that the American political system is justified, since there was and is no economic constitution. The people did not formally vote on the system, nor did they formally accept it. Is the onus on those who attack or on those who defend the system?

If we consider economic transactions to be the result of the free exercise of individual people, then we emphasize freedom. Freedom initially requires no defense; restraints on freedom do. The adoption of a new economic form—such as socialism—would also require defense; but since freedom is initially primary, to the extent that the free-enterprise system embodies freedom, the system need not be explicitly justified, except to show that it does not restrict freedom or cause harm. Rather, restrictions on the system require justification. This onus has historically been accepted by those who wish to counter some of the tendencies of the system towards doing harm or some of the tendencies of unrestricted economic freedom which some use to promote monopolies or cartels that aim to restrict trade. Just as the introduction of an income tax into the joint politico-economic system required defense and eventually a constitutional amendment, statutes that limit the rights of actors on the economic scene also require defense.

The authority structure can be challenged, however, if it fails to promote the freedom upon which it is built or if it fails to benefit all of those who are subject to the system. The source of the system's authority is the people, and they can revoke it.

The people gave initial authority to small, competing businesses. The theory of competition and of the "invisible hand" applied to a market that had many buyers and sellers. But some small businesses have grown into giant conglomerates.

Under our political system the people give the government a monopoly of force in return for guarantees of freedom and safety. The government is made sovereign to keep order and to be above all the individuals, whose disputes it adjudicates. It is restricted by laws, which guarantee the rights of individuals against the government. In a democracy the government is made responsible to the people by making the officials of the government accountable to the people. Disclosure enables the people to see what is being done, to evaluate it, and to remove from office those whose actions the people do not like.

In the economic system, none of this is the case. Someone might reply that this is because, in the economic sector, we are concerned with private transactions. This is not always the case, however, especially where large corporations are concerned. Economic decisions that seriously affect large numbers of people can be made secretly and arbitrarily for the benefit of those making the decisions. Public accountability is not required, and there is no possibility of removal by public vote. Private corporations have become quasi governmental in the importance of the roles they play in people's lives; but they are not open to the constraints put on public officials and public institutions.

The questions are: What kind of authority was given to corporations? How much do they at present have? Do the people still want to allow them such authority? The increasing amount of legislation being applied to corporate action may indicate that the authority of corporations has exceeded what the people originally intended, or at least what they presently intend to give to corporations.

Although historically businesses were supposed to be in competition, it soon became apparent that in some ways they were not. Business and workers were both supposed to gain by bargaining; but businesses were in a stronger position than were the workers. No worker was forced to work for any individual business, but he was forced to work for *some* business in order to live. And if all businesses offered him the same wage, he had no option but to accept one of the offers. The worker attempted to increase his bargaining power, to make himself equal to the employer by forming unions, and by giving the union representatives the authority to bargain for him. His efforts have been only partially successful. For instance, during periods of depression or recession, unemployment tends to rise; and during periods of full employment, the unemployment rate is between 4 and 5 percent. No individual firm is required to hire people or to keep on the payroll those whom it can no longer use or support. As free entities, firms have the authority or right to protect their interests by laying off employees. If there is not enough work for a firm, this can be blamed, not on particular employers, but on the system. The authority that is given by the people to the system is not given to any particular individuals, such as is the case in the political system. There is no economic president or legislature to hold responsible or to recall. The system indirectly grants authority to firms and to individuals who seize the productive or entrepreneurial initiative; but the delegation of authority by the people to the system was a delegation that was based on the faith that the system would serve their needs. What happens when the total effect of implementing the system turns out not to serve the needs of all?

A number of alternatives are possible. One is to seek a political remedy to the defect of the economic system. A second is to seek economic remedies, perhaps enforced by government. A third is to change the system, perhaps replacing it with another. The people have the right to revoke the authority that they give to and through the system. If they allow a system of their own choosing to assume independent status, they become alienated from and eventually dominated by it. The use of authority by some people within the system to dominate others to the detriment of the latter is unjustifiable. A system that fails to be responsive to the people who are the source of its authority is likewise unjustifiable.

Systemic economic authority derives from the people. In the free-enterprise system the authority that is mediated through the system is not specifically allocated. It is available freely and may be seized and used by some to the detriment of others. This is a defect in the allocation of authority. For whenever authority is unallocated, it creates a vacuum that tends to be filled by authoritarianism. If the people yield authority to a system that does not directly allocate it, the people have difficulty holding accountable those who seize it.

Yet the free-enterprise system has resources that have not been adequately developed. Just as labor has organized, consumers have slowly become aware that they can organize to counter big business, big labor, and big government.

If the authority to conduct business comes from the people and if legislation represents the view of the people, then the defenders of business cannot legitimately claim that governmental actions infringe upon their rights or that government and the people should stay out of their private affairs. Their affairs are not private when they seriously affect the lives of others.

From an external point of view, a moral evaluation of the economic system can be made in terms of the results of the distribu-

177

tion of goods, work, opportunity, and wealth. If procedures that are internally justifiable produce unacceptable results, perhaps because of inequalities in the initial position, then the results are unacceptable. However, attempts to demonstrate the soundness of this external critique have not generally been successful in the United States. Internal remedies still seem to be sufficient to produce results generally regarded as acceptable. No panacea, no other system, has been tried elsewhere and shown to be clearly superior. The American people are not yet prepared to withdraw their authority from the economic system of free enterprise, although they would be justified in doing so in the name of freedom, if and when this should become necessary.

Socialist systems generally are intertwined with government to such an extent that the authority present within the system is, from the start, a mixture of economic and political authority. In some cases the government is the sole employer. The government also decides how resources are to be allocated, which jobs are to be created, which goods are to be produced. The concentration of authority in such a system is greater than in a situation in which the political and the economic system are to a large extent separate. The danger in the free-enterprise system is the lack of control and accountability in assigned authority through the system. When political and economic authority both reside in the government, the people know whom to hold accountable for damage to individual or common good. But the people have little recourse if the government is not responsible to their will. The more authority is concentrated, the greater is the danger of authoritarianism.

OPERATIVE AUTHORITY IN BUSINESS

Under the free-enterprise system, authority is allocated through the system to firms. Within firms, operative authority, which is sometimes reinforced by political authority, dominates. The general rules for evaluating the justifiability of operative authority apply in individual firms, just as in any other freely formed groups. Because firms are part of the total economic system and because they benefit from that system, however, we cannot consider the authority of individual firms as if they did not form part of the system. Businesses are not human individuals; businesses are ultimately to be judged justifiable in terms of the good or the harm that they do to individuals. The freedom of individuals does not necessarily translate into equal freedom for the firms that they establish. The freedom and authority that are exercised within a firm may be justly curtailed to offset defects of the system of which they are a part. Systemic authority influences the operative authority of firms.

Authority within a firm may be held and divided in numerous ways. There is no one best way. Within a university department, authority is frequently shared among faculty members, each of whom is responsible for his own classes, students, and research. Together the members may democratically set departmental policy. One of them may serve as chairperson; but his duties may be strictly clerical and administrative. The university as a whole may operate similarly and collegially. Such collegial sharing of authority is frequent in partnerships and in firms that have a large number of professional people. Hospitals frequently have a dual authority structure: one collegial among staff doctors; the other hierarchical among administrative personnel.

Worker self-management has been tried with some success in Yugoslavia, and cooperatives operate in many countries, including the United States. Yet the typical business in the United States is structured hierarchically. Such structuring of operative authority poses a number of problems.

Those who organize a service type of group specify the conditions and the advantages of membership. Those who join have no control and no authority to make changes. By joining, the members give the organizer the authority to act for them. It is not a right to command them, though he may make hypothetical demands on them: if they wish some *a*, they must do some *b* (e.g., pay a fee). If the organization is a free one, there is no reason to object to it on moral or other grounds, at least none that bears simply on its mode of organization. But if it is not a truly free organization, such as an electrical association that withholds this necessity of modern life from nonmembers, then the bearer of authority should not be free to set any conditions that he wants to for his service.

There is nothing inherently objectionable in having some people supply others with goods or services. The authority for the entrepreneur (whether cooperatively or otherwise internally organized) comes from the people to the extent that he satisfies their needs by providing the goods and services they desire. If the enterprise is to be justifiable, it must remain free and responsive to the needs and desires of the people. If monopolies develop, if one group corners the

179

market, or if cartels set the price of some good and eliminate competition, then the authority of the enterprise no longer comes from below but is imposed from above for the benefit of those above. The result is the authoritarian model, antidemocratic and unjustifiable. Governmental, voluntary, or public restraints are then required and justified.

The authority that is exercised internally by cooperative and managerial groups can be morally defended, according to the principle of authority from below, as being freely given by those who join it. Isolated cases do not pose any particular problems of justification. On the other hand, the entrepreneurial group is organized by the entrepreneur who hires others to do what he wants done. Since those who are subject to authority are not the organizers, they do not confer authority in the way that they do in the other two kinds of groups. The justification is not by means of the principle of authority from below but by means of the moral justifiability of a limited contract that has freely been entered into. Free people are not morally free to sell themselves into slavery; they are free to enter into contracts in terms of which they work for another in return for compensation. Any individual case is justifiable if the terms are fair, acceptable to both sides, and free of coercion. The worker accepts authority in a limited domain, which he understands and agrees to. If ever the conditions are not to his liking, he is free to terminate his participation, since it has been freely given. He is then no longer subject to the authority of the entrepreneur. May an employer, who finds that he no longer needs or wants the people whom he employed, terminate the arrangement, providing there is nothing in the contract to preclude his doing so? For a long time the accepted answer was yes, according to the doctrine of employment at will; but this doctrine has come under legal challenge in many cases.

Under what conditions is it reasonable and justifiable to accept such an entrepreneur's authority to hire or fire at will? To say simply that both parties to the employment arrangement are free is not enough. In market terms, both parties should have access to information about other opportunities: the availability of jobs and of labor, the rates being paid for different jobs, the conditions of employment, the extent and kind of activities that are subject to the imperative authority of the entrepreneur, and the amount of profit that the employer will get from the labor of the employee. The principle of freedom does not entail that each person is free to exploit others when he can get away with it nor that the principle of caveat emptor prevails.

If the condition of freedom is to have meaning, two other conditions should be met in addition to full information on both sides. First, the two parties should be relatively equal in their bargaining position. If more knowledge or greater ability to manipulate the situation makes one party considerably stronger, then the agreement is less likely to be fair and justifiable. The second condition is similar. Though nominally free, neither party should be in a forced position, where the alternative of not entering into the agreement is clearly unacceptable. If one either must accept a position on the offered terms or starve, then there is little real choice or freedom. The bargain is so one-sided that the employer can offer increasingly worse conditions, as long as they provide subsistence.

This provides a capsule version of Adam Smith's justification of the capitalist system in terms of freedom and of Marx's critique of it in terms of a supposed but nonexistent freedom.

Recent years have produced signs of an awakening to the limits on legitimate authority within a freely organized group. Management does not generally see its authority as coming from below, nor does it decide policy democratically. Within the goals of the group as set by those who form it, managers exercise their authority to commit firms in various ways, and they expect their implementing orders to be obeyed. They assign tasks to be done, evaluate the results, and reward or penalize on the basis of their evaluations.[1] Although the government has built-in checks and balances on its authority, business usually does not. In its own domain, business is free to organize itself hierarchically and to operate dictatorially if it so chooses. It is restrained by law, possibly by its competitors, and by its ability to earn a profit and to succeed in the marketplace. Government represents many interests which it attempts to balance for the general good. Business may represent mainly the interests of its stockholders, possibly only the interests of management, with its primary concern being profit. With respect to democracy and authority from below, business is more like the military than like the political realm, the educational realm, or the religious realm. Like the military, business's end must at some point join that of the common good; if it does not, it becomes a threat against which a society may defend itself.

---

1. See Sanford Dornbusch and W. Richard Scott, *Evaluation and the Exercise of Authority* (San Francisco: Jossey-Bass Publisher, 1977).

An entrepreneurial type of organization is one of the many kinds of possibly legitimate groups. It need not involve exploitation, even though in some cases and circumstances it does so. Frequently the interests of the workers are bound up with the interests of the firm, providing that they can receive some of the increased rewards. Through unions, labor has forced management to share its increasing profits, to prevent arbitrary dismissal, to assign tasks clearly, to keep what is expected of the worker reasonable, to limit the work week, and to make employers somewhat accountable in their evaluations. Although workers' self-management appeals to many, if Peter Drucker is correct, workers in factories, who frequently have the capacity to establish self-management plants, just as frequently do not care to do so.[2] Making work interesting continues to be a problem in any industrial society; it is not eliminated by worker's self-management or shared authority.

Authoritarianism is the coercive use of authority for the benefit of the bearers of authority at the expense of those who are subject to the authority, regardless of how one enters the authority situation. Anyone who is subject to authority should accept such subjection only to achieve his own good. This is true in regard to political authority, parental authority, epistemic authority, and operative authority, including operative authority in the economic realm. The submission to authority is not simply a matter of agreeing to submit in return for pay. Certain parts of oneself cannot legitimately be sold. Selling one's labor does not include selling one's self-respect or one's rights. The corporate employer frequently imposes respect for authority through exercising the fear of being fired. Fear as a motive for obeying authority is no more a justifying factor in the economic realm than it is in any other realm. Accountability to workers for tasks that are set and for evaluations that are made keeps authority responsible and prevents it from being arbitrary. But this is only a first, and not the last, necessary step.

Authority in an organization is frequently allocated to positions. Those who fill the positions have the authority. Those who fill subordinate positions are expected to obey those in superior positions. Legitimate authority extends only as far as the legitimate operation of the corporation. It cannot legitimately command any-

---

2. Peter F. Drucker, *The Unseen Revolution: How Pension Fund Socialism Came to America* (New York: Harper & Row Publishers, 1976).

thing that is immoral. Nor can it legitimately command what is outside the scope of the organization and the position involved. It should be fair and reasonable in assigning tasks and in evaluating performance.

If the worker is not in a truly free position because of the system and if the power of the corporations is vastly superior to that of any individual, it is reasonable for the worker to expect and demand certain guarantees. He should not be subject to arbitrary dismissal. He should properly expect a certain increase in wages as the cost of living goes up or as he gains more experience and expertise at his job. His safety on the job should be protected. He should receive certain periods of rest and vacation. Generally, his self-respect should be recognized, and he should be treated as a person.

Though a corporation can be owned by individuals who manage it, this need not be the case. Even when it is the case, the corporation cannot function without workers. That they have no rights within the corporation and that they are simply subject to the authority structures within it can be legitimately questioned. To hold that the corporation owes nothing to the employees is to see the corporation as somehow belonging only to those who own title to it; but owners or managers cannot use the factory as they do personal goods. Furthermore, the factory is productive only if it has employees. The good of the factory is not completely independent of the employees, whose futures are bound up with it. Though subject to authority, they should be given some understanding of the reasons for orders, the purposes of the authority, and the effectiveness of management. It is not true that because management is in a position of authority, it owes nothing to those in inferior positions. Legitimate operative authority requires that authority not be used at the expense of those who are subject to it. Those who enter the relationship should obtain some good for themselves, together with the good of the entrepreneur.

Most contemporary corporations of any size are not managed by the owners, who are the many shareholders in the corporation. A fair portion of certain corporations is owned by workers through their pension plans and through insurance policies, the assets of which are invested in corporations. A company's authority resides in large part in the owners of the company. In many cases the owners became owners after the corporation was established and flourishing. Yet the authority for the company cannot be kept from the owners. This is acknowledged by shareholder meetings, at which important questions are put to a vote. In most instances, however, these are simply formalities.

Management has the controlling vote through its shares of stock or through the proxy votes of other shareholders. For the most part, shareholders are poorly informed. Some information is made public by law, and more disclosure is being sought; nevertheless, the items to be voted on are rarely presented with clear arguments pro and con. Simply the position and the fact that it is either supported or opposed by management is given. It is assumed that management has both the responsibility and the authority to run the company and that shareholders should be interested only in whether the company is making a reasonable profit. They should not concern themselves with how that profit is being made, with the effects the company is having on society, with honesty, or with efficiency.

This view implicitly holds that the operative authority to run the company rests with management; yet management gets its authority hierarchically from the shareholders through the board. If management is grossly inefficient, the board may replace it. The board supposedly represents the interests of the owners; but if the board is appointed by management, it cannot effectively represent the owners. Management holds its authority in virtue of its filling positions to which authority is assigned. If such authority is to be justified, management should be accountable for the use of its authority to the owners, to the workers, and to the consumers, as well as to those others whose lives it seriously affects. It should be accountable at least to the extent of being ready and able to justify its actions by giving its reasons for those actions which seriously affect others, when those people seek the reason or challenge the legitimacy of certain decisions or actions of the company.

Corporations are formed with the consent of the people. The laws of their incorporation have the basic aim of limiting the liability of the corporation to protect those who invest in it if the corporation should fail. The corporation is a legal person and is recognized as having a certain limited end. It is not a natural person. And since it affects natural persons, it should be kept in check. A corporation often has at its disposal vast resources that are not available to individuals. It is appropriate to limit its authority and to limit what managers can do in the name of the company.

Since the authority of corporations comes from society, society can rightly determine what corporations have the authority to do. The limits that can and should be put on corporations vary from society to society. Corporations in the United States were given authority according to an initial view. With time the corporations have grown and have taken on tasks that have come to affect the general community in unanticipated ways. The authority that they have assumed in order to act in these ways has in some instances been explicitly denied or curtailed by legislation; but no systematic reconsideration of the authority of corporations has been undertaken, and changes have been for the most part ad hoc.

The internal authority of the corporation is both entrepreneurial and managerial. In a few cases it is cooperative. The justification for the exercise of authority by management has frequently exceeded the usual norms for justifiability in that management has not been held sufficiently accountable to those whom it seriously affects, either to shareholders, employees, or the general community. The trend towards increasing social accountability is one earmark of a changing social mandate.

There are many ways of organizing social life, just as there are many ways of owning and managing production and distribution. Which is best from a moral point of view cannot be decided a priori, nor can a plausible case be made that anyone knows better than the people themselves the kind of system that they want. If we are to speak of morality, certainly that must be considered. How much a government should or should not be involved in the economy should be decided by the people, not by abstract principles or supposedly enlightened prophets.

Ultimately, the authority to do business, like the authority to carry on any other social activity, comes legitimately from the members of society and only from them. As a people, we know that the mandate we have given to business in the past to supply jobs and to produce goods for us at the best competitive price is too simple a mandate. We can no longer afford such simplicity. The social consequences of such a mandate are too high, and remedial action of government is doubtfully adequate. Both the authority in and the authority of the corporation and the economic system as a whole need reconsideration and rethinking.

PART 3

Authority and the Private Realm

9

Morality and Authority

The complex relation between morality and authority is multifaceted and intertwined. Both are necessary for any society and help constitute it as a human society. Although morality grounds and limits legitimate authority in the public sphere, it operates in the private realm as well. The relation between morality and authority has three aspects (1) the authority of morality; (2) the concept of moral authority; and (3) the function of authority within morality itself.

THE AUTHORITY OF MORALITY

Morality is the set of norms and rules which all people should follow, and it incorporates the goods and values worth pursuing in life. The specific content of what is thought to constitute morality varies somewhat with the age and the society. All known societies have recognized some set of rules and norms, the most basic of which form their morality. The existence of morality is not a matter of serious doubt or debate, and the degree of relativity among the moralities found in various cultures is not of central importance here. As long as there is the institution of morality, we can speak of the authority of morality. For the sake of clarity and to prevent confusion, I shall call this the authority of moral obligation.

The authority of moral obligation is the right of each person to act as he or she is morally obliged to act. Since all persons have the moral obligation to act as morality commands, each of them has the right to so act. To act in this way is to act in a manner authorized by morality. The authority of moral obligation provides the justification for any morally obligatory action.

Moral principles, values, and ideals form the ultimate ground of the authority of moral obligation and the power of moral justification, just as knowledge and truth constitute the ground of epistemic authority.

We can distinguish actions that are morally obligatory from those that are morally prohibited, and we can distinguish both of these from actions that are neither obligatory nor prohibited. The latter are morally permitted, but since they are neither obligatory nor prohibited, they can also be considered morally neutral. The authority of moral obligation gives one the right to act as required and to refrain from performing prohibited actions. For this reason, each person has the authority to act as he or she morally ought, even in the face of political, legal, or other obligations to act to the contrary. With respect to morally neutral acts, morality does not provide an excuse for failure to comply with nonmoral obligations. Problems arise from the discrepancy between what morality demands and what someone thinks morality demands.

Although everyone is obliged to act as morality demands, no individual and no collective is infallible as to what these demands are. An action has subjective moral worth only if the agent acts as he thinks he ought to act. His action has objective moral worth only if he acts as he ought. His action has both subjective and objective moral worth if he acts as he thinks he ought to and if this coincides with his actual moral obligation. From a practical point of view, if he wishes to act morally, he should never act in a way that he believes to be immoral. If he comes to believe that an action is morally wrong and chooses it nonetheless, he chooses what he believes is morally evil, and such a choice is a choice to act immorally.

Where views conflict as to the morality of an action, no authority other than morality itself can settle the dispute. Both parties to such a dispute should give rational consideration to all the facts, principles, and values at issue. Whether or not all moral differences can be resolved in principle, clearly they cannot all be resolved in practice. When the conflict is between a person or a group and the laws of a society, the authority of moral obligation is overriding. In these instances an individual has the moral right or authority to act counter to the law. He need not declare his actions openly or necessarily attempt to change the law; nor need he be willing to suffer the legal consequences of his actions; for this authority is moral and not legal or political. It is not the same as the claimed right to civil disobedience. Civil disobedience is a political act, though it is based on the premise that each person has the authority to act as morality demands, together with the claim that some individual law or laws may be immoral and should be changed. If the aim of a civil disobedient is to question the legitimacy or the morality of certain laws or governmental actions and if he has attempted to work through the established channels, governmental authorities interested in morality should seriously consider his claims, as should other members of the society. However, since the disobedient may himself be mistaken in what he thinks morality obliges, others are neither legally nor morally required to pardon any or all such disobedients simply because they claim to be acting on the basis of their conscience or to be acting with the authority of moral obligation. When no substantial harm is done to others, the disobedients' moral purpose and intent should distinguish them from those who break the same laws without moral intent.

The authority to act as one is morally required to do is consistent with others' so acting and with each person's protecting himself and refraining from doing injury to others. Moral authority is overriding in the sense that one's moral obligation is the basis on which one should act, despite possible legal or other rules to the contrary. Only the foolish person or the fanatic ignores the possibility of mistakenly perceiving what morality actually requires when tradition, rules, laws, values, or principles weigh against his own perceptions or preconceptions. These should all be considered.

A larger unit, group, collective, organization, or a state also acts with the authority of moral obligation when it does what is morally required of it. A morally justified government has no right to legislate what is immoral. Nor do all of its actions or laws carry the authority of moral obligation, since not all of them are required by morality. Moreover, since it cannot possibly do so, a government has no obligation to legislate and enforce all that is required by morality. The extent to which a government should legislate and enforce what is morally required depends on what type of society it is, what type of executive (nonmoral) authority it has, the quality of life and the moral development of its citizens, its own moral knowledge, the amount of disruption the society can stand in allowing free rein to a diversity of moral views, and similar considerations.[1] Yet we can and should

---

1. For a development of this point see my articles "The Enforcement of Morality as a Function of Law," *Annuario de filosofia del derecho* 17 (1973/74): 533–38; and "Law and Ethical Pluralism," *Archiv für Rechts-und Sozial Philosophie,* supplement no. 11 (1979), pp. 281–91.

distinguish what a government does with the authority of moral obligation from those actions which it performs that are neither immoral nor morally obligatory.

THE CONCEPT OF MORAL AUTHORITY

The concept of moral authority is closely related to the authority of moral obligation. Because I have both the duty and the right to act as duty commands, when I so act, I can be said to be acting in a manner that is authorized by morality. A person who acts in this way acts with moral authority. His actions are authorized by the demands of morality. This approach to moral authority defines it as legitimate.

This sense of the term underlies the phrase 'moral authority' when it is used to characterize the actions of those who act with confidence and assurance that their actions are morally correct; and in these cases it describes the psychological state of the agent, rather than the action itself. Someone who is convinced of the morality of his action, whether or not his action is actually objectively moral and whether or not he has the right to force it upon others, may in an authoritative manner perform some given action or may attempt to enforce his view. He may act as if he had the moral authority to so act whether he has such authority or not. His assurance and the strength of his belief may be sufficient to render him a de facto epistemic or exemplary moral authority and for others to consider that his actions have moral authority and to accept them. But legitimate moral authority accrues to moral actions and only to moral actions, irrespective of the psychological confidence or lack of confidence of the agent.

We also speak of countries acting with moral authority or of authorities within a country acting with moral authority, sometimes in the performance of their regular duties, sometimes in actions that are not specifically designated by the rules that govern their office. To speak in this way is to judge that their actions are morally justifiable, whether or not they are acting precisely as prescribed by law (though not usually in opposition to it).

'Moral authority' can also refer to the character and quality of the holder of an office in government, such that it amplifies his legal authority and justifies the trust of office that he bears. It signifies more than a justification according to some law or constitution; it also signifies a feeling on the part of those who are subject to him that he is not only a legal ruler but a legitimate ruler who can be trusted. If a leader or an official has moral authority in this sense, he commands greater respect than otherwise; when it is lacking, his reign and influence are impeded. For this reason not only Caesar but also Caesar's wife should be above reproach. Scandals in government, even if they involve no illegality, weaken respect for the officeholder who is involved, weaken his ability to lead, and so frequently weaken his ability to influence people and to wield his power in noncoercive ways.

The basis of such moral authority is morality itself; it grounds both the action and the actor's character. The most appropriate virtues to establishing moral authority in the political domain are honesty, integrity, truthfulness, selflessness, and dedication to duty. We can define de facto moral authority as the respect given to X and to X's actions by Y (who stands in an inferior position to X in R) because of Y's belief in X's morally upright character and in the morality of X's actions in R. Such an authority is legitimate when X does in fact have the moral character that is being attributed to him and when X's actions are morally grounded. Such legitimate moral authority gives the bearer no special right to command, but it may well incline Y to obey X's legal commands, follow X's suggestions, or implement X's policies more willingly and readily than Y otherwise would. These are not things that the bearer can rightfully demand; but they are the natural, expected results of such de facto moral authority, other things being equal.

Such moral authority can accrue to leaders in realms other than the political, as, for example, to religious leaders; but it should be distinguished from exemplary moral authority. If an exemplary moral authority did attempt to give orders or to influence people, moral authority might attach to his orders as well. The moral authority of political leaders results not from extraordinary virtue but from public virtue together with public position. The same person who had the same qualities without the office would not have the same moral authority, because it typically becomes effective as well as de facto when it is joined to a role of leadership or public trust.

THE FUNCTION OF AUTHORITY WITHIN MORALITY

The third aspect of the authority/morality relation concerns the legitimate function of authority within morality. The domain of morality is a fruitful testing ground for the thesis that nonexecutive authority does not carry with it any right to command. This thesis marks out the limits of authority in the moral domain and makes the proper function of authority in the moral domain compatible with morality itself.

In one common meaning of the term, someone is a de facto moral authority if he dictates what men ought to do insofar as their actions are right or wrong and if he rewards or punishes them according to whether or not they act as he commands. Thus, someone is an executive moral authority if he is the author of morality, in the sense that his decisions or commands make actions either right or wrong. The paradigm of such a moral legislator and executive is God, though in certain eras and in certain social systems it might be the king, the ruler, the government, or the party. Thus X is a de facto executive moral authority for Y if Y believes that whatever X enunciates as a command or prohibition for Y (as an individual or as a member of a class) becomes Y's moral duty. The range of such authority may be unlimited, as in the case when God is the moral authority. If the state were a moral authority, the range might extend only to certain public acts. The extent of God's moral authority might be thought to extend legitimately to all of mankind, though in one de facto sense it would extend only to those believers who consider him such an authority. The extent of a state's moral authority might reach to all citizens or to all those within its borders, or it might include only a subset of these. The de facto range and extent might therefore be less than the legitimate range and extent. X could also be Y's parents, and the range could be a rather limited number of actions that are open to a young child. Or some Y might feel morally bound by some X's commands for any of several possible reasons, in which case X would be a de facto moral authority for Y. This is one important sense of a 'moral authority'; it is the one that is most frequently criticized by moral philosophers. It is not the only sense, however.

In a second sense, someone might be called a moral authority if he were an authority on morality. If, as many claim, morality involves knowledge of right and wrong, then someone might be called a moral authority if he were an epistemic authority in the field of morality. This would not be a distinctive kind of authority but would be a subclass of epistemic authority, and the principles of justification and of limitation that apply to the latter would apply equally to the former. In this sense, X would be a de facto epistemic moral authority if there were some person Y who, because of Y's belief in X's greater knowledge of morality, holds some proposition p, which X enunciated (or which Y believes X has enunciated) in the moral domain, to be true or more probably true than before Y believed that X enunciated *p*.

Providing the same person is not taken as a moral authority in both the first and second senses, the difference is that in the second sense, Y does not believe that X is the author of morality or that X has the right to reward or punish Y, at least not in the same sense that the author of morality does. Y may believe that the moral authority in the first meaning of the term has delegated the right of reward or punishment to the epistemic moral authority; but such a right is distinct from the simple belief of *p* by Y, which constitutes X as an epistemic moral authority.

Individuals or groups of individuals often find their moral values exemplified in a particularly dramatic, moving, or inspiring way by some holy person, saint, or moral hero. In this sense, X (the holy person, saint, or moral hero) is a de facto exemplary moral authority for Y if X's actions (or at least some of them) constitute for Y a model of appropriate or of morally praiseworthy behavior which Y attempts to emulate.

If there were no cognitive content in moral statements, it would not be possible for X to be a legitimate epistemic moral authority unless X simply reported what people believed; but it would be possible for X to be a legitimate exemplary moral authority, because what is conveyed to Y by X is not a set of principles or any explicit statements at all, but is feelings, reactions, patterns, and modes of behavior, which it may or may not be possible to make explicit. To the extent that morality is emotive and to the extent that it involves certain ways of living, an espousal of certain values, and a reaching for certain ideals, X can be a moral authority for Y without being either the author of morality or a teacher, scholar, or sage in the moral realm if X has the appropriate exemplary effect on Y. Though the same person may be both an exemplary and an epistemic moral authority, an epistemic moral authority communicates through propositions that are believed; an exemplary moral authority communicates through actions or the results of actions that appeal to the emotions and provoke a positive response. A legitimate exemplary moral authority must be holy or must act morally, but it need not have explicit knowledge of principles or be able to articulate them.

Can anyone be a legitimate moral authority in any of the above senses? The preponderant view among contemporary philosophers is that there can be no legitimate moral authority in the first sense,[2] though a good many religious people think otherwise. Two major arguments have frequently been used to show that no one can be a legitimate executive moral authority. The first is based on the source of morality and of moral norms and values; the second, on an analysis of moral autonomy or freedom. Each makes a valid point. Nevertheless, the conclusions of these arguments do not end the investigation of authority and morality, they simply provide a beginning for it.

(1) The first argument, whose long history can be traced back at least to Plato, depends on what it means for someone to be an executive moral authority. According to this view someone is an executive moral authority if he is the author of morality in the sense that his decision or command makes actions right or wrong. What can it mean for the rightness or wrongness of an action to be determined by such an authority? Either the decision about the moral quality of an action is arbitrary and dependent only on his will or whim, or he has some criteria by which to decide which actions are right, good, or moral and which are not.

Suppose that an action is right or wrong only because someone in authority says this is so. Then an action is right or wrong if it is judged so by the authority. This is not what most people mean by 'good' or 'bad', 'right' or 'wrong'. Even if someone were to mean this by these terms, would he continue to do so if he analyzed what this entails? A reasonable person could not, for he would need some good reason for accepting the fiat of the one in authority, and no such good reason is available. The most plausible reasons, and the ones that are usually given for such acceptance, are either that (a) the moral lawgiver is powerful and will punish those who do not follow the

---

2. Thus Charles Hendel noted: "The moral philosopher will have no truck whatever with authority. For to allow of any possible role for authority in the moral life of man is to take away its properly ethical character, no matter whether the authority be divine or regal, because morality consists in actions of an individual's own authentic choice, choice in the light of his own knowledge, appraisal, and conviction, without any external inducements or sanctions" ("An Exploration of the Nature of Authority," *Authority*, Nomos 1 [1958], p. 7). This has been the position of most moral philosophers, at least of this century, who have been concerned to preserve the autonomy of morality from metaphysics, and who have defended a morality independent of religion.

commands or that (b) the moral lawgiver is good, can command only what is good, and therefore should be obeyed.

(a) The first reason involves the fear of punishment, here or hereafter. However, such fear is not an adequate moral basis for obeying an authority's commands. If someone who is powerful were to command an immoral act, the subject of that command might well perform it out of fear; but his performance of an immoral action, though itself an instance of obedience, would not change the nature of the performed act. According to the view being considered, however, an action commanded by the moral authority could not be immoral, because what it means for an action to be wrong is for it to be held wrong by the one who is in authority. The result of this view is that any action—no matter how vile by any reasonable standard—would be moral as long as it was commanded, arbitrarily or not, by the one in authority. The murder of millions, the wanton infliction of pain, the senseless maiming of the innocent—all of these would become moral actions that must be performed when commanded by the authority if one wished to act morally. No enlightened person could accept this view as a serious account either of what most people mean or of what they should mean when they speak of morality. The power to force a subject to act in the way that one demands is insufficient, therefore, to make an action moral, if "moral" is to be understood in any ordinary sense.

(b) The other alternative holds an action to be good because it is commanded by someone in authority who is good and so would not command what is evil. Since God is all good and incapable of commanding what is evil, God's commands are good and moral. This claim again presents two choices. For either (i) what God commands is good simply because it emanates from him and because he is good; or (ii) God is good because he always commands what is in fact good independent of his command; this implies that he has some criteria for deciding what is good and what is bad.

(i) Consider the first alternative. What could the claim that God (or some other moral authority) is good mean to the person who is searching for the basis of morality? If whatever God commands is good and if we are not to fall back into the previous case in which even the most heinous crimes become good because they are commanded by God or by some other authority, then some other sense must be given to the statement that God is good. The ordinary means of judging whether someone is good is by examining his actions. This is precisely what, in this case, we are precluded from doing, because according to this view what the authority commands is good simply because it is commanded. There is thus no independent way to judge the goodness or badness of the commands, because any criterion outside of the authority's commands is denied. As a result, there is no way to judge that the authority is good, yet the argument depends on this judgment. It thus assumes precisely that goodness that it aims to explain.

One might attempt to save the argument in two ways. The first would be to maintain that on some independent grounds one can judge that the authority is good; once this judgment has been made, then it can be held with confidence that anything that the authority commands is good, even if we do not see why it is good. This argument presupposes the validity of some judgments based on criteria other than the goodness of the lawgiver or the moral executive. If this is so, however, then first, there are independent means of determining what is right and wrong, good and bad, which are logically prior to the criterion of the authority's fiat; and second, the meaning of the terms is not dependent on the lawgiver. If the independent judgments are valid for deciding that the authority is in fact good, can they not be used to decide in each case whether or not he is good? It may be reasonable to hold that his judgment on a given moral issue is correct even though the reasons are not clear. This acknowledges him as an epistemic moral authority, though this is not the same as saying that what is commanded is right simply because it is commanded by the authority. The possibility of independent judgment must be available if one is to have legitimate grounds for assuming that the authority is judging on the basis of greater insight into the available criteria. Hence this version of the argument fails to substantiate the view that what is right or good is made right or good simply by the arbitrary decision of an authority.

A second way in which one might attempt to save the argument is to claim on faith that the lawgiver is good and to accept whatever he says in this regard. If no rational defense is made for this leap of faith and if no claim is made for its rationality, then argument and reasons are to no avail. This move takes morality beyond the realm of rational consideration, and someone who is defending this view cannot at the same time maintain it and consistently claim to be holding a rationally justifiable position. Such arbitrary morality becomes indistinguishable from the arbitrary decisions of the lawgiver. It thus collapses into the first type of case which we examined. An alternative version of the argument asserts that the lawgiver, if he is in fact also the maker of the beings that he commands, has the right to command his subjects as he wills. This also collapses either into case (a) or into a view in which the term 'right' and the criteria for moral goodness are in some sense independent of the lawmaker's whim.

Either variation of this view of a moral authority presents a further difficulty. Suppose one holds that the fiat of a moral authority determines right and wrong and that somehow this can be given a consistent interpretation. How could moral agents ever know what actions to perform? How could they know which actions were right and which ones were wrong? If all actions were right or wrong only by the decision of an authority, then that authority would have to pass judgment on each action. A general set of rules would be insufficient, since at any time he might change the rules and make what was right wrong and what was bad good. Hence, we could never know which acts were right and which wrong. Furthermore, since no rules can cover all situations, we would need to interpret the rules in different situations. Unless we were told the correct interpretation in each specific instance, we would not know how to act in order to behave morally. No human authority could possibly give each of us his interpretation, even if, like Big Brother in *1984*, he constantly surveyed each of our actions with his electronic equipment. If the moral authority is God, it is claimed that he can keep track of all our actions and dictate what we should do. To maintain this view consistently, however, God must do more than issue the Ten Commandments, establish a church, or authorize some body of interpreters to communicate his views. God must have a direct line with all moral men. Whether we consider a special group to be the interpreters of God's desires or whether each person has a direct line to the moral authority through something like conscience, we must make clear how the authority communicates decisions in each case. Some people claim to know directly how the moral authority evaluates a situation, calling it inspiration or moral intuition. How such claims to knowledge can be verified, if equally sincere and believing people frequently disagree on the moral quality of a particular action, remains an unanswerable question if the authority's fiat is the only allowable criterion.

(ii) The second alternative fares no better. If we argue that God is good because he always commands what is in fact good independent of his command, we are forced to acknowledge some criterion for his deciding what is good and what is bad. The arbitrariness of God's commands is thus denied. The attempt is both to say that God is not arbitrary and yet to maintain that morality, at least in some sense, comes from him. A standard argument claims that God is rational, and so he made things and the rules by which they are governed, not arbitrarily, but for good reasons. Another maintains that he made the world and human beings according to certain laws of his own choosing. These laws of nature can be discovered by human beings; but since the laws are dependent on God in the first place, he could have made them differently. Whether the appeal is to the nature of reason or to natural law, this argument acknowledges a criterion that is independent of an authority's command, even if it maintains that metaphysically the criterion is dependent on the authority.

The argument concludes that the moral authority designates certain actions as good because by some criterion or criteria he knows they are good. It is because they *are good* that he says they are; it is not the case that they are good *because he says so*. But if actions are good independently of his saying so, if they are morally independent of his command, then the source of their goodness must be something other than his fiat or command. Furthermore, the criterion or criteria must be available to others. Otherwise they could never judge that the moral authority and his actions and decisions were good, and so they would not know that they should accept what he says and act as he says. If what is good and what is bad are not dependent on his fiat, then we should attempt to uncover the grounds for the goodness and badness of actions. The difficulty of discovering what the authority says, of interpreting it, and of deciding whether it is in fact moral is greater and involves more chance of error than discovering simply whether the action is moral or immoral. Because this can be dis-covered independently of the moral lawgiver, the moral lawgiver becomes superfluous for this purpose. God, the Church, the govern-ment, or the rulers of the state may know better than the ordinary man what is right or wrong. Nonetheless, this is beside the point, because neither the meaning of 'good' and 'bad' nor the morality of any action is dependent on the command of the lawgiver or of the moral authority. As a consequence, the moral person stands in no need of an executive moral authority. Morality is autonomous; it does not depend on authority.

(2) The second argument that is generally brought against authority in morality is based on a view of the freedom and autonomy of the moral agent. It goes briefly as follows. A moral agent freely chooses an action and accepts responsibility for it. Though he may

seek advice from others, ultimately he must decide for himself how he is to act, and he should take responsibility for his action. Only in so doing is he a full moral agent.

In the Kantian version of this argument, the moral agent's autonomy involves his being his own lawgiver. This does not mean, however, that he can create any moral laws that he wishes; he must follow the dictates of reason and the universal laws that reason prescribes. He is to act on the moral law because it is his duty to so act. Strictly speaking, only then is he moral. Thus, to act simply on the command of another, to give over one's responsibility or to give up one's moral autonomy, is to cease to be a fully moral agent. According to the Sartrean interpretation, to give up one's moral autonomy in this way would be to act in bad faith, that is, to act as if one were not free.

In any version of this argument a moral action is not simply one that coincides with what is morally obligatory. If an action is to have subjective moral worth, it must be performed by someone who freely chooses to do it, which precludes his doing it simply because it is commanded. To act on the command of a moral authority is to withhold judgment as to the moral worth of an action or to assume its morality simply because it is commanded. In this case, one is not legislating for oneself but is giving up his autonomy, and to that extent is no longer a full moral agent. Children may have the obligation to obey their parents; but this reflects the fact that they are not fully developed rational beings. If mature adults are to exercise their full moral capacities, they cannot do what another says merely because he commands it. This would make obedience the only moral commandment. Every act would be only an act of obedience, without taking into consideration the nature of the commanded action. The agent would thereby relinquish responsibility for the morality of the commanded action, and to that extent he would fail to act morally. Hence, the argument goes, the moral autonomy of the individual is incompatible with moral authority in the sense of a moral lawgiver.

Both of the preceding arguments have a valid point. First, morality is autonomous, in the sense that it is not simply the arbitrary fiat of someone in authority; actions are right or wrong, good or bad, because of something other than the word of an authority. Second, all rational men can, in principle, arrive at a determination of moral rules, values, or particular obligations. The individual rational being is morally autonomous in the sense that ultimately he must choose for himself how to act and must accept the responsibility for such actions; but it would be a mistake to conclude that there is no legitimate moral authority in any sense or that authority and morality are antithetical. To do so would fail to consider carefully enough either the nature of authority or the actual moral situation in which people find themselves acting as moral agents.

The force of the first argument was that actions are not right or wrong because they are commanded or forbidden by some moral legislator; there is no legitimate universal executive moral authority. The concept of a moral executive authority is only one of the senses of moral authority, and we have seen that it is the wrong paradigm for considering the true function of authority in morality and for making sense out of ordinary usage.

The second argument defended the moral autonomy of the truly moral individual. There may be few truly moral human beings in this sense, just as there are or may be few fully rational men; and even fully rational and moral individuals did not spring into being fully grown. Autonomous morality is an achievement and the result of an individual's building on what is supplied by conventional morality, by society, by saints, by sages and philosophers, and by one's parents, teachers, and friends. If an agent knows what it means to be moral and if he wishes to be moral, he may well seek guidance. To act morally involves attempting to form one's conscience correctly. The autonomy of conscience does not mean that it is *sui generis* and cut off from the moral experience and knowledge of others. Though conscience should not be forced or coerced, its autonomy is consistent with information and guidance; in this sense it is compatible with recognizing and following, not an executive moral authority, but rather an epistemic or exemplary moral authority.

EPISTEMIC AND EXEMPLARY MORAL AUTHORITY

Since an epistemic moral authority differs from other epistemic authorities only in the field of his knowledge, the legitimacy of such authority is established by the same general argument, and an epistemic moral authority is someone who has knowledge in the moral realm. It may be knowledge of moral principles, expertise in moral reasoning or in the application of such principles to specific cases, or knowledge of conventional norms—that is, of what is generally held to be right and wrong by a community or society. Y's belief of p as uttered by X, when p is in the moral realm, is sufficient to constitute X as a de facto moral authority. X might be an individual person or a group (such as a church or the ruler of some society) or a book (such as the Bible) or an ethics text. In each case the person who is subject to authority (Y) believes what the authority (X) says and so constitutes X as a de facto authority. But such an authority may be legitimate or not, depending on whether, in fact, X has the presumed knowledge and whether or not what X says is actually the case. Someone could be a de facto epistemic moral authority even if there were no such thing as moral knowledge. He could also be a legitimate epistemic moral authority, providing that he had knowledge of conventional morality or of what was generally held to be moral.

If parents are de facto epistemic moral authorities for their children, the children believe what the parents say in the moral realm to a greater or lesser extent. In the moral as in other realms, children do well to learn from their parents as well as from their teachers and other adults. As they grow older, children become more discriminating in what they believe in the moral as in other realms. When authorities disagree, children rightly attach less credence to their statements than when the authorities agree. This in part accounts for the difficulty in transmitting moral norms and values in a dynamic pluralistic society as opposed to a traditional monolithic one.

Epistemic moral authority, by its very nature, is substitutional, as is all epistemic authority. Others can, in principle, achieve the knowledge that the epistemic moral authority has; as the one who is subject to authority acquires more of that knowledge, he has less need for the authority. In the moral realm a proper aim of a moral teacher is to enable the subjects of his authority eventually to think through moral problems for themselves. Parents tell their children what is right and wrong and counsel them until they are able to make the necessary discriminations, carry on the moral reasoning process, and make moral evaluations on their own.

Epistemic moral authority is substitutional in a second sense. Adults also need help at times with their moral reasoning. They seek advice and moral guidance. Because adults are not subject to anyone in the sense that a child is subject to his parents and is dependent on them, they choose a moral authority from a wider range of possibilities than is open to a child. Epistemic moral authorities may be formally designated in a society, or they may be informally identified by an individual on his own. In each case the logic behind the identification is similar.

Applying to moral epistemic authority what is generally the case for any epistemic authority, the one who is seeking a moral authority must have at least some knowledge of the field if he is to make the identification himself. He must know something about what is moral and what is not, he must know what moral knowledge is like, and he must believe that he has some such knowledge. Otherwise he will not be able to recognize someone who has it. He must be able to verify, by some independent means, at least some of the moral statements of the person whom he will accept as an authority. He must also be able to follow, at least to some extent, the reasoning by which the authority arrives at his conclusions. If he is able to do that much, he can feel—rightly or wrongly—that he has good reason for accepting the authority's conclusions even if he is unable to follow the authority's reasoning or principles. He will, in this way, have some grounds for believing the authority to be a legitimate authority and for making him a de facto authority. The amount of credence the subject gives to the authority may vary from very slight belief in what he says to complete belief, depending on what else the subject knows; the other opinions, statements, or beliefs pertinent to the moral situation he has encountered; or the satisfactoriness of the advice that he has received in the past. Many correct utterances in an area build up a basis for confidence in authority; even a few discovered errors undermine such confidence.

The situation is similar for a formally designated epistemic moral authority. An informal moral authority for an individual might be a more knowledgeable friend or loved one or someone who is more morally sensitive or objective. A formally recognized authority is someone whom society or some portion of society designates as having more than usual competence in an area because of study or training of a certain type. Thus, moral philosophers or ordained ministers are certified as having spent a certain number of years studying moral theory, casuistry, or other pertinent materials. Society's stamp signifies that some process, similar to the one described above with respect to an individual, has been gone through for a class of persons. Just as doctors or lawyers are certified, so are ministers or moral philosophers. Such certification designates an individual as a member of a class. The acceptance of the pronouncements of a clergyman by his flock is a typical example of an officially certified epistemic moral authority whom many accept as a de facto moral authority.

203

Tradition reinforces and builds up increasing respect for certain authorities: for example, for the Bible, for the moral writings of Aristotle or Kant, or for other similar works. Tradition also reinforces the belief that certain things are either right or wrong. Unless circumstances have pertinently altered their applicability, the fact that they have withstood the test of time can be an indication of their validity, even though it does not prove it.

Disagreements among authorities tend to undermine their authority. This is clearly seen when formal epistemic moral authorities within a given church or society differ as to the morality—for example, of birth control, abortion, or divorce; and it is also the case when different sects or segments of society hold varying views on the morality of an act or on moral values. Despite these limitations, however, to the extent that morality has cognitive content, some X can be a legitimate epistemic authority for some Y.

Exemplary moral authority presents a similar situation. Since morality is a realm of practical activity, virtue—as well as knowledge—can make one an authority. An epistemic moral authority should have knowledge in the moral realm; however, he need not act in accordance with that knowledge: that is, it is not necessary for him to act virtuously or in an exemplary manner. One might well question the depth of his knowledge or the sincerity of his belief if he were consistently to act in opposition to his stated beliefs on moral issues. Such an authority, however, need not be especially moral in order to be good at moral reasoning. Weakness of will and knowledge of moral principles are compatible.

An exemplary moral authority, on the other hand, is one whose actions inspire others or one whose actions become a model for the behavior of others. Saints and the recounted lives of saints, holy men, and moral heroes—such as Christ, Saint Francis, Gandhi, Martin Luther King—all serve as exemplary moral authorities for many who are inspired by their actions or are guided by their behavior. Someone may see exemplary moral conduct in the actions of a friend, an associate, a neighbor, or a loved one; he may choose to act as that person does, follow in the causes that he champions, live in his style. He may also seek him out for moral advice and may follow what the other one says, not because of any reasons or principles that the latter articulates, but because he has accepted the authority's judgments and actions in previous circumstances. Officially designated exemplary moral authorities are usually persons who are outstanding because of their moral actions. They have not only fulfilled their ordinary obligations but also either have surpassed the demands of morality (if such is possible) in self-sacrifice or have otherwise distinguished themselves by their moral courage or insight.

Moral values and attitudes are often communicated more effectively by example than by preaching; moral reasoning is communicated more effectively by teaching and explanation than simply by action. Although epistemic moral authority and exemplary moral authority are in many cases distinguishable, they are very closely related and are frequently found together. The great moral teachers have most often been moral exemplars as well.

Epistemic and exemplary moral authority can play a legitimate role in the moral realm. This does not imply that a moral authority in these senses can legitimately absolve a moral agent of the responsibility to make moral decisions. Such an authority does not have the right to command the actions of another in the sense that he has the right to tell him what to do and to punish him for not obeying. Neither epistemic nor exemplary moral authority entails any form of executive moral authority. I have argued, when discussing epistemic authority, that knowledge alone entails no right to command; similarly, neither epistemic nor exemplary moral authority (nor the two together) entails any right to command, in the sense of morally binding the actions of another. Hence, executive moral authority cannot be justified or rendered legitimate in terms of one's moral knowledge or virtue alone.

An epistemic or exemplary moral authority may give commands in the sense of uttering imperatives (e.g., Thou shalt not steal). He may tell others what to do, and he may act on or for them. His actions may be accepted and his commands obeyed. He thus may be a de facto executive moral authority. However, we should distinguish between enunciating an actual moral imperative that should bind any person who is appropriately situated, whether he happens to hear it or not, and X's attempting to bind Y morally by some command simply because X commands it. The latter case is not justified either by knowledge or by virtue. If someone either believes or knows that a certain action is right or wrong, this knowledge by itself does not bestow on him any *right* to force an action on others. He may himself have an obligation to act in a certain way or to try to inform others of the proper way to act and to exhort them to do so; but this real or purported knowledge *by itself* does not give him the right to coerce the actions of another.

This assertion must be correctly understood. Knowledge of one's obligation entails the moral duty to fulfill that obligation. On the other hand, knowledge of someone else's obligations or knowledge that some action that is going to be performed by someone else is wrong does not by itself give anyone the right to interfere with the action or to force a different action. If some harm is to befall a third party, then one may have the obligation to protect that person; but this is different from having the right to force another to act in a certain way *simply* because of one's moral knowledge or virtue. If, for instance, someone knows that serving in the army, practicing segregation, or engaging in prostitution is wrong, he does not, simply by virtue of this knowledge, have the right forcibly to prevent anyone from doing these things. He might speak against such actions, attempt to get legislation enacted to outlaw them, or take other steps by virtue of his rights as a citizen, but not by virtue of his knowledge alone. The preacher or the prophet may have the duty to exhort others to act in certain ways; but neither virtue nor knowledge gives him any special right to act on or for others. To the extent that interference with the actions of others is morally justified or required, he shares with everyone else the right to engage in such interference or to the use of force. He acquires no special rights because of his status as an authority. The words and actions of a de facto epistemic or exemplary moral authority may draw followers who do as he says simply because he says so. They may so act because they accept the correctness of his statements for some valid reason other than his saying so; they are not so much responding to his command as they are acting in response to the moral imperative that he clarifies or enunciates for them to do so. They may, on the other hand, act simply because he commands them. In both instances their right to act should not be confused with the authority's right to command, which cannot legitimately be based only on his knowledge or virtue.

Someone may approach an epistemic moral authority for moral guidance. If the enquirer receives such guidance, he may be immoral if he does not act on it. But the one who gave the guidance has no right to force anyone to act as morality demands: that is, he has no *special* right as an epistemic authority to do so. An epistemic moral authority can legitimately only inform a person of the moral nature of the act in question, explain the reasons that substantiate the judgment, and exhort him to act morally. Similarly, the saint or holy person who inspires actions may exhort others to act in the same way; but neither authority has any special right to force them to so act. This follows from the nature of morality and from the freedom due to an autonomous moral agent. A moral agent can rightly seek advice, and he should act on the best advice and insight that he can find. Nevertheless, the action remains his, and he retains the responsibility for it.

If we see the legitimate function of a nonexecutive authority in the moral realm as being that of one who teaches what is right or who exemplifies what is good, then the model of such an authority is not that of an executive giving orders but that of a teacher showing the way. The better he does his job, the less he is needed.

An individual's conscience is the proximate and, in that sense, the ultimate personal authority in moral matters. This simply means that in the end, the moral agent must decide for himself how he is to act. The moral teacher can say what he believes to be right and wrong; and a good teacher of those who have reached moral maturity will also explain why and how that judgment was arrived at, what rules or principles were pertinent, and what values were involved. The reasoning can thus be followed and checked.

In a society of mature moral individuals, a church might well be a legitimate epistemic or exemplary moral authority whose adherents learn from it or who find in it examples of virtue. Frequently, members of a church find examples of wisdom and virtue in the church despite its obvious defects, while nonmembers, who focus on the defects, are not touched by the examples of virtue and are not persuaded by the moral reasoning of its leaders. Though no church has any legitimate *executive* moral authority, it may legitimately function as *an* authority in the moral realm.

The autonomy of one's conscience is compatible with learning from an epistemic or exemplary moral authority and with denying the right to command morality as a function of moral knowledge or virtue. Each person is morally obliged to act in accordance with the dictates of the moral law. Practically speaking, the moral person acts according to the dictates of his conscience when he acts on the basis of the best moral deliberation he is capable of at the time, taking into account all of the pertinent facts, values, principles, and circumstances. However, no one's conscience is incorrigible or infallible. Each person has the obligation to determine his duty to the best of his ability, which may involve seeking someone else's guidance or example. Ultimately the action has subjective moral value only if he follows his conscience, which can itself be considered an executive moral authority, issuing commands. Because the commands are subjectively perceived, they are binding on oneself but not on anyone else.

Is it rational and moral to set oneself up as the interpreter of the moral law and to trust one's own reasoning even when it goes against tradition and generally recognized moral authorities? If we admit the legitimacy of epistemic and exemplary moral authority, do we not in fact seriously weaken the defense of moral autonomy and thus open the way for the moral executive?

Kierkegaard, in reflecting on the Biblical story of God's command to Abraham to sacrifice Isaac, describes the command from God as being unique and as going beyond the ethical realm, which is concerned with universal laws. Abraham thus becomes a knight of faith, whose actions result from a leap of faith that cannot be explained rationally or justified.

Another possible interpretation of this event, however, keeps Abraham's actions within the moral realm: he is following the universal injunction that whenever God issues some command that countervenes the Ten Commandments, this command should take precedence. God, in his omniscience, knows better than anyone else what is really right and wrong; since he is all good and has nothing to gain by lying or issuing immoral commands, he can be trusted when he issues commands that are contrary to the Ten Commandments.

The point is not Biblical exegesis. Rather, because within the described limits it is rational to believe and to follow what a legitimate epistemic moral authority says, it is rational to believe his statement that some particular action is immoral (or moral). Some churches and some governmental leaders make this claim for themselves: they claim to know better than the average member of such a society what is right and what is wrong, and so they issue pronouncements on the morality of certain acts. If the members of the communities do, in fact, accept such leaders as epistemic moral authorities, the members should take their leaders' statements seriously. But if the members wish to be fully responsible moral beings, they cannot simply accept what they are told without engaging in reflection and thought and without considering opposing arguments and other pertinent material. A pope, for instance, may try to guide the members of his church on moral issues, after seeking the best advice that he himself can obtain. Many members of his church, who may think that the pope has more resources at his disposal and has paid greater attention to the implications of the act, may take seriously what he preaches. If there are important dissenting voices, however, to some extent the individual relinquishes his moral responsibility by relying on authority instead of using authority to arrive at his own understanding of the situation.

The person who wishes to be morally autonomous should make every effort to establish a correct conscience, and he may legitimately utilize moral authorities to do so. He should also take into account public opinion on the question and the built-up wealth of tradition which forms a backdrop for many individual moral decisions. Just as tradition represents an accumulation of authority in other branches of knowledge, so it does in morality. The tradition may be mistaken; but one should have very good reasons for countering it in the moral as in other realms. Because the actions may seriously affect others and may produce irreversible results, more care should be taken when one goes against the weight of tradition in practical moral matters than in theoretical moral matters.

OBEDIENCE AND MORAL AUTHORITY

Though I denied the legitimacy of executive moral authority over fully adult moral individuals because such authority was incompatible with their autonomy, parents have the right to command their young children and legitimately to expect obedience. Does this constitute legitimate executive moral authority? If so, how is it justified, what is its proper domain, and, by extension, can it become a model for some individual or group to exercise such executive moral authority over others—perhaps masses of people—who have not achieved moral maturity?

In the case of parents and young children, executive moral authority is both a function of the position of the bearers of authority and a result of the incomplete moral development of those who are subject to such authority. Childhood is a training period, and obedience is the initial virtue through which good habits are formed. As children become fully autonomous moral persons, the legitimate moral authority of the parents diminishes and ultimately disappears. This is justified by the moral growth and development of the child.

We should, however, consider a little more closely what it means for a parent to be an executive moral authority. Parents have the right and the obligation to care for their child in his early years. This obligation involves teaching him or helping him to learn. He must be protected from danger, he must learn what he can and cannot safely touch, and he must eventually learn to respect the rights of others. In this process, parents are generally considered to have the right to use the necessary means for training their children, including the use of reasonable rewards and punishments. The right to do this is a constituent part of parental authority. For the benefit of all the members of a family or household, parents may justifiably establish certain rules or delegate certain chores. We can say that such authority is justified without saying that it is executive moral authority, which involves the right or power to dictate morality, in the sense of making something right or wrong simply by one's fiat. A clear limitation on a parent's executive authority, therefore, is that he has no right to command his children to do anything that is immoral. He cannot make what is immoral moral simply by commanding it. The child may feel some obligation to obey his parents simply because they tell him to do so; but if the action is immoral, he cannot be morally obligated to act as he is commanded. Children who have been taught not to lie intuitively feel this when they are commanded by their parents to tell a lie for the parents' convenience.

Secondly, when a parent commands his children to act in a morally correct manner—for example, by telling them to speak the truth or to return stolen goods—the real moral obligation comes from the nature of the act. The intermediary of the parent and the reward or punishment that is used place only a secondary moral obligation on the child; the primary demand is the morality of the action itself. When parents command children to do what is moral, the moral quality comes from the nature of the primary act, rather than from the fact that it is commanded. Thus far the parent is not an actual executive moral authority.

There are other actions, however, which are in themselves neither moral nor immoral. A child is told to be home at a certain time; he chooses to disobey that injunction and comes home at a later time. Has he acted immorally? Since coming home at that hour might be morally neutral, it is immoral only because it is an act of disobedience. In this instance, what is moral depends on the parent, on the one who is in authority or in a position to issue commands; the parent is then an executive moral authority. Although the extent of his legitimate ability to make actions right or wrong is limited, he does exercise such authority legitimately within those limitations. If the right to issue such commands is a function of the parental position, the right to administer some appropriate, reasonable punishment to encourage future adherence to such commands or rules is an instance of parental authority.

Everyone—this includes children—has an obligation to work for the general good and to promote the general harmony of the community, including the family community; and this involves abiding by the reasonable regulations that govern that community. In a family these regulations may be made by parents, especially for young children. Such rules or commands are specific instances of a child's general moral obligation, though he does not fully realize this and is not completely competent to translate from the general to the particular case. Parental authority is substitutional, and the child's moral obligation to obey is a substitute for the more complex moral demands he is still incapable of handling. But the obligation to obedience, though both real and comprehensible to the child, is only indirectly a moral obligation; it is also an imperfect obligation, binding someone who is not yet a fully moral being.

The claim that a child has a moral obligation to obey his parents in legitimate matters has historically been extended, implicitly or explicitly, by both states and churches, which sometimes claim that the leaders of these institutions are comparable to parents, while the members are comparable to children. These institutions claim that the members are not fully capable of reasoning correctly in regard to their moral obligations, which must be spelled out for them, and that members must turn to an authority in order to gain security and confirmation of the fact that their consciences are correctly formed. If the members of a state or of a church are in fact comparable to children in their moral insight and development and if the leaders have the knowledge and insight they claim to have, then, strictly speaking, the argument from moral autonomy is inapplicable, and the parentalistic argument has some cogency. There were perhaps stages in society's development when this was the case; there may be some societies or groups for which this is still the case. However, the people of many societies feel that they are mature adults, not children, and that they are not to be protected and commanded as if they were children. In the former societies, one might extend the analogy and maintain that citizens have the indirect and imperfect moral obligation, obedience within the limits set by the demands of morality, to obey the laws established by the leaders of the society, whether religious or civil. Yet even where the parental type of relation is not the model that is being followed, the question of whether citizens or members of a society are morally obliged to obey the laws of that society, simply because they are laws, can be answered in part on the basis of the parental analogy.

Because the state and the church are not the authors of morality, what they legislate cannot be morally binding simply because they legislate it. Also, one cannot be morally bound to obey a law that is immoral; otherwise one would be morally bound both to perform and to abstain from performing the same act. Nor when the same act is forbidden by both morality and the civil law does it make much sense to say that if one does the forbidden act—for example, if he commits murder—then he has broken a law of the state and two moral laws, one the law against murder and the second the law that one is to obey the laws of the state. It would suffice to say that he had broken both a law of the state and the moral law against murder. So the question of whether one has the moral obligation to obey the laws of the state refers most appropriately to those laws that are not in themselves either counter to what morality demands or are the same as what morality demands, and it might also cover the question of whether one is morally obliged to accept the punishment that is meted out by the state.

In many instances what parents command is simply a specification of a general moral obligation, which the children do not clearly perceive on their own, or a rule to foster the good of either the children or the family as a whole. The moral obligation of obedience is therefore an indirect one, as well as an imperfect one.

Similar reasoning applies to those laws that are regulative and that, though arbitrary in one sense, help to promote social order. Whether traffic is to move on the right side of the road or the left is arbitrary; but all motorists must follow the same convention if they expect to move in comparative safety. Obeying such laws is a matter of prudence rather than of morality, but to ignore the prudential and deliberately to endanger ourselves or others without good reason may well be immoral. Still other laws are procedural, and their aim is to settle disputes in an orderly manner. None of these cases violate one's autonomy, even if one had no say in the original passage of such legislation. The status of income-tax laws or conscription laws is more ambiguous. I will leave open the question of whether or not and under what conditions they are moral, rather than only legal, requirements. If there is a moral obligation to obey them, it is not because all legally promulgated laws are morally binding. Disobedience to such laws is at best indirectly immoral: for example, once a convention or rule has been adopted, injustice will be done to others unless each assumes a fair share, assuming that the laws are fair and equitable. If no harm is done to anyone by an action that is against such a law, the action may be illegal but not immoral. Suppose I overpark where others are neither deprived of a place nor inconvenienced. I can be cited for overparking, and I can be fined; but have I acted immorally? For an action to be indirectly immoral, the action must in some general way be immoral, though it would not be immoral unless the rule or law had been passed; but it is a specification of some general moral imperative. Inconveniencing others or taking an undue amount of parking space might be considered immoral insofar as it is inconsiderate of others or is unfair (assuming that consideration and fairness are morally obligatory); but in this instance, neither of these factors is at stake. The only other plausible reason for saying the action is immoral, even indirectly so, would be that breaking even this minor law ruptures the fabric of society in a small way, lessens one's respect for law, makes it easier next time to overpark when someone else's rights might be infringed. Such cases would determine the morality of the action, and reasonable men may differ. Insofar as there is a moral obligation to obey laws of this type, the moral obligation is an indirect and an imperfect one.

What of the acceptance of punishment? Anyone who disobeys an immoral law may still be legally liable. It would be odd to be morally obliged to break the law and also to be morally obliged to accept punishment for breaking the law. If the law is unjust, then it is unjust to punish someone for acting morally by doing what the law forbids or by refraining from doing what the law commands. Yet it does not follow that any means becomes morally legitimate in order to escape punishment.[3] One is, in general, indirectly obliged morally to accept and submit to just legal punishment insofar as such punishment forms part of the social fabric and framework on which the society is organized. This leaves open the question of what punishment is just (and not merely legal), and it assumes that some general moral justification can be given for the organization of the society.

The situation is similar with the class of actions that are otherwise morally neutral and that some statute makes legally obligatory. The obligation to accept punishment is an indirect one, and the gravity of

3. The consideration here is not the same as in the case of civil disobedience in which someone breaks another law in order to protect an unjust law. The civil disobedient is morally obliged to accept or to submit to just punishment for his lawbreaking.

it depends on the gravity of the damage done to the society, on the means one takes to avoid punishment, and similar considerations. If one parks overtime, inconveniences no one, and is not cited by the police, then most people would feel no moral obligation to turn themselves in, and the police would be astounded should anyone do so. But if one is cited and given a ticket, then the legal and moral obligation to pay the fine is different from the original obligation. The punishment, if legal, is justifiable if the state or other groups have some morally justifiable right to pass laws, such as parking laws.

If some type of executive authority can be justified for some group within a church, then that group may pass rules that, by analogy with the legal situation, can be said to be religiously binding. These rules are binding on members of that church only, unless they reiterate moral rules that are otherwise binding; and they must not command what is immoral. But actions of a third class are morally neutral. Dietary laws are an example. There is nothing intrinsically immoral about eating certain foods or about eating at certain times; yet a variety of religions observe fasting or abstinence of some kind. Similarly, attendance at religious services might be binding on members of a religion. Are such laws only religiously binding, or are they morally binding? Since we have argued that actions cannot arbitrarily be made moral or immoral by any supposed moral executive, it would follow that they are religiously binding, and they may be indirectly morally binding in the sense that I described with respect to parents and children. If, for instance, there were a moral obligation to worship God, then a religion that specifies a particular type of worship or a particular time for worship might be seen as specifying conditions for a general obligation. Whether any church or its leaders stand legitimately in a place that is analagous to parents and their children is left open here, though religious language frequently uses the analogy of God as Father of all, and churches sometimes claim to speak in God's name, and sometimes with his authority. The present point is not to analyze these claims or the nature or legitimacy of religious authority or of authority in religion but is simply to point out that the concept of indirect moral obligation might apply to religions as well as to a family and to a state. It might also apply to free associations and the rules thereof—for example, to universities, clubs, or corporations. A member might be said to have an indirect moral obligation to obey those rules that are not immoral so long as he remains a member.

To the extent that any of these organizations are free, a person may also say that he is indirectly morally obliged to obey the rules or laws in question. If one has promised, agreed, or contracted to obey them, then not to do so breaks the promise, agreement, or contract; this may be immoral, and hence breaking the rule could be indirectly immoral. This line of argument is more obvious in the case of joining a free association and explicitly entering into an agreement than it is in a family, a state, and, in many cases, a religion.

Neither an epistemic nor an exemplary moral authority has any special right to command, since knowledge and virtue by themselves do not carry with them or legitimately ground executive moral authority. Yet once we admit the legitimacy of an epistemic or of exemplary moral authority, as well as the indirect moral obligation to obey certain executive authorities, the line between these and executive moral authority becomes very thin. Since moral knowledge is frequently put in imperative form, an action that is done by some person in response to the imperative of someone else might seem to be the same whether the first person correctly took the second one as an epistemic moral authority or incorrectly took him as an executive moral authority. Nonetheless, the distinction is important, because the first is compatible with moral autonomy and is legitimate, while the second is not. Thus, if God or one of his spokesmen (be he prophet or church) is taken as an epistemic moral authority, then what he enunciates as moral commands may be justifiably accepted as such. The reason for accepting the Ten Commandments, for instance, would not be that they express the arbitrary command of an executive but that they enunciate moral laws which are promulgated by someone who knows more than does the one who is subject to the authority, who in turn has good reason to trust the knowledge and veracity of the bearer of the authority. The reasons would of course have to be specified; but if people have a moral obligation to do what is right and if they have a moral obligation to find out what actions are right, then there may well be cases in which they have an obligation to accept epistemic or exemplary moral authorities and have a moral obligation to act in accordance with what such authorities say and how they act. This can apply as well to traditions or to imperatives contained in the laws of a state.

The autonomy of the individual is crucial in the moral realm, but this does not deny the fact that morality, like language, is a social product. We learn what morality is only by living and interacting with others. The authority of tradition plays some role in passing on to us the content of morality as well as its general principles. Unless in some ways we initially accept on authority what morality is, most of us would never become morally autonomous beings. We all naturally pass through several stages in our moral development.[4] Some people may never get beyond the stage of conventional or conformity morality. If they do rise to the level of reflective morality, the level at which they become the autonomous persons whom philosophers are so interested in, then they arrive at that stage only after passing through the earlier stages. To the extent that tradition, customs, conventional mores, and the law—rather than principles or abstract values—determine the content of morality, we can say that the content is defined by the authority of tradition, custom, or law. To this extent, authority plays a direct role in laying the groundwork for its ultimate transcendence in autonomous morality.

Despite the autonomy of the individual moral person and despite the independence of the moral domain from the control of any executive moral authority, epistemic and exemplary moral authority are, under certain circumstances, compatible with morality. As a backdrop, they make personal moral development possible. Persons who accept either the commands of God or those of a church or who feel morally obliged by the laws of a government or a society have frequently misstated the basis for their obligations; but they cannot be easily ignored or shown to be as misguided as the traditional arguments maintain.

Authority and morality are intertwined in a variety of ways, yet at crucial points they are neither as close as some have maintained nor as antithetical as others would have us believe. Authority is sometimes compatible with morality and moral autonomy; sometimes it is not. Although in some instances we can decide the compatibility or incompatibility by a priori reasoning based on the concept of morality or of moral autonomy and on the concept of executive moral authority, in other instances we cannot, and we should then proceed by making a careful analysis of the circumstances and of the kinds of authority at issue.

---

4. For a developed view of the stages see Lawrence Kohlberg, ''The Claim to Moral Adequacy of a Highest Stage of Moral Judgment,'' *Journal of Philosophy* 70 (1973): 630–46.

10

Religion and Authority

According to many religions God is the creator of the universe. As the creator, he exercises legitimate executive authority over the earth and all human beings. His authority is ultimate in all domains, and therefore absolute. Many religions believe that God is all-knowing and truthful. Hence, if he speaks to human beings, he is an epistemic authority whose statements are eminently worthy of belief.

Is God's authority religious authority? Does he exercise his authority directly, or does he delegate it? The authority that religions, their members, or their representatives exercise within a secular society can often be distinguished from the authority found and exercised within established religions. If any of these is religious authority, how is it related to other kinds of authority in religion? How is it justified?

The answers to these large and complex questions cannot always be answered in general terms, because religions differ in their beliefs, in their structures, and in the authority that is exercised by or within them. I shall deal with some issues on a general level, but I shall attempt to give more detailed answers by taking Christianity as an example of an organized religion and by looking at the exercise of religion in the United States, where there is a constitutional separation of church and state. The relation of religion to the state is clearly different in the United States from what it is in England, Vatican City, Israel, and Iran.

DIVINE AND RELIGIOUS AUTHORITY

God's authority over the universe can be conceived in terms of power. As the creator of the universe, he established the laws of nature. He made human beings in certain ways. Exactly how we are to understand these statements, which are asserted by many religions, is a matter of interpretation; but if we assume the existence of God and that he created the universe, his authority over it is a function of his power. If we further assume that human beings had no right to be created and that they have no rights against God except those that he gives to them, then although human beings may wonder why God acts as he does, his actions require no justification. He is free to act as he chooses. His authority and power are such that human beings cannot affect them. He exercises his authority over them, whether or not they recognize him and his authority. We can call God's authority divine authority.

By recognizing or acknowledging God's dominion over them, human beings make God a de facto executive authority; and de facto divine authority exists whether or not God exists. However, divine authority is not religious authority. Divine authority is exercised by God; whatever religious authority turns out to be, it is exercised by human beings.

Religion is a relation between a person and God, in which the former acknowledges his dependence on and subservience to the latter. Religion, to this extent, is a personal matter and a personal relationship. But the relation in formal or organized religions is not only individual and private but is also public and communitarian. All of the generally recognized religions involve a community of believers, who are bound together by their common beliefs, joint practices, and some organizational structure. Organized or formal religions involve several kinds of authority. To what extent is the authority found de facto in organized religion compatible with the private and personal aspect of religion? What are the limits to the authority that is found in organized religions?

Some religions do not claim a divine origin. They consist of worshipping God and perhaps of seeking his intercession in the order of nature. If executive authority is exercised within the religion by some members, it may be by virtue of special powers these people claim and are recognized as having. Some individuals may be thought to be vehicles through whom God speaks or to be especially effective in seeking God's intervention. Others may have exceptional knowledge about God, his will, and his relation to human beings. Still others may be particularly holy, or they may dedicate their lives to God or to his service in special ways. Because of such special relations, power of invocation, knowledge, holiness, or dedication, the members of a religious community may give these individuals special authority. These individuals then become de facto epistemic or executive authorities within the field of religion. Although we might call the authority that is so granted religious authority, there is nothing special about it, other than the field in which it is exercised. Its source is the people, and it should be used for their good. It is, in principle, revocable by them and is subject to the principles of justification and limitation, which we have already described in dealing with the various types of executive and nonexecutive authority.

The same is not true with respect to those religions that claim divine origin, because the authority of these religions and at least some of the authority that is exercised within such religions comes, not from the people or from a community of believers, but from God. Because it is not of human origin, its justification and limitations may be considerably different from those for any other kinds of authority; and because such authority is exercised by human beings, it is not divine authority. We might call such authority religious authority. But not all authority that comes from God is religious authority, as the doctrine of the divine right of kings shows. Having God as its source is necessary but is not sufficient for us to call authority religious.

Nor can we define religious authority by saying that it is the authority exercised in or with respect to religious matters. A professor of the history of religion may be an expert and a legitimate epistemic authority in that field for his students. A professor of theology may be a legitimate epistemic authority in his field as well. Both are epistemic authorities concerning matters of religion; but neither one is a religious authority, and neither one has religious authority simply by virtue of his knowledge. Nor is all organizational authority within a church religious authority.

Religious authority comes from God, is exercised by human beings in the context of a church or religion, and is limited to religious matters—usually questions of belief in God, man's relation to God, the actions derived from these beliefs, and the morality implied by or contained in them. Just as belief in God is central to religion, so the basis and justification for religious authority is found in religious faith or in belief in God and his revelation. A necessary though not sufficient condition for such authority's being legitimate is that the religion in question be legitimate.

Over whom is religious authority exercised? The answer depends in part on who the bearer of authority is. When Abraham was prepared to sacrifice Isaac because God so commanded him, Abraham could claim the religious authority to do so. If he was actually given this authority by God, it was legitimate. If Isaac recognized Abraham's religious authority to sacrifice him, then Abraham had de facto religious authority to perform the sacrifice, whether or not it was legitimate.

For those who hold direct, personal revelation, God is the source of their knowledge. Their knowledge is not necessarily religious knowledge, nor does the possession of such knowledge give them any right to command others. X is a de facto religious authority only for those who believe in God and believe God has given special authority to X. This authority may be either executive or nonexecutive in nature. Religious authority may reside in an organized religion or in a church as a whole; it may be possessed by certain specific members of the church; it may rest in each individual member or corporately in all or the vast majority of the members taken together; or it may rest in a certain group. If religious authority rests in all the members corporately, then it is exercised over individuals only when they are in disagreement with the corporate body. Many questions arise here about the size of the consensus necessary and how such matters are appropriately determined. If authority rests in each individual, it is difficult to see over whom he has authority, unless we say that he has it over himself, in the sense that anything he holds or believes on the basis of his religious authority takes precedence over any other knowledge or inclination. The third, and probably the most common, interpretation is that some members of the church—namely, its ministers, priests, or hierarchy—hold authority over the other members of the church in matters concerning religious belief, practices, or morality.

Religious authority is structurally similar to other kinds of authority. Indeed, for it to be totally different would be something of a puzzle, because we use the same term 'authority' here as we do in speaking of other forms of authority. Its family resemblance is demonstrated by the fact that it is a special kind of relation of the bearer, with respect to those who are subject to authority, over a particular field by virtue of some specific justification.

Religious authority is de facto, whether or not God exists. It is legitimate only if God exists. Even if God exists and if he does authorize certain people to act for him, it may be difficult for others to know this. Ultimately the justification for acknowledging that any authority is religious must be based on faith. To claim otherwise would be to claim that both the knowledge of God's existence and the knowledge that he has given certain people or bodies special authority can be arrived at by the ordinary means of gaining knowledge. Most religions do not claim this, even though some claim that religious belief is compatible with scientific knowledge and that people can have good reasons for religious belief. The good reasons, however, are not compelling; hence the need for religious faith and the justification for speaking of religious belief.

If religious authority depends on faith, then those who exercise religious authority (X) cannot expect those who do not believe in religious authority or those who do not believe that X exercises legitimate religious authority either to believe what X says or to do what X commands when X exercises his religious authority. X is a de facto religious authority only for those who acknowledge X as such. X is a de facto epistemic religious authority if Y believes what X says in matters of religion because Y believes that X either has received this knowledge from God or that X has been authorized to interpret it. X is a de facto executive authority for Y if X acknowledges that X has the right to act on or for Y in religious matters. Y may acknowledge X's right to perform rites or rituals that others are not allowed to perform. Y may also acknowledge that X has the right to command Y to act in certain ways or to do certain things.

Although the sphere of religion is in one sense limited to one's relation to God, it may infuse and embrace all of one's activities. Are there limits that can be placed on religious authority? We have already noted that Abraham was prepared to sacrifice Isaac because God commanded it. Religious justification for the sacrifice was subjectively sufficient for Abraham. It would not be sufficient for others unless they believed that Abraham had been given this special command. How could they know this? They could not have been sure; but they may well have believed what Abraham told them because of his virtuous life, his known love for Isaac, and other such factors. They would ultimately have to believe Abraham's word. Within a certain society and community of belief such claims carry more weight than they do outside of the community. The members of organized religions share a body of beliefs and frequently believe that God has intervened in human affairs in some direct way, granting special power to his representatives and revealing certain truths.

Many believers claim we cannot put a priori limits on the extent of religious authority. A religious authority (X) is not a de facto authority for a nonbeliever (Y), in the sense that Y does not acknowledge that Y is subject to X, even though Y may acknowledge that X is a religious authority for others. If X believes that he has a mission from God, however, he may attempt to fulfill that mission by forcing certain actions on Y, even though Y does not acknowledge X's authority. History is full of examples of this type. The crusades were fought in the name of the holy mission of freeing the Holy Land. Religious wars have been fought over territory, as well as over conflicting religious beliefs. Some religions have identified political with religious authority, and politico-religious authorities have enforced religious belief, persecuting those who did not believe, attempting to force religious belief on them, or executing them for unbelief, heresy, atheism, or false belief. Are there limits to the legitimate exercise of religious authority with respect to believers and nonbelievers?

ORIGINAL AND DERIVED RELIGIOUS AUTHORITY

Original religious authority comes directly from God. This is the authority held by such figures as Moses, Christ, and Mohammed. We can ask both how the individuals themselves knew they had received authority from God to say or do what they did and how those who followed them could know this.

We can say that, in one sense, Moses, Christ, and Mohammed each founded a religion. Moses dramatically experienced God in a burning bush and thereafter became the leader of the Israelites. He received directly from God the stone tablets containing the Ten Commandments. We cannot say how he knew his experience was authentic, but we have no indication that he doubted it. His claims were believed by those who followed him. There were external signs that reinforced their acceptance or provided the motivation for their acceptance. Both the parting of the Red Sea as Moses led the Israelites out of Egypt and his ability to supply them with water and manna from heaven were signs. The authenticity of his life and virtue were additional grounds for believing what he said. He wrote the first five books of the Old Testament, which were accepted as the word of God.

Mohammed also had a significant religious experience in which the archangel Gabriel revealed to him the word of God. Despite an initial period of hesitation and doubt, Mohammed soon came to accept the authenticity of the revelation and of his divine call. He answered it and was followed by others. He penned the Koran, but he attributed its authorship not to himself but to God. Just as the Bible is God's word for the Jews and Christians, so the Koran is God's word for the Muslims. Mohammed preached not only a religious message but also an organizational one; in Islam, religious and political authority became identical. The Koran includes instructions not only on prayer but also on fasting, taxes, and the law, which are incorporated into political legislation in Islamic states.

Christ is unique. While Moses and Mohammed were prophets, Christians believe that Christ was not only a prophet but was also God incarnate. He not only received his religious authority from God, but as God, he exercised divine authority. He founded a church, and he gave religious authority to his apostles to carry on his work. The New Testament is the record of his acts and words. The basis for belief in him is not only his message but also his miracles, which are signs for the faithful.

Moses, Mohammed, and Christ initially had no political power or designated authoritative position of established power. They rose from the populace by the force of their personalities and of their messages. They had charismatic authority, and they acquired a following because of their personal qualities, their faith, their message, and the way in which they lived and acted. They had the authority of authenticity and the ability to convey this and to inspire followers. In each case they enjoyed religious authority as direct representatives of God, who were in direct communication with him. Through them their followers received authority from God and thus exercise derived religious authority. In each case a holy book embodied the word of God and carried direct religious authority. In each case, followers were faced with the task of institutionalizing the religion that they received through the original prophet or source. The preservation and spread of the religion fell on others, some of whom had charismatic authority themselves. Saint Paul, in the Christian tradition, experienced God directly in a bolt of lightning and went on to preach the gospel with authority. Eventually, in all three religions, the religious authority became routinized and formalized. Interpreters of the holy books took on epistemic religious authority. Those who were authorized to perform rituals took on performative executive religious authority. Those who were empowered to set rules and to issue commands took on imperative executive religious authority. All such authority was derivative and was justified internally by the line of authority and delegation that extended from the source of authority in the tradition, which was traceable ultimately to God. The authority is legitimate if it does, in fact, come from God.

Some religious authority, both epistemic and moral, is nonexecutive. Insofar as religious authority is executive authority, it is operative authority when it is not identified with politico-legal authority; otherwise it is both operative and politico-legal. Those within a religion accept such authority because of their faith in the authenticity of the initial revelation, the initial direct delegation of authority from God, and because of their belief in the legitimacy of the continuous transfer of that authority. Although Christians do not doubt the authority of Christ, nor do Muslims doubt that of Mohammed, there is room even for believers to doubt the authenticity of some of the actions of those who wield derived religious authority. The revealed books, which carry direct religious authority, provide an independent measure and test of the actions and preachings of those who have derived religious authority. Eactly how the test is to be applied and whether it can be applied by any individual or only by duly constituted bodies which have the appropriate operative authority varies from religion to religion. But the duality of authority within any specific religious tradition is significant and leads to many controversies. Heretics, schismatics, and dissidents within religions often claim to follow the true teachings of the religion as found in its holy books, while they are simultaneously condemned by those who claim orthodoxy and have the power to enforce their condemnations.

THE LIMITS OF RELIGIOUS AUTHORITY

We cannot set limits on God's authority. He does not receive his authority from us, and nothing that we could do would limit divine authority. Even though religious authority comes originally from God, it is limited. We cannot decide what God has authorized or will authorize human beings to do; but if God works through human beings, certain limits automatically impose themselves. Unless God gives individuals the power to change the laws of nature or to intervene in a nonnatural way in that order, religious authority is limited to the sphere of human action. Since religious authority works through human beings, there must be some way by which human beings can know that they have received their authority from God to do certain things; and if they have executive authority with respect to others, there must be some ways for those who are subject to religious authority to know this.

If the religious authority happens to be Moses or Mohammed, he knows that he has been chosen by some sign or experience that he interprets as having come directly from God, that seizes and transforms him, and that gives him the charisma necessary for him to be accepted by others both as an epistemic and as an executive religious authority. Many people have believed that God has spoken to them directly, but no one else has believed or followed them. If they received some divine message and were authorized by God to act for him or in his name, their authority was legitimate. If no one believed or followed them, their authority was ineffective. Some fanatics also have charisma, and sometimes they speak and act as if they have been chosen by God to carry out their mission. How can third parties distinguish the authentic bearer of religious authority from the fanatic and the fraud?

Several tests are appropriate; they relate to the kind of being that the religious person believes God to be. One test is the holiness of the religious authority. The great religious leaders have been exemplary moral figures, and this is part of their charisma. Other people perceive them not only as holy but also as authentic, trustworthy, and dedicated. The content of their doctrine forms a second test. Those who believe that a religious authority speaks for God must have some idea of what God is like. They must perceive in some way that the words could plausibly be God's and could plausibly express his will. If these believers have absolutely no idea what God is like, they could have no way of telling whether or not they should believe what they are told. They might first be brought to believe in God by believing what the religious authority tells them. They might then somehow resonate to that description or message and, by using some criterion, see it as revelatory or enlightening, as being worthy of belief. They may be persuaded by the vigor of the authority's own belief. Those who believe that God is good would not believe the words of a supposed spokesman for God who preached evil. A third frequent, although not necessary, test is some visible sign of the divine imprint. This might consist of miracles or extraordinary good works or the ability to secure a large number of dedicated followers. A fourth and standard test is the test of veracity. Is there any reason to suspect fraud or that the religious figure is pursuing his own wealth or power at the expense of others? Religious leaders generally seek the good of their followers, rather than of themselves. Unless this is so, many may question whether they should follow a self-proclaimed religious leader.

There is no way to prove that one's authority comes from God. Hence religious authority, like religion itself, demands and is based

225

on belief. Both the bearer of authority and those who are subject to it must believe that God exists and that he has given authority to speak or act to certain human beings, who may have the authority to pass that authority on to others.

We have already seen one principle of internal limitation to any individual's religious authority. If within the religion there is a sacred book—such as the Bible or the Koran—that contains God's word, then the actions of any derived religious authority can be measured against that book. Legitimate religious authority comes from God. De jure religious authority is passed on by some formalized means within the religion's organized structure. Members of a religion can distinguish the de jure status of the authority exercised by religious authorities from the religious authority that is contained in the sacred writings. Members may give more weight to the truth of the writings than to the preachings of a de jure religious authority. Each religious tradition has examples of de jure religious authorities who claimed doctrines that are either contrary to the sacred writings or are contrary to the interpretation of those writings that is held by the majority or by those with special teaching, interpretative, or executive authority.

Because religion has both a personal dimension and an organizational and public dimension, we can distinguish the authority operative in the two dimensions. Many religions believe that all individuals can directly communicate with God, pray to him, do his will, or dedicate their lives directly to him. If God is a judge who rewards and punishes human beings, that relation may be a personal, direct one between God and each person. What an individual believes may or may not exactly coincide with what the leaders of the religion preach. The individual may or may not feel that the official organizational authority of a religion supersedes his personal relation with God as taught and described by that religion. The amount of authority that any Y grants in the sphere of Y's private life to any religious authority depends on Y. A religion or church or religious authority may claim the right to enter into each member's private life; but the possibility of doing that is restricted by each individual's control of his own thoughts, regardless of his outward expression of belief.

A religion that has executive authority can ostracize members whom it deems unworthy or seriously mistaken in their beliefs. If the religion also has political power, it may imprison, torture, kill, or in some other way punish or intimidate the wayward. But none of these external sanctions need be taken by a believer as more authoritative than his personal belief. The believer may take his perception of the religion as correct, despite the orders and instructions of formal leaders. An executive authority cannot force belief, even though such an authority may impose physical sanctions or demand an outward expression of belief. We can at least doubt whether such attempts are ever justified, even though, within some religions, such actions are defended as justifiable.

From an external point of view we can defend many limitations on religious authority. When we judge from outside, we can question whether any religious authority is legitimate. We cannot prove that it is not, any more than the believer can prove that it is; but since it is a matter of belief, we can set certain limits on it. Religious authority appropriately applies in the realm of religion. There are many views on what that realm includes; but if it is based on faith, there is no apparent reason why religious authority can be exercised over nonbelievers. Freedom of religious belief or nonbelief is a widely recognized human right. It was and is not always acknowledged. When religious authority is identified with or is closely linked to political authority, people who do not belong to the state religion are often denied certain rights and privileges. For the most part, however, people today acknowledge that religion cannot properly be forced on anyone. At best, people can be made to conform outwardly. Even the right to force such conformity is dubious in most societies. If any religious authority attempts to violate a person's safety or life, that person has the right to defend himself. Similarly, nations have the right to defend themselves from the religiously motivated attacks of other nations.

A religious leader of one religion may, by his holy example, become an exemplary moral authority for members of another religion. Mahatma Gandhi set an example of passive and peaceful resistance that has been emulated by many Christians in the West. Albert Schweitzer was an exemplary moral authority for many non-Christians. In some of his pronouncements, the pope is an epistemic moral authority for some non-Catholics. In all of these cases, those who are exemplary or epistemic religious authorities cannot demand that people from other faiths follow them or accept what they say. The general principles of limitation that apply to moral epistemic and exemplary authorities apply as well to such religious authorities.

THE AUTHORITY OF RELIGION

The divison between political authority and Christianity has a long history in the West. During the early centuries of Christianity, the followers of Christ had no political power and were persecuted by the Romans. The Christians gradually increased in number. When finally the emperor Constantine was converted to Christianity, Christianity became closely tied to political power. The development of the role of Christianity in the Holy Roman Empire led to disputes over jurisdiction between church and state. The church claimed the right to invest the emperor with his authority, which came from God. Temporal power was exercised through the state; but the church had great influence in temporal affairs and had great wealth as well. It had its own system of courts and its own recognized sphere of jurisdiction in which it could carry out sanctions, such as burning heretics at the stake. The break between the secular political realm and the religious realm accelerated as the Holy Roman Empire was transformed into nation states. The Protestant Reformation marks a break within Christendom, an important part of which was the rejection of papal authority. The Protestant sects claim to be as authentically Christian as the Roman Church.

Religious persecutions and wars continued for centuries. The Maid of Orleans heard voices that she attributed to God, and she charismatically was able to lead French troops against the British army so as to enable the dauphin Charles to be crowned at Rheims. Why God preferred the French to the British and therefore intervened in this dramatic way is not clear. But clearly Joan of Arc possessed charismatic religious authority and was followed by many, even though she was eventually burned at the stake by the English for heresy.

Today in the West, religion no longer lays claim to political authority. However, it does wield religious authority among its members and moral authority in many of its pronouncements. In the United States the Constitution establishes a separation between church and state. The right to practice the religion of one's choosing is guaranteed. The forming of a state church is precluded. The extent of religious authority is not clearly spelled out.

Within the American political scene, organized religion can act as a pressure and lobbying group, just as other groups can. Spokesmen for organized religions frequently have great prestige and command great respect. Some churches are able to influence their members to vote in certain ways and for certain candidates. Political candidates seek the Jewish vote or the Catholic vote, just as they seek the vote of blacks, Hispanics, or labor.

There is considerable disagreement about the proper role of religious authority in the United States. When ministers or priests take public office, some people worry whether their allegiance is to their religion or to the state, should the two conflict. When John F. Kennedy became the first Catholic president, he consciously put to rest the fear of some that the Vatican would dictate his political decisions. But that did not end discussion about the authority of religion in nonreligious matters.

The Christian churches in America do not attempt to wield political authority directly. Yet they do preach morality; and many churches have taken positions on such issues as the right to life, abortion, the morality of nuclear war, prayer in schools, federal aid to church-supported schools, and welfare. Churches lobby for what they believe is the morally right position on these issues. They try to convince their members of the correctness of the church's view on them, and they attempt to marshal their members to take part in mail campaigns, donations, or other actions to foster what the church or sect believes is the right action. The Christian churches do not always agree. They have no authority to force their views on nonmembers, and they have no right to have their beliefs enacted into law. Nor do most churches have the power or the ability to force their members to act politically as the churches wish. Churches exercise no overt coercive power; they nonetheless carry weight and religious authority that influences secular life. The Judeo-Christian tradition infuses the value system of most Americans, and the churches are still a very strong influence in the formation of the moral consciences of young and old alike. The influence of religion in contemporay society is present both on the institutional level and on the level of personal action. Its operative authority does not extend directly into the political realm, although its moral and persuasive authority influence public policy. Religion often enters the political realm indirectly through influencing leaders of government or through lobbying and pressure either by the churches as institutions or by their members.

Although one's religion is a private matter, religion has an external, a public, face. The authority and influence of the Catholic Church in Poland is enormous, even though the church has no political power or political authority. No church fills a comparable role in the United States. The authority that any church exercises in

American politics is properly moral and persuasive; it is never legitimately executive authority. No church has the right to impose its views or beliefs on nonbelievers, although every church—just as any organization—has the right to speak out, explain, and defend its views on public-policy issues.

AUTHORITY WITHIN RELIGION

Religious authority is properly exercised within a religion. Each believer, however, has a dual relation within religion. One is a direct relation with God. The other is a mediated relation through membership in a church. A person's religion is a private area and a matter of individual conscience, but there is an inevitable tension between the private, individual practice of one's religion and the public practice as a member of an organized church. What is the proper use of authority in religion? Are there limits to the legitimate use of religious authority within a church? The answer to these questions depends partially on the religion in question and on the claims made by those who exercise the religious authority.

In most cases a church is not a contractual organization in any of the usual senses, even though it is a free society. Members of a church are not members simply by birth, and their continued membership is contingent. They may dissociate themselves from the church and leave it if they so wish. Coercive membership is antithetical to the present concept of a church. Yet this freedom of membership does not involve a contract. One does not join conditionally, with some agreement about what the church must do if one is to continue to be a member. Rather, continued membership is contingent on belief concerning what the church *is.*

If a religious faith includes the belief that membership in that church is necessary for salvation (however defined), then membership is not entirely free, even though there is no coercion by the church in question. The coercion is exercised by one's religious belief. If one truly believes that membership in the church is required for salvation, then one cannot easily decide not to belong to it. Any church that has such an article of belief as one of its tenets precludes from salvation any believer that it excludes from membership. The power of expulsion—which is often called excommunication—is the most potent weapon a church has against its members. Although not a physical sanction, it can be extremely effective. Since excommunication in some Christian religions is equivalent to eternal damnation, the power of excommunication is a threat that can be and has been used to force believers to act in certain ways. Does any church have the right to do this? Many have claimed the right. Yet in civil society we have argued that no group that is necessary for the good of others, such as the group that sells electricity, can preclude membership to anyone desiring it. By what right, if any, can a religion do this?

If a member of a religion believes that through the church he is given both special help in living a good life and special blessings from God, then he may wish to take part in the rituals and practices of the religion. In many Christian religions, special help is given through sacraments, which are administered by priests or ministers. A church may deny the sacraments to members who act in forbidden ways. This is another method of enforcing rules and bringing pressure to bear on members to conform to the religion's standards.

If a believer desires salvation and believes that it can be acquired only through a given church and its practices, then he is bound by the rules and practices of that church. He may feel that he gains more by remaining a member, despite the injustices he suffers or the corruption he sees in the exercise of authority within that church. If he sees some of these rules and practices as being unjust or arbitrary and as being promulgated for the good of those who are in authority rather than for the good of those who are subject to religious authority, his recourse will be difficult if the church is authoritarian. Those who exercise authority will not listen to complaints about their abuse of authority. A church may even use its operative authority to extend the scope of its authority, or it may claim that its operative authority is religious simply because it is exercised within the church. It then claims immunity from criticism, because its authority comes from God. The areas of potential abuse are many, and there is little recourse for believers who are subject to such abuses.

The dilemma that many believers face sometimes leads to reforms within a church or to reformers who attempt to change a church or who break off from it in order to establish a rival sect. In contemporary society the authority of most Christian churches is no longer as powerful as it was during the Middle Ages. For some believers, one recourse to abuses of authority within a church is to continue to practice their religion, privately assenting to those aspects of the church that they believe to be valid but ignoring those aspects they believe to be dubious or wrong. Officially a church may not condone such attitudes, and it may insist that a member believe all that the church teaches and that he submit to all of its rules. Practically, however, if a church lacks political authority, it usually also lacks the operative authority to enforce such demands.

Although we have already seen some limits on religious authority and some of the ways validly to distinguish religious from operative authority, the dilemma of many believers cannot easily be resolved. In some instances they must choose between doing what their conscience tells them is right and doing what the religious authorities in their church demand. Their dilemma is especially acute if they believe they have a duty to do what the church commands and if they wonder whether they can, in fact, be correct and the church wrong. The situation is exacerbated if a church teaches its members to distrust their own opinions and reasoning, while extolling the church's own holiness, insight, infallibility, or authority. When believers think they have the right not to obey what they see as arbitrary rules or pronouncements made by those who have authority within their church, they are torn between obeying and exercising their human right to follow their conscience. In a pluralistic urban society, such people may remain active members of a church and, at the same time, privately do what they consider to be appropriate. In a small closed or nonpluralistic community this solution may not be possible.

Analysis will not help resolve all of the tensions that religious believers may feel between their personal practice of religion and the requirements of their church. But at least in those religions in which God grants religious authority for the good of the people who are subject to that authority and not for the good of those who exercise it, we can state some principles of limitation.

For Christians the apostles and those who come after them were entrusted with both knowledge and power. For the believer, witnesses to the events of Christ's life and teachings are legitimate authorities on what he said and did, in the same way and at least to the same extent that other witnesses to other events and sayings are. For some believers, the Bible alone is the epistemic authority on what God has revealed, unless he further reveals himself directly to each of them or to certain others. In the Catholic tradition the Catholic Church is an epistemic authority in the realm of faith and morals. It has the authority to interpret and guard the purity of the truth which is revealed both in the Bible and in tradition. If a church or its members not only have or guard the content of faith but also are charged with teaching it, we can say that it or they have the authority to preach, or preaching authority. If Christ instituted sacraments to help the faithful reach salvation, then the authority to administer the sacraments is different from the authority to preserve the truth or to preach it. This is the right or power to perform certain kinds of actions within a certain domain. Within the Christian domain the successors of the apostles—either all of the faithful or the bishops and priests— have the right, power, or authority to administer the sacraments. This is sacramental authority. In order to organize the church on earth, the apostles obviously needed organizational or operative authority to enable the Christian community to achieve its common goal. Moreover, just as parents have parental authority over their children because of the need and incapacity of their children, the Christian church, in an analogous sense, is sometimes said to have paternal or maternal authority.

A tension arises from the analogy of religious authority and parental authority. In the case of Christianity the few people who were given special access to God's revelation had both the authority to protect it and the obligation to pass it on as they had received it. Because the knowledge was not available except through revelation, they had to teach it to those who are willing to listen, learn, and believe. But because some of the precepts and truths concerned action and the proper way to live, these people had the task not only of imparting knowledge but also of teaching people how to act. The tendency to assume parental authority came easily. In a period in which the religious authorities were the learned members of the community, it was appropriate for the unlearned to defer to those who had knowledge and religious authority. The inclination of religious athorities to act also as parental authorities makes some sense in a society in which they truly know more, are perhaps the only ones who are able to read, and act out of solicitude for those who follow them. But parental authority is only temporary and is substitutional. Parents no longer have parental authority over their children when those children become adults. Prior to that time their authority diminishes with the increasing maturation of their children. At some point, parents can tell that their children are indeed adults. How do church authorities determine that its adult members are no longer subject to the church's parental authority? One key is the religious maturity of those who are subject to authority. At some point, mature adults have learned enough about their religion to practice it as adults, not as children. Those who do so may question practices that have been taught to them and claims that have been made by religious authorities. Discipline of children has as its end the guidance and good of the children. Unless willingly accepted and sought, the discipline for adults is punishment. Many believers do not accept that religious authorities have the right to impose punishment. In part, this stems from the believers' view of what religious authority is and what its purpose is. If religious authority is indeed given for the benefit of all believers, there are clear limits to the exercise of religious authority. There are also clear limits to the justifiable exercise of parental authority over adults.

A church has religious authority in some sense over its members, but what does it have the authority *to do*? In the Christian tradition the church (however defined) has the authority to preach the Gospel, to administer the sacraments, to establish ecclesiastical procedures, to admonish and correct when necessary, and possibly to punish by exclusion. These are all functions of religious authority. Many of them are found mixed with other kinds of authority. Strictly religious authority may be either nonexecutive or executive. Whether any of it is imperative and whether it involves the right to command and the correlative obligation to obey are topics on which there is much confusion.

We shall assume that religious authority is given by God for the benefit of the people as a whole and for the benefit of each believer. It is not given for the benefit of those who exercise religious authority. There is a strong tradition that sees the life of the ministry as being one of service to others, not as one of exercising any right to command.

The analysis of epistemic authority, which carries no right to command, can be applied to the religious authority that Christian religions possess to preach the Gospel. The right to preach entails no right to force anyone to believe. If the Gospel is the word of God, those to whom it is preached may have a religious obligation to receive it; but attempts to force belief, besides involving a logical mistake, become counterproductive if the point and value of religious belief consists in its being a willing assent to God's word. Historical attempts to force belief by torture or threat must be regarded either as misconstruals of the nature of belief or as politically and socially motivated. They have little to do with religious authority or religion, even though representatives of religious bodies have exercised such authority. The Inquisition was a de facto exercise of religious authority, but it was an illegitimate use of such authority.

234

Another aspect of the religious authority to preach is interpreting, preserving, transmitting, and safeguarding the truth of revelation. Since early times, Christian Councils and other gatherings have established which texts are to be included in the Bible. Certain readings were condemned as being wrong or heretical, and certain beliefs were formulated into creeds as well as developed by scholars, theologians, popes, bishops, and the body of believers.

No sharp line divides those tasks of interpretation, preservation, and transmission that are strictly religious from those that are similar to the interpretation, preservation, and transmission of other documents and bodies of knowledge. Yet if we admit the validity of revelation, the situation *is* different from other instances of epistemic authority.

Someone is an epistemic authority by virtue of knowledge and trustworthiness, which can, in principle, be checked independently. The authority is substitutional. Knowing what is true entails no right to command others and no special right to prevent others from speaking, even if what they say is false.

Divine revelation, however, communicates what cannot be checked independently, because it cannot be arrived at through ordinary reasoning and experience. Reason cannot establish many of the doctrines of Chrisitan belief, such as the Trinity or the Incarnation, even though reason can operate within the system of beliefs. The latter task constitutes theology. But there is a crucial difference between the direct communication of the word of God, as found in the Bible, and the interpretations and explications that have been developed by theologians. The development of theology allows room for dispute, and our previous discussion of epistemic authority applies. Those who believe that revelation is the inspired word of God, however, accept it as true and not falsifiable.

The Protestant revolt against Roman Catholic authority and the abuses that were present within the Christian Church led some Protestant denominations to emphasize individual interpretation of the Bible, the accepted and established religious authority. Some Christians hold that each individual has a right to make a private interpretation of the Bible; they submit to no authority that seeks to impose its own interpretation, even though they listen to ministers and others who have studied the Bible especially carefully and who may bring out insights and aspects the individual did not previously see. Individual interpretation, however, could be bought only by giving up a unified single interpretation, which was, by definition, orthodox. If the Bible does indeed state God's message to man, is that message validly open to diametrically opposed interpretations? If passages can mean both x and non-x, they are contradictory and meaningless. But if not every interpretation is allowed, who decides which is and which is not, once the authority to do so is denied to any special body or interpreter? Believing that each person's interpretation is acceptable, some demoninations have been willing to give up any notion of orthodoxy. They have also given up any attempt at systematic theology. Other denominations believe that the interpretation of a congregation is what is correct. The Catholic Church claims that the bishops and the pope have the authority to decide on the meaning of the Bible and on dogmas concerning doctrines of faith and morality. From the outside one might invoke the principle that because the various churches disagree, the authority of all of them is questionable; from the inside a believer may know that the churches disagree but still believe that only his church is correct.

The authority to preserve the text must come either from God or from the members of the religious body, if such authority exists and is to be legitimate. Otherwise authority over the text is simply assumed and imposed on others. If the authority comes from the members of a religion, it must be given to someone or to some group because of his or its knowledge, integrity, or interest. And the final decision as to what constitutes the tenets of the religion's belief—whether written or verbal—is left to that person or group. In this case, other qualified people can evaluate the way in which they perform their task. Because the authority comes from the people, they can also revoke it.

The other alternative is that the authority to preserve the text comes from God. He might give the task to a whole people, as the Jews preserved the Old Testament, with God's prophets appearing periodically to continue the revelation and keep it correct. Or he might give the task to certain individuals, as Christ is said to have given it to his apostles and, in turn, to their successors. God might also guarantee the continued accuracy of the transmitted revelation in a variety of ways. How this is, was, or could be done is not of concern here; but the question of the legitimate extent of any such authority is of concern here.

If one has the religious authority—the right and duty—to preserve the integrity of revelation, a central question is the recognition of that authority by other members of the religion. If it is recognized, then those members of the religion who wish to know the content of revelation will turn to the acknowledged authority. If they do not recognize or consult the authority, then they run the risk of believing falsehood. Does the authority to preserve the text involve the right to silence those who, in the view of the authority, are falsifying it?

If the falsifiers are outside of the religious body, religious authority by itself gives the holders of that authority no right to do anything but to speak against the falsification and to take the necessary means to protect themselves and their doctrine from the incorporation of error. This is true even if the religion is joined to political authority. State censorship or the silencing of error in religion, as in any other sphere, is the exercise of political authority, which is properly restrained by safeguarding the rights of all members of the community. If the falsifiers are within the religious body, the religious authority can condemn error as error and make this known to its members. The preservation of truth is distinct from the silencing of error. Condemnation of a doctrine is different from doing anything to the holder or the promoter of error.

The argument that error has no rights presupposes knowledge of what is erroneous. The liberal tradition believes that the best way to determine truth is to allow the free interplay of argument. The same principle applies in the religious as in any other realm. If some religious leaders fear that the members of their church may become confused if many doctrines are propounded, they implicitly either believe that the members are children, or they doubt the members' belief in and allegiance to their church.

If a church has an organized structure, by virtue of its organizational authority it will not give the holder or promoter of what is considered error any position or power, it will not allow the erroneous work to carry its seal of approval, and it will not in any way aid the publication or distribution of that work. Such action is justifiable. Nevertheless, a church's religious authority to preserve the sacred text is distinguishable from its organizational authority.

The authority to guard a religion's doctrine—whether it lies with the pope, councils, bishops, the teaching magisterium, or a whole church—also carries with it the right to make decisions about what is and what is not held to be true within the religion. This is a power of decision, not simply a matter of knowledge.

The discovery that someone who is considered to be an epistemic authority has said something that is false justifiably diminishes that authority. To protect itself against any such possibility of diminished authority in certain areas, a church might insist that its teaching is infallible under certain conditions. The Catholic Church, for instance, distinguishes those truths that are defined from those that are not. Defined doctrines are not open to change, whereas others are. By making this distinction, it can remain credible; for if it claimed at one time with certitude what at another was found to be not true or not quite true, its credibility would be correctly diminished. It is also for this reason that its theologians, though they are epistemic authorities, do not in any way bind the church; for the fact that they have knowledge or make claims to knowledge does not commit that church; and when they disagree, this in no way diminishes the teaching authority of that church. Theologians may have epistemic authority, but they do not have religious authority to determine what members of the church must believe.

If certain members of a religion have the religious authority from God to preserve the integrity of his revelation, by indirectly determining what members of the church must believe, they determine who is a member of that church. This follows if a member of a church is one who believes what that church teaches. This indirect authority to determine membership is separate from the authority officially to exclude someone from membership through excommunication or some other means, which is a facet, not of the preaching function of religious authority, but of organizational authority.

As in any other area of authority, a clash among those who claim to have religious authority cannot be resolved by appealing to authority unless a competent higher authority is in a position both to decide and to have his decision accepted. This in part explains religious wars (power is brought into play when authority fails to reign), as well as the growth of many religious sects within Christianity.

In speaking of the religious authority to preach the gospel, we have thus far concentrated on matters of doctrine or articles of faith, not on matters of morality. We have already seen that there is no legitimate executive moral authority and that neither epistemic nor exemplary moral authority carries with it the right to command. By a similar analysis, when religion demands certain actions that are comparable to or identical with moral actions, the same limitations hold for epistemic and exemplary religious authority as apply in the moral realm. Executive religious authority does not legitimately become, except indirectly, executive moral authority.

Because actions are not made moral or immoral by anyone's fiat, they are not made so by the fact of any church's fiat. Churches frequently teach a moral code and moral ideals as well as religious ideals; they may well be recognized as epistemic moral authorities. They also frequently produce exemplary members, who are worthy of emulation by others. Such members are sometimes called saints, and their lives serve as models of moral and religious activity. The epistemic and exemplary moral authority of a church, however, is not different in principle from any other such authority, and it is subject to the same limitations. Moral commands should be distinguished from religious commands, even when churches do not do so and claim that violations of either are sinful. Moral commands bind everyone, whereas religious commands bind only those who belong to the religion. For instance, dietary laws are religious laws and carry with them religious sanctions if they are violated. These laws operate within the framework of the religion but are not binding on those outside of it. On the other hand, the religious command to worship God on certain days in certain ways may be indirectly moral, if there is a general moral obligation to worship God and if this instance of it is prescribed for members of the religion. Such indirect moral executive authority on the part of some members of a religion is comparable to that of the state in its legislation and that of parents with respect to their children. The limitations are also similar.

People have a moral obligation to determine what morality prescribes and to act as morality prescribes. The leaders of a religion, the holy men, the sacred texts or traditions, or the whole community may guide and help the members to determine what is morally right and morally wrong. To that extent they are morally required to consider seriously what a church says on moral issues. This is different from believing that any religious body makes actions moral or immoral by its fiat.

There is another important difference between the teaching of a church on matters of faith and its teaching on matters of morality. Matters of faith are based on revelation, and they concern doctrines that cannot be known in ordinary ways. Principles of morality, however, can be known on independent grounds as well as on the basis of revelation. The Christian churches may rely on the Bible, tradition, the Fathers of the Church, papal pronouncements, the councils, and the magisterium for many questions of morality; but many areas of morality are new either because of new technology or new circumstances, and definitive answers in these areas are simply not yet available. Under such circumstances a church may attempt to reason out the morally correct thing to do, given both the sources of faith and of tradition and the light of reason. But moral epistemic authority is subject to the limits of any epistemic authority, and exemplary moral authority is deficient when the exemplars are not as exemplary as they might be. The ability to reason about moral issues, independently of faith, and the consideration that epistemic authority carries with it no right to command show why attempts on the part of persons in some churches to command morality do not work. The rationale for such attempts is frequently paternalistic, but paternalism with respect to competent adults must be freely accepted in order to be justified.

Knowing what is right is not equivalent to making it right. Similarly, knowing what actions are necessary for salvation is not the same as making those actions necessary for salvation. In itself the preaching authority contained in religious authority contains no special right to command.

The content of faith is one aspect of religion. Ritual is another usual aspect. In the Christian religions, the administration and reception of sacraments is a third. These are religious acts, defined within the context of religion and forming part of it. The authority to perform religious rituals and to administer sacraments might belong to all members of the religion, or the authority might be restricted to specially designated classes of individuals within the religious community. These persons may be chosen and given authority to perform the rites or to administer the sacraments by virtue of their holiness, their training, or their family ties and lineage. The conditions under which their authority is de jure is a matter of internal rule, law, procedure, or tradition within the religious context and the organizational scheme.

Part of the belief of a religion might be that certain rituals are to be performed in certain ways, that certain sacraments are to be administered in certain ways, and that participation in these is necessary for salvation. This does not mean that the rites or the sacraments carry with them any right to command other members of the church. The rites and sacraments may be defined in certain ways within the religious context so that the performance of certain actions is what counts as the rite or the sacrament. This means that anyone who wishes to perform the rite or to administer the sacrament must do certain actions and say certain words. But this is not a command. The authority to administer some or all of a religion's sacraments may be restricted to certain authorized individuals. If two people wish to marry and to receive the sacrament of matrimony, they must appear before an appropriate minister and must exchange certain vows. On the part of the minister the executive authority to perform the ceremony is performatory, not imperative, executive authority. Similarly with baptism and the other sacraments. The sacraments, by their nature, are believed to give grace or power to the recipient to do certain things or to live in specially sanctified ways. Even though by baptism one is cleansed of original sin and brought in a special way into God's grace, family, and church, the administering of the sacrament of baptism involves no right to command on the part of the minister or church. The authority to perform rites and to administer sacraments is part of religious authority, and although executive, it is not imperative authority.

In the central areas of belief and ritual, therefore, religious authority carries with it no right to command. This may seem contrary to ordinary practice. Yet in some ways it is not, and under at least one view of religion, it should not be unusual. If God did in fact reveal to mankind truths about himself and the way to salvation and if he instituted rites and sacraments, he did so for the benefit, not of himself, but of mankind. To the extent that religious authority entails the right or power to do certain things such as preach and minister and to the extent that it comes from God, it exists for the benefit of the people who are subject to authority, not for the benefit of the priests, ministers, or bearers of authority. Although the authority does not come from the people, the authority is bestowed for their good. And if bestowed for their good, help, and guidance, then there is no intrinsic reason why it should carry with it any right on the part of the bearers to command those who are subject to religious authority.

The bearers of religious authority may be honored, reverenced, or respected for their holiness, their service, or their dedication. Because they have the authority to safeguard God's word, to preach it, and to perform the sacred rites and rituals, they may carry with them some of the mystery that religion and religious belief involves. They may be acknowledged as separate and special. This may form the basis for those within the religion to grant them executive imperative authority, but this should not be confused with the question of whether such authority comes by right as part of the preaching and ministerial aspects of religious authority.

Where then, if at all, does the right to command and the correlative obligation of obedience legitimately lie within a church? Obedience involves some agent (Y) doing what some X tells Y to do or commands Y to do, simply beause X commands it. In every case, obedience involves either an explicit or an implicit command to perform some action. The value, worth, or quality of the action commanded will necessarily affect the value or worth of the obedience.

Obedience cannot legitimately be blind. It is justified in the case of minors and incompetents when the commanded acts are for the good of the minor or for the good of the community and are commanded by appropriate people in appropriate realms. A similar justification holds for mature adults: obedience is legitimate when it does not involve doing what is illegitimate or immoral, when it is either in the interest of the individual for his own good or in the interest or good of the community of which he is a part, and when it is obedience to one who is appropriately placed in a field. Authority in religion, as elsewhere, becomes authoritarian when the orders given and the obedience demanded or coerced are in the interests and good of the commander at the expense of the commanded. When the justification for the obedience and acceptance of religious authority is either the benefit of the subject or the benefit of the community, a certain trust in the authority—in his knowledge, in his concern for the individual or the community, in his virtue, or in the legitimacy of his position—is necessary. Counterinstances tend to break down the necessary trust. Obedience and submission to an authority for one's own developmental good are frequently referred to as discipline. Submission to the discipline of another can promote self-discipline and develop one's powers. In religion, such obedience is justified on the part of an adult who freely follows the example or instructions of a religious master or who joins a religious order that he sees as exemplifying outstanding virtue. Obedience is justified if it is a freely chosen means to attain a legitimate end. Continued obedience is justified by the continued mastery that the master demonstrates or by the individual's or the community's progress toward a certain end. But obedience is justifiably limited when either of these is or becomes deficient or when participation ceases to be free. When obedience to authority is justified by the good of the community, the good must be perceptible or perceptibly approached, and the submission of one's own good to the good of the community must be proportional.

A church's religious organizational authority is mixed. It is religious insofar as it has to do with the function of organizing a structure to carry out the religious mission of preaching and ministering to the people and insofar as the principal ministers carry their religious charge. As an organization, a church is bound by the same rules of organizational structure and efficiency as are other organizations. It is subject to the same limitations on the use of its authority. Even a church's divine origin cannot protect it from administrative excess baggage. If a church's bureaucracy impinges on justice and on the welfare of some of its members, others may legitimately seek to provide remedies. Authorities within a church should not ignore such abuses.

Due process, public and speedy judicial consideration, and the right of defense and appeal are concepts and practices that have emerged in secular society. They have proved to be potent means for fostering justice. This recommends them for fuller adoption in any church's juridical system. Discipline is not a safeguard of faith; nor is secrecy a sign of inspiration.

Organizational authority that is essential to certain functions can be distinguished from what is simply peripheral. The tendency to make the peripheral be central undermines the willingness of believers to obey, for it makes the insistence on the peripheral seem meaningless, it serves only to bolster the ego of the bearers of authority, and so it appears authoritarian.

The organizational authority that the hierarchy in some Christian religions exercises over the clergy is backed up with religious and nonreligious sanctions, which are more severe than those that the clergy can impose on lay persons. Excommunication remains a church's strongest weapon; it is not only a religious sanction but also, in at least some communities, is a social sanction, carrying with it shame and, possibly, social ostracism. Whether it is a religious sanction or an operative sanction applied by religious authorities is at least open to question.

Our analysis of authority within religion has drawn heavily on authority within Christianity. The analysis is appropriate to many aspects of other religions as well, even though different religious beliefs will raise some different issues. Although many churches and religions confuse epistemic, moral, disciplinary, and organizational authority with religious authority, the many kinds of authority exercised in an organized religion can be fruitfully sorted out. Religious authority is itself plausibly a special kind of authority. But it carries with it no right to command those who do not freely submit to it, and rational limits can be set to its legitimate use.

11

The University and Authority

Many kinds of authority—epistemic, paternalistic, operative, politico-legal, moral, charismatic—are found in a university; it therefore provides an ideal subject for testing the fruitfulness of our analysis. Though a university is often state supported, the justification for its authority is different from the justification of state authority and the state apparatus. Even when not state supported, its usual nonprofit status makes it different from a business or entrepreneurial organization. It claims the authority to run its own affairs, no matter who supports it. Its history goes back to the Middle Ages; its long tradition gives it not only the weight of authority but also many authoritarian trappings. Because it is not for everyone and because it courts bright students who can benefit from its offerings, it is elitist. It encompasses a class system—the inequality of master and apprentice, teacher and student—making it ripe for authority relations of superior to inferior.

The contemporary university is typically large, complex, and in some ways fragile. It was seriously shaken during the 1960s and early 1970s when students around the world chose it as the focus for their attacks. They often lashed out, without thinking through their specific grievances. In their eyes the university stood for the establishment and for established authority. They sought, if not to topple it, then to seize it, to turn it from an authoritarian institution into a democratic one, and, in any event, to change it from what it was. Though the university withstood the attack, few universities remained totally unchanged. Now that the protests have subsided and changes have been made, we can fruitfully investigate the justifiable place of the many kinds of authority in a university.

THREE VIEWS OF THE UNIVERSITY

According to the bureaucratic view of the university, it is a formal organization which has a legal foundation and structure and has

244

service and support components. It is organized in a hierarchical pattern: the administration is at the top, the faculty is in the middle, and the students—the clientele to be served—are subordinate to both of the higher levels. The professorial view of the university is considerably different from, though not incompatible with, the bureaucratic view. The faculty sees the university as a group of scholars, who, because of their expertise, attract students and young scholars to study and to learn from their collective store of knowledge. The university makes it possible for the faculty not only to transmit knowledge but also to carry on research and push forward the frontiers of what is known. In the student view the university is a place where students can be educated for their own development and enjoyment and can be trained for desirable positions of employment when they graduate. Each view captures something of the university, and each constitutes a model that is approached by some universities. Most universities, however, embody all three models and suffer from the tensions that arise when one is championed to the exclusion or neglect of the others.

There is no special authority called educational authority. The authority within the university is both executive and nonexecutive—primarily epistemic, operative, and legal. In each model, authority operates differently. The administration, the faculty, and the students all make some claims about authority, and each does so with some justification from its own perspective. Can the competing claims be sorted out and adjudicated?

The bureaucratic model is exemplified in most American state universities. The legislature has the authority to establish the university and the authority to fund it at various levels. Usually in the United States, as opposed to some countries in Europe, the legislature does not attempt either to run or to oversee the university directly; instead, it establishes a board of regents or trustees to do so. The board receives its authority from the legislature. It in turn appoints a chancellor or president to run the university. The president has the authority to appoint deans to oversee schools within the university. The deans, in turn, hire faculty in a sufficient number of departments and in sufficient quantity to provide instruction for the students who attend the university. The physical plant of the university is provided through state funds, which are voted by the legislature. The legal structure of authority is hierarchical, coming from the legislature down through various levels.

Although the authority exercised by the president is created by statute in a state university, the administrative authority within the

245

university is operative authority. A university bureaucracy develops. The running of the physical plant and the hiring and firing of clerical and maintenance employees are similar to these activities in other governmental agencies and private firms. The faculty has its own sphere of authority. Nonetheless, the faculty are employees and are subordinate in the hierarchy to the administration's operative authority.

The faculty model does not deny the legal structure, but does not give it much prominence. For although the legal structure determines the level of support and is important for the university's organization, it is not of central interest to the university's mission. Not all universities are state supported. And a university could carry on its primary functions, as it sometimes has in the past, without the structure of a separate administration.

According to the faculty view, most important is the group of scholars, learned in various disciplines, who preserve past knowledge, who pass on their knowledge to those who are interested in learning, and who push forward the frontiers of knowledge through their scholarly work. They consider the authority of knowledge to be the most important kind of authority. They bow to facts and arguments that are rationally and cogently presented, they acknowledge the great thinkers of the past and perhaps of the present in their fields, and they generally accept the framework of their disciplines. A faculty goal may be to make students into peers, but students are initially subordinate to those who know more than they do. Epistemic authority has a legitimate and important place in the university.

Epistemic authority is held primarily by the faculty, not by the deans, not by the president or chancellor, and not by the legislature. Administrative competence is desirable but does not yield epistemic authority. Faculty members are the experts in their various domains of knowledge. Deans may handle administrative affairs to help the faculty do its work, but from an academic point of view or from a point of view of knowledge, the deans are not above the faculty. Similarly, the president of the university may be more or less effective in getting funds from the legislature or the alumni to enable the faculty to carry on its work. He is not above them from an epistemic point of view. Nor is the legislature. The consequence, according to the faculty view, is that if the faculty members are to perform their tasks effectively and efficiently, they cannot be controlled or commanded as the organizational model might suggest. Within their disciplines they claim to be superior in knowledge to those who are legally and administratively above them, and they claim they cannot be told what it is proper for them to teach or to pursue in research. They are subject to the professional evaluation of their peers within their discipline. Those who do not have knowledge and expertise in a field cannot judge what is and what is not sound within that field unless this has certain repercussions that nonexperts can evaluate. Those who are outside the field cannot determine what should be investigated or what should be taught in the subject area in question. If the university as a whole is an institution devoted to the development, preservation, and transmission of knowledge, then those who do not have proper knowledge cannot appropriately limit it. The argument for academic freedom on the professional level is an argument for the autonomy of the university vis-à-vis outside forces such as the legislature.

The faculty is usually divided into departments, headed by a chairperson. Authority within the department may be hierarchical but is more often collegial. Often each faculty member has an equal vote, and the faculty sets departmental policies by consensus or by majority vote. Each also has a voice in setting degree requirements for students. The faculty has the operative authority to do so. The operative authority of the faculty in academic affairs of the university runs parallel to the operative authority of the administration in the university's organizational affairs. The two lines of authority cross at various places, and when they do so, which kind of authority takes precedence is often controversial.

Faculty members are professionals who have peers and colleagues in their field at other universities. Faculty members sometimes have more in common with those colleagues than with their colleagues at the same university. They feel allegiance to the academic field, as well as to their institution, and they react to epistemic authority in their field as much as to operative authority in their university in deciding what to teach, what research to pursue, and what to publish. Because of their ties to a discipline that cuts across universities, faculty members often see themselves as parts of a larger community than a single university.

The student model acknowledges professors as epistemic authorities. For students, the chief function of faculty members is teaching. Research in order to teach better is appropriate, but the faculty's research function is properly subordinate to its teaching function. Student authority, either actual or claimed, varies according to the school. At some European universities students claim the right

247

to hire and fire the faculty, since the faculty's main function is teaching and since students, parents, or the state provide the money for the university. Those who pay have the right or the authority to fill the offices of the institution with those whom they deem to be best. The authority to hire and fire, however, clashes with epistemic authority. By the very nature of their status, students are not epistemic authorities and are not able to judge the extent of the learning of their professors, at least not until they themselves have advanced greatly in knowledge. Students at most American universities admit this and do not claim the right to hire or fire faculty members. However, they believe they can judge the effectiveness of a teacher, which is not a function solely of epistemic authority. They can also judge the ways in which a professor uses some of the other kinds of authority that he has. Students frequently defend a popular teacher who has been denied tenure and attempt to have the teacher reinstated.

In the United States, students do not run the university to the extent that they do in some parts of Europe, but students in the United States have sought and frequently have been granted authority to run their own affairs. The running of student housing, student organizations, and extracurricular matters does require operational, not epistemic, authority. Some structure is more effective and so is usually more advantageous to students than no structure. Whether students, professionals, or the university's administrators handle student housing makes little difference, as long as the operational authority is properly used for the benefit of the students. When it is not, they have legitimate grounds for complaint. Whether they run their own activities or hire out the operation of these activities is not a matter of great issue.

In the past, many parents expected universities to act as parent substitutes. They transferred to the universities some of their parental authority to make rules for the protection and care of their children. Many universities accepted this role. The authority came in this instance from the parents, to whom the students were at least in theory still subject. The present student view tends to deny paternalistic authority to universities. When students are independent and not subject to their parents, the exercise of parental authority is not appropriate.

According to the student view, students are subject to the epistemic authority of their teachers. In the student model the faculty alone should not decide the amount and kind of operative authority that it rightfully exercises, since the students are subject to that authority. An epistemic authority may know a great deal about a field and how one learns about it. His epistemic authority extends that far. But whether there should be grades and what the nature of grades and of certification that are given by a university should be are not matters that have to do with a faculty's expertise in particular disciplines. They are not decisions the faculty or administration should make without involving the students. Similarly, a professor who is an expert in physics is not thereby an expert in general or liberal education; his knowledge of physics does not automatically give him expertise on course distribution or general requirements for graduation. Students have less experience and therefore are usually even less knowledgeable on these matters. Nevertheless, these matters of operational authority do not fall automatically to the faculty, and the student view maintains that those who must live with and under these rules should have some role in determining them.

No one of these models is correct and the others wrong, and each of the models reflects some aspect of American universities. Although a given university will probably not follow any one model, it will very likely have within it people who operate in and on it as if one of the three models were the only appropriate one.

Universities are social institutions; they are the products of those who make and use them. Every university, as an institution, requires the allocation and use of operational authority; as a place of teaching and learning, it requires epistemic authority. How the various kinds of authority are balanced, justified, and limited depends in part on the kind of university that it is, its mission, its social setting, its financial support structure, and other relevant considerations.

Each of the three models of the university suggests that authority within the university should be divided in a certain way with the administration, the faculty, or the students being dominant. Prior to the question of how authority should be allocated within the university is the question of whether the university is rightfully an authority unto itself, as it often claims to be. Is the university rightfully subject to the authority of others—for example, of the legislature or parents, if they financially support it?

THE AUTONOMY OF THE UNIVERSITY

In some countries, universities are subject to the authority of the government that supports them. They are subject not only legally but

249

also operationally. The government has the right and the power to appoint not only the president of the university but also the faculty, and it has the right and power to determine what shall be taught and how. It determines what is proper research, and it prohibits what it dislikes. It sets standards for entrance, as well as for graduation. A university that is so structured receives whatever authority it has from the state and is subservient to the state in its internal activities.

Such universities are organs of the state and can be used by the state for its own purposes. The state can prescribe the ideology that is to be taught students and can specify what courses in the ideology are mandatory for graduation. It can proscribe research it finds threatening to its ideology, and it can dismiss professors whom it finds threatening or who do not teach or write what or how they are told. The rationale for these actions is the same as for any other governmental agency. The people within the university are employees of the state, paid to do a specified task in the manner assigned. If they do not wish to do so, they can resign or seek other employment. As paid employees, however, they are expected and required to do what they are told. They are appropriately subject to the authority of those above them. The same sort of analysis would hold for a university that is organized along proprietary lines, with the authority being held by those who provide the funding or who pay for the operation of the university. If a university is simply an entrepreneurial service type of institution, the rules for justifying authority within it pose no special problem.

Although such universities exist, they are not the typical American university, either private or state. The typical American state university claims by right a certain distance from and independence of those who fund it—especially from the legislature and other organs or members of government. It claims this despite the fact that the legislature is superior to it in the hierarchy of legal authority and is the source for most of its funding. The American state university claims autonomy, which means both independence from state authority in the running of the university's internal academic affairs and the authority to run these affairs.

Police departments, fire departments, state and municipal hospitals—all may claim autonomy in the same way as the university does. They are experts in running their own specialized affairs and so, on that basis, would claim distance from and independence of the legislature. Is there a significant difference between these other state institutions and a university, such that a university can support a special claim for autonomy?

The answer seems to be clearly no. There is no great difference between universities and such other institutions, if the university is run along lines that are comparable to other organs of the state. In such universities the issues concerning authority are not unique, nor do they require special discussion. There is one exception, however, and it is an exception that most American universities claim. A university is different; it is properly not subordinate to the state or to the group that creates it or to those who support it, if it is dedicated to the pursuit and transmittal of objective knowledge. Such universities—which I shall for brevity's sake call objective-knowledge universities—claim that the state should not exercise its legal control over them and should allow them to operate autonomously, despite the fact that they are state supported. Their claim to such autonomy clearly requires defense. Objective-knowledge universities have a long tradition; they can also play a unique role in a free society. Such a university, moreover, requires certain kinds of authority structures, which society must accept if it wishes to have such a university. The justifiable authority in the university is a function of the nature of that university, which also dictates the limits to the internal use of authority.

In the United States the claim of the state-supported university to autonomy is bolstered by the claim to autonomy of the privately supported universities. Despite the different sources of basic support, both kinds of university are very similar. Private universities claim academic independence from parents and donors, just as the state universities claim independence from the state.

The objective-knowledge university has as its primary end the traditional trio of discovering, preserving, and transmitting objective, systematic, and unified knowledge. A university that does not pursue objective, systematic, and unified knowledge, just as a university that does not simultaneously engage in discovering, preserving, and transmitting knowledge, will probably require different authority structures from one that does. The authority that is found in a university is a function of its organization, its ends, and its view of the knowledge that it pursues.

To call knowledge objective underlines the fact that it is communal—shareable and open, not personal or individual—and the fact that it is possible in some way to demonstrate or cogently to argue for it. Its validity does not depend simply on someone's believing it, desiring it, or finding it pleasant. Objective knowledge stands on its own; it is descriptive or representative of the way things are or the

251

way they are apprehended by human beings. The highest authority in the realm of knowledge is shared by facts and by reason. If knowledge is objective in this sense, then the earlier discussion of the justification for and limitations on epistemic authority applies.

Objectivity involves critical creative thinking, a testing of what is known, and a constant evaluation of accepted fact and theory. As knowledge is reevaluated and developed, the authority of tradition is either respected or rejected, as appropriate. This aspect of knowledge makes it inappropriate for any authority—epistemic, politico-legal, or administrative—to dictate what its content is or must be. This aspect of knowledge makes its pursuit sometimes conservative, sometimes radical, vis-à-vis the conditions of the society in which it is developed. In itself such an objective pursuit of knowledge is neither necessarily radical nor necessarily conservative, though its pursuit involves elements both of preservation and of change.

The argument for the state's granting autonomy to a university that is dedicated to objective knowledge is based on two claims: first, autonomy is necessary if such a university is to achieve its ends; second, the state benefits by allowing such a university to achieve its ends.

The first claim is based on the previous description of the knowledge that a university pursues. The automomy of a university consists of its academic independence from the control of any person, body, or portion of society outside of itself. It has the authority to run its own academic affairs. Its authority entails that courses and content, curriculum, degree requirements, research, and the academic evaluation of both students and faculty are to be decided by those who are competent to do so within the university without interference from those outside of it. In all of these areas the determining essential ingredient is knowledge, and judgment in each of these cases must be based on knowledge. The knowledge involved, moreover, is the knowledge preserved and developed at the university, especially by the faculty. Knowledge, not anyone's dictate or desire, should be the ultimate guide to decisions taken in these areas.

The claim that an objective-knowledge university should, in academic matters, be free from political intervention derives from the nature of knowledge and the necessary conditions for its pursuit. For anyone to dictate what must be pursued, what must be ignored, what is appropriate for publication, and what should be censored and prohibited, on any basis other than the criteria of knowledge and its objective pursuit, is to preclude the objectivity of the knowledge obtained. The search for objective knowledge demands freedom from imposed ideology. Intellectually honest debate and controversy, a common desire to uncover the truth, and a respect for reason, logic, and fact are the lifeblood of the search for knowledge. Uniformity of view, when imposed upon a university under the guise of promoting the truth, leads to the stagnation of any truth that such an imposed view may contain. If a society does not cherish the university's goals, it may not want such an institution; but society cannot both cherish the end and consistently deny the means for attaining it.

Can the second claim to a university's independence from state authority be supported? The state has the power and the legal authority to control the university. Does an enlightened, free society derive more from a university devoted to the objective pursuit of knowledge than it does from one that it controls? The answer is yes. Society receives three important things: (1) objective knowledge, (2) a haven within society from which society can be objectively evaluated, and (3) a body of citizens who are trained in the critical thinking necessary for a continuing democratic society.

(1) Society derives benefits from new knowledge in the sciences and from imaginative developments in the liberal arts and human-ities. Because new knowledge and intellectual developments are unpredictable, research and thought cannot be dictated. Those who are pursuing new knowledge must be allowed to pursue it freely, constrained only by the discipline of the field, not by political aims.

Pure research in mathematics, logic, physics, or chemistry em-braces those pursuits for which the researcher sees or imagines no immediate and, perhaps, even no remote application. Scientists in technical laboratories operated by industry or in government-con-trolled laboratories are usually paid not to do this type of research but to do research that is pertinent to particular domains that have pragmatic and fairly immediate application. These scientists are subservient to the operative authority of those who hire them. Yet pure research has been extremely important in the develu͡pment of science and technology. A society that supports an objective-k. ʻl-edge university is more likely than is another society to have such basic knowledge developed within its universities.

The realm of the humanities is even clearer. The practical application of history, literary and artistic appreciation, or theory of knowledge is tenuous and receives little attention in the training programs set up by most corporations or by other university sub-

253

stitutes. Nor could the token Shakespearean scholar, the colonial historian, or the political philosopher who might be present in such institutions be expected to function without a body of colleagues with whom to discuss and argue, without the ambience of scholarship, and without the respect for humanistic knowledge, all of which are found at universities. Arts, letters, and philosophy have flourished outside of university walls; but the preservation, the critical study, and the transmission of a cultural heritage have flourished best within them.

Only an autonomous university can be a true haven for the objectivity of knowledge. An industry or a government that hires scientists and scholars to carry on research usually tries to maintain control over the knowledge produced, over its dissemination, and over its use. The research represents vested interests, is subordinated to particular points of view, and is governed by political or economic factors. Yet there can be no arbitrary bounds or limits placed on what can be known; the pursuit of knowledge cannot fruitfully be subjected to any authority other than the canons of knowledge and reason; nor can criticism of the status quo in science, economics, or politics be legitimately stifled. Any enlightened society, and especially a democratic, open society, has only in its universities a potential seat of objective knowledge, which it tries to control intellectually at great ultimate cost to itself.

(2) A democratic society allows dissent. It typically is governed by a political party that allows opposition parties. It does not believe that any person or group has all of the answers to society's needs. The people have the ultimate authority to remove from power, by prescribed means, those who do not serve them well. Freedom to criticize all aspects of government and of society provides the most efficient way in which government and society can improve.

By permitting the free discussion of all ideas in a university, society makes it possible to determine and provide the reasoned justification for the truths that it holds and the values that it supports. Errors are uncovered and brought to light. Dangerous ideas and values are objectively discussed and safely vented in a nonpolitical atmosphere, and students are trained in the critical thinking processes that are so necessary to a self-governing people.

Only a university that is not politically controlled can provide a forum for people rationally to examine, criticize, discuss, and debate theories and policies without fear of reprisal or loss of position. Epistemic authority and respect for argument and facts prevail there, rather than any kind of executive authority. We would not expect a company training program to teach its employees how to criticize the company; but we should expect an autonomous university to teach its students how to criticize radically and how to evaluate appropriately all aspects of society. It is not the direct function of such a university to change society. Objectivity demands a certain distance from the practical decisions and the immediate action that are characteristic of politics and business. The university has no executive or operative authority outside its own walls.

An objective-knowledge university in some ways can act as the conscience of society and as the source for its continued improvement. It can fulfill neither function if it is not free from external political control.

(3) Society rightfully expects that any university will produce graduates who can do the various tasks necessary for society's functioning. A modern society needs teachers, doctors, engineers, accountants, lawyers, and technicians. These skills require knowledge that has been developed, preserved, and passed on from one generation to the next in a nonending continuum. An objective-knowledge university transmits knowledge that has been received from the past but is critically rethought, which provides the basis for further development.

A democratic society expects that those who have a university education will have two other attributes. First, they will have prepared themselves for continued personal and social growth, for taking part in the intellectual, cultural, and artistic aspects of society, which make life worthwhile and attractive. A liberal education frees and broadens the mind of those who pursue it; it is different in kind from technical training.

Second, a democratic society profits from having a large number of liberally educated citizens who can adapt to changing conditions, who are able participants in public affairs, and who are critically trained to question authority and to participate intelligently in their own governance. A democratic society especially needs citizens who respect facts and arguments, who have a creative imagination and a critically developed intelligence, and who are not easily swayed by a crowd. They should have a sense of their own worth and importance, a consciousness of their rights, and the ability to act as a counterweight to the exercise of power in the political or in the economic realm. An objective-knowledge university helps produce autonomous citizens; a critical mass of such citizens is what prevents a democracy from succumbing to despotism or totalitarianism. A free, democratic society, therefore, has a great deal to gain by supporting an objective-knowledge university that it does not control.

The argument in defense of the university's freedom from the authority of government leads us to a conditional conclusion. If a university pursues knowledge objectively, freely, and as a unified whole, then society benefits by supporting, but not by controlling, its academic functions. An assumption thus far has been that the university we have been describing is nonpolitical in two respects. First, in academic matters it is not subject to the political authority of the state; and second, it is nonpolitical in its actual operation. A university that is either political or politicized ceases, to that extent, to be an objective-knowledge university, even if some of the people within it do seek knowledge objectively. Because a university may be deflected from its objective pursuit of knowledge in a variety of ways, society and government can demand that the university be accountable in some way.

ACADEMIC ACCOUNTABILITY

A university may be politicized in many ways. A political end can be its primary goal, either in theory or in fact. During the late sixties many students claimed that the implicit goal of universities was the defense of the status quo: they said that universities cooperated with the military-industrial complex, provided docile white-collar workers for industry, and served as apologists for the existing structures of society. Students claimed the universities were subservient to the political aims and authority of the state and were no longer being objective. They claimed further that the operative authority of the university and the faculty had become authoritarian and was being used for the benefit and enhancement of the interests of the bearers of that authority, rather than for the benefit of students. Radical groups tried to politicize the university differently: they used it in an attempt to effect radical change, launched antiwar and antiestablishment demonstrations from the campuses, and entered directly into the mechanics of social change, instead of simply discussing such change. To the extent that universities made either the defense of the status quo or the attack of the status quo a primary end, they were and are correctly said to have been or to be politicized.

The student argument was partially correct and partially mistaken, for the students claimed that since the university was politicized in defense of the status quo, it should be politicized differently so as to achieve the students' aims. If the universities had been politicized, however, they were no longer objective-knowledge universities. Their claim to autonomy could then no longer be supported. The appropriate alternative would have been for the university to be controlled by those who were funding it. States would have directly controlled the state-supported universities and would have used them to achieve the state's purposes. Private universities could have set their own ends if they had had the means to do so and could have admitted students who wished what the university had to offer on the terms it proffered. Otherwise, those who supported such universities would have controlled them. It was only if the politicized universities became depoliticized and became once again objective-knowledge universities that any claim to autonomy or immunity from political control would have been justified.

An externally politicized university is run by the direct decree of the state, which sets the university's internal policy, tampers with its internal decisions, or uses it as a means of suppressing criticism or mobilizing support. An internally politicized university subordinates the pursuit, preservation, and transmission of knowledge to other ends. Internal factions of a university may decide various aspects of university policy, from graduation requirements to promotions and tenure, on the basis of vested interests. Lines may be drawn between departments or schools, between faculty and students, or between either group and the administration.

How is a society to know whether a university is dedicated to the objective pursuit of knowledge or whether it has become internally politicized and so has implicitly forfeited its right to autonomy? If a university openly engages in political activities, of course, there is no problem of detection. It must not only avoid political activity; it must earn the trust of society and be willing to explain and defend its actions in terms of its ends and the objective pursuit of knowledge. Those who give authority in any realm can legitimately demand that those who use it be kept accountable. Only accountability makes it reasonable for a society to support an autonomous university. The university should be held accountable for fulfilling its function and for achieving its end. This is clearly different from financial accountability, which has to do with the level of funding and the proper use of funds. The external accountability that justifies autonomy is the clear explanation of academic policies and decisions, when these are reasonably challenged as being either politically motivated or counter to the good of society.

Operative authority within a university can be divided and exercised in many ways; hence, those who are subject to it can legitimately ask that it be justified. Internal accountability requires that those who are subject to authority can expect those who exercise any kind of authority to explain and defend their use of it to those who are subject to them. Operative authority within a university should be used for the benefit of those who are subject to it, consistent with the ends of the institution. Just as the nature and ends of a university dedicated to the pursuit of objective knowledge can justify autonomy and define its limits, they can also justify the use of authority within the university and can supply the appropriate limits of such authority. Departments, schools, faculties, and individual professors within a university claim autonomy under the name of academic freedom in the exercise of their epistemic and operative authority. The price for autonomy in each case is appropriate accountability. Neither the autonomy of the university as a whole nor the autonomy of the faculty or of students gives them license to do whatever they please.

Administrators in a university have legal authority as well as operative authority. In matters of administration, epistemic authority is usually not pertinent, though competence is. Their operative authority is both to represent and to act for the university vis-à-vis those outside of the university and to oversee, direct, and administer the internal workings of the university. They are responsible for the efficient running of an inefficient institution. They should be held accountable for making possible the growth, preservation, and transmission of knowledge. Students and faculty should hold the administration accountable for its policies towards them. Accountability, here as elsewhere, means that decisions, rules, expenditures, and allocations must be open and defensible. The criteria used in justifying needs should be directly related to the function of the university, not to political considerations. The faculty may wish to govern itself, or it may wish simply to have channels of input to the administration. This depends on the traditions of the institution, the wisdom of the decisions made, and the character of the faculty. Administrative authority clearly does not extend to the area of knowledge, and administrators have no right to decide what does or does not constitute knowledge within a discipline. If an administrator believes that a faculty member is deficient in knowledge of his subject or that a department or unit as a whole is deficient, he must base his belief on epistemic grounds. The truth of what is taught is a function of the nature of reality and reason, not of administrative fiat.

The administration of a university is complicated by the dual status of faculty members as employees of an institution and as autonomous epistemic authorities. Knowledge, expertise, and legitimate freedom of inquiry and of teaching must be balanced with administrative rules concerning the number of hours worked, the number of courses taught, the amount of pay received, the fringe benefits granted. How much voice faculty members have in these matters varies greatly. Nevertheless, administrators have the responsibility to see that the university functions with reasonable efficiency within its financial means and that it fulfills its overall mission. It has the operational authority necessary to meet its responsibilities. If its authority comes from the state, it may still delegate much of its operative authority to the faculty. If the university is a private institution, the faculty usually authorizes the administration to act as the arbiter of disputes and as the administrator of nonacademic affairs. Faculty members may be especially articulate in demanding accountability, and a wise university administration should be ready to explain its decisions to the faculty.

Many different models describe the role of a university administrator: an entrepreneur in a competitive market; an elected official in a democratic society; an equal among equals, who has temporary operative authority; or a dictator. Each model may describe individuals at different institutions or the expected role of the administrator at different institutions. The different models produce different justifications for and limitations on the proper use of authority by an administrator at a university. Most of the analyses we have already given can be taken over and applied, depending on whether we have in fact an organization that is run like a business; an institution that is run democratically, by the faculty, by the faculty and students, or by the students; a university in which the administration exercises its legal rights autocratically. In each case, accountability is part of the appropriate price for the exercise of authority. In a university, if anywhere, reasons should be given for actions; and if challenged, decisions should be defended rationally, even when they are made unilaterally.

The faculty is subject to the operative authority of a university in both the administrative and academic lines. The faculty of a university is accountable primarily for the development and transmission of knowledge, which are frequently equivalent to doing research, publishing the results, and teaching students. It is proper that each faculty member's retention, advancement, and monetary remuneration be dependent on how well he does these things. Beginning teachers go through a probationary period during which they are judged by those who are more established in the field. During these years, habits of teaching and research and of dedication to the pursuit of knowledge and its effective transmission should be developed. For those who earn it, tenure carries with it the right not to be dismissed unless there is proof of incompetence or moral turpitude. Tenure does not, as some seem to think, carry with it freedom from all accountability, pressure from or review by one's peers, or the right to automatic promotion or merit increases regardless of performance in teaching, research, and publication. The faculty should, however, be exempt from political judgment of their work; their accountability must be to the university and to those who are qualified to judge their performance on academic grounds.

A tension exists between operative and epistemic authority in judging faculty. Departments usually have the operative authority only to recommend promotion and tenure and are required to evaluate the academic achievements of the colleagues whom they wish to have promoted. The departmental task is to be objective about a colleague who may be a good friend of some departmental members and an enemy of or a threat to others. For this reason, departments rarely have the operative authority to make promotions. Their recommendations are reviewed. Faculty committees at the school or the university level usually review departmental recommendations and make their independent recommendations to the administrators, who have the operative authority to promote, to fire, and to grant tenure or raises. Administrators must judge the objectivity of the recommendations they receive and the overall needs of the institution. Although knowledge in itself gives no right to command, departments often think that their expertise and prestige provide a basis for the automatic acceptance of their recommendations. If rebuffed, they may seek to challenge the administration's operative authority and to bring pressure for the administration to reverse its decision.

Colleagues form the most rigorous body by whom a faculty member can be held accountable. They are the ones who are most keenly aware of the demands of the academic discipline, of its pitfalls and difficulties, of the difference between the superficial article laced with technical jargon and the solid contribution to scholarship. As people who are knowledgeable in their field, they are attuned to the flashy rehash of old ideas, they are sensitive to the slipshod, and they are remarkably well informed (most often by way of students) about the quality of their colleagues' teaching. Colleagues' decisions on tenure and promotion, if fair and impartial, are based on the best professional evaluation available. No other body outside the universities has the same competency to review such decisions; therefore, any reversal by legislators or boards of trustees must be considered political and inimical to the possibility of an autonomous university's fulfilling its function. This assumes that faculty review and evaluation are done honestly and rigorously. Only then can a university expect outsiders to accept such review as satisfying the demands of accountability. Legislators, boards of regents, and other outside groups may legitimately question the clarity and adequacy of the criteria, seek explanations of what is not clear, and ask for a defense of what seems improper. If internal reviews are properly carried out, there should be no difficulty in explaining the procedures. Departments and their procedures should also be open and defensible to students, to members within the department, to members of other departments, and to those in the higher administration.

The faculty are the chief discoverers, preservers, and transmitters of knowledge in the university. They are the epistemic authorities in their fields. They teach for the benefit of students, and they publish for the advancement and preservation of knowledge. No one can legitimately tell them what is acceptable or unacceptable in the pursuit of knowledge. They should be unrestricted in what they teach within the field of their competence, providing that they can rationally justify and defend any theory or view they propound and providing that they are intellectually honest and unbiased. The qualifications and knowledge of a teacher may limit his teaching to a given area; only the availability of necessary materials limits his right to carry on research.

In a classroom a teacher's primary authority is epistemic authority based on knowledge. This authority is compatible with the autonomy of students, whose intellectual freedom can be fully respected. The teacher should not expect or encourage uncritical acceptance or suspension of judgment. His de facto epistemic authority comes from the students, because they accept what he says as true or because they are inclined to hold some proposition as more

261

probably true because he asserts it. Many students are prepared to grant such authority to their teachers; but the teacher may make mistakes or have lapses in his argument. Independent and outside confirmation tends to justify the acceptance of the teacher's statements. The discovery of errors tends to undermine such acceptance. A teacher is accountable to his students for what he teaches; but the *final* evaluation of teaching, as of research, requires more than a student's perspective.

Since epistemic authority carries with it no right to command, teachers cannot legitimately command a student to learn or to believe what they say. But universities give teachers de jure operative authority to carry out the tasks that they are expected to achieve. If they must treat a certain topic or cover certain material in a course, they have the operative authority to structure that material, to organize the course. Because of his knowledge of the field, the teacher is given the operative authority to choose texts, to make assignments, to require reading and term papers, to give tests, and to evaluate the students' work. Because of his knowledge he is given the operative authority to grade his students.

This operative authority is not essential to teaching or to learning. Students need not be required by someone who has operative authority to read or to work. They might follow the suggestions of someone whom they accept as an epistemic authority. They need not be graded in order to learn. The justifications for the use of operative authority in the classroom are not found in knowledge but are found in other functions, such as the certification of students for society. The legitimacy of these functions is a separate issue; but if they are conceded to be appropriate, the operative authority of teachers must be circumscribed by fairness and reasonableness. Some teachers structure a class and tell students what they are expected to do and how they are to do it. If clear and reasonable, such an approach can be legitimate. Other teachers prefer an unstructured class, or they let the students structure or help structure the class, with the teacher acting as a resource person. From the point of view of the exercise of authority, neither is preferable: both can be effective; both can be abused. The structured approach can turn into tyranny, with the teacher assigning unreasonable amounts of work, changing requirements, and setting impossible goals. The unstructured or student-structured approach can lead to a teacher's abdicating any instructive role, by allowing students to try to teach each other something that none of them knows much about. Each type can become authoritarian if it is used by the teacher for his convenience and for his own purposes, instead of for the good of the students. Because his operative authority is justified by the good of those who are subject to it, students can expect a faculty member to be able to justify his use of that authority.

The university has taken on the dual function of education and certification, the latter being a task that is useful for society. The operative authority of the faculty frequently involves setting requirements for a major or for graduation. The faculty's knowledge is directly relevant for the former, since it is an area in which the members of a department have expertise. With respect to graduation requirements, faculty members jointly have more experience and relevant knowledge than do the students and may be less self-interested. To the extent that faculty members are self-interested (for instance, in requiring their own courses), they should be checked by peers in other departments.

Students sometimes distrust the motives of faculty members in setting requirements and feel that students should have a say in the conditions that they are expected to meet. A wise university will hear valid arguments, will consider relevant data, and will adopt reasonable regulations. Although students have not been through the educative process and have come to the university to learn, this does not settle the issue of whether students should by right have a voice in the development of requirements or even whether they might not do just as good a job as, and possibly in some instances a better job than, the faculty. Most students are prepared to admit that the faculty are more knowledgeable and have more experience and time to devote to these topics than students do.

Because the faculty has knowledge, its certification of students is accepted by society. If it does not have knowledge, then its operative authority is misplaced. Teachers may have knowledge but not have other qualities necessary to use their knowledge well. They may have no interest in organization, administrative detail, or liberal education. They may lack qualities of honesty, impartiality, and fairness. They may be unable to communicate effectively. They may substitute coercion for instruction. They may lack imagination and be unable to think on a student's level in their field. These are all good reasons for not giving such persons operative authority in a university or for restricting such authority.

Though students are correctly held accountable in academic matters by their teachers, the teachers are accountable to their students for knowledge, fairness, and pedagogy. The faculty has the authority to prescribe a curriculum; but because it exercises this authority for the students' good, students' desires and interests in curricular matters should be considered and implemented whenever possible and whenever such implementation makes educational sense. The means to make these matters known should therefore be provided. If both faculty and students are cooperatively engaged in the search for knowledge, their interests in academic areas should coincide. When curricular decisions are challenged, they should be defended with sound educational principles. The vested interests of either students or faculty should not play a decisive role in academic matters, even if presented under the guise of some reasoned argument.

When knowledge is central to a decision, those who have the appropriate knowledge should carry greater weight than those who have less, regardless of who has the operative authority. If those who have the operative authority cannot defend their decisions, there is good reason to think they are not using their authority effectively for the good of those whom their decisions affect. There may be grounds for charging authoritarianism, for seeking to remove their authority, or for not obeying them.

Although both professor and students may have and may exercise power, the exercise of power does not legitimate any authority. It may well undermine it. Professors have some coercive power over their students, if one considers that grades or recommendations are tools of power. If they are justifiable in a university, they should not be used without justification. Students have the power of numbers and the ability, through their numbers, effectively to disrupt the university. The university is not typically organized to control mass demonstrations or physical violence. When confronted with these, it can use its operative authority and administer such sanctions as suspension and expulsion—sanctions based on the assumption that the student wishes to continue at the university. When laws are broken, the appropriate social organs that handle such violations can be called upon.

Accountability precludes the need for violence and for the use of power. A university that exemplifies the use of reason, which it teaches, is less likely to need force or power than are other elements of society. However, if accountability is absent, if abuses are numerous, or if the institution is not responsive to reason, then nontraditional ways may be needed to obtain a fair hearing and legitimate changes. The arguments for civil disobedience and strikes, as well as the use of these techniques, have been and can be defended.

University education should be freely undertaken. The student must enjoy a certain amount of autonomy. To force university education on a student either by leglislation or by social pressure is to undermine the university and its goals. Some who attend college because of social pressure learn what knowledge is and what its pursuit involves. Others never do learn this. The love of knowledge and the desire to pursue it systematically cannot be forced on a student. Exposure is a first step to knowledge, which is communicated most fruitfully by gifted teacher-scholars. Overworked teaching assistants often fail to convey the zest for knowledge and the mastery of the discipline that they themselves are still cultivating.

University teaching does not simply transmit information; careful reading and study does it better. What does not emerge from books alone is an appreciation of what they contain: a living example of a mind interacting with the material, developing, questioning, elucidating, and illuminating the text. Method, as well as facts, is conveyed and taught; but developing quality of mind is more important still. Ideally a student should be free to pursue this quality of mind at his own rate, rather than at a fixed pace. Such freedom is compatible with accountability.

To pursue knowledge is to submit to the discipline of its acquisition. Knowledge may be pursued intensively in one area or extensively along a broad spectrum. Colleges by virtue of their operative authority usually require students to take a variety of courses in the sciences, humanities, and social sciences, both for their own development and for their understanding of the diversification and unity of knowledge. Students major in a discipline so as to get a feel for a specific branch of knowledge in some depth and so as to begin the mastery of its techniques and methodology. Faculties know which courses are necessary for mastery of particular areas such as mathematics, chemistry, or philosophy. They know less well how the curriculum of a liberal-arts education should be structured. The different points of view become evident when one compares various college catalogues and when one investigates the requirements for the same degrees at different institutions. Those within the academic community may share some uncertainty in this matter, but their ideas are usually tempered by discussion, tradition, and experience. Their operative authority is informed by experience and reflection. They are better informed on this topic than are state legislatures or other

265

nonacademic bodies and are better able to circumscrie the student's autonomy in curricular matters.

The university sometimes uses paternalistic authority to make rules governing nonacademic student conduct. Some students consider this to be coercive, but it also protects students from the larger society and its more stringent rules. In the United States, parents of students, or students themselves, have frequently given the university parental authority which has been incorporated either into operative practices or into the university's legal authority. We can distinguish paternalism in curricular matters from that in noncurricular matters.

The university may accept parental authority and may make rules to protect students in some special way. It may also require observance of certain rules of behavior. These are not a necessary component of a university and are usually not directly related to its end.

The basic aims of the university do not involve nonacademic discipline, the moral training of students, or their moral supervision (though they may involve the cultivation of the intellectual virtues of honesty and of having the moral courage of one's convictions). Students must obey the rules of conduct of society at large, plus any rules that are necessary for the fulfillment of the university's primary role. The maintenance and supervision of dormitories, the provision of meals, and the establishment of codes of student conduct, as well as all extracurricular activities, can be the responsibility and preserve of the students. If the students seek help, members of the faculty or administration may provide whatever does not interfere with the primary end of the university. These are not academic matters. Whether or not they are found at a university has no bearing on the fulfillment of the function of an autonomous university. A university need not have any responsibility either for punishing or for protecting students in their daily lives, independent of their academic pursuits. Unless they jointly so desire or unless some similar justification exists, students should not be accountable to the university in these matters, nor should the university be accountable for the extracurricular activities of its students.

The private university might defend its autonomy in terms of a service type of entrepreneurial operative authority. A state-supported university may make a similar claim. But are those who support either type of university to have no say in how the university operates? Though the answer is not an unqualified no, they can have no say that goes against knowledge or the means by which it is pursued, preserved, and transmitted, nor can they legitimately interfere in any of the practices that are necessitated by the primary ends of an autonomous university.

The student is a privileged financial supporter of the university because he shares in its basic end. The university is not simply a service type of organization, offering knowledge to those who seek it, because it allows students to be a part of its operation in a way that service businesses do not. Its operative authority must include an active concern for the students' good. If ever a student fails to find what he is seeking at the university, he is of course free to withdraw; more importantly, as a member of the university and in the spirit of the university, he should try, by means of rational argument, to effect whatever changes he thinks desirable. The operative authority of faculty and administrators should allow this.

As far as business and industry go, if they are dissatisfied with what and how the university teaches, they are free to set up their own screening, teaching, training, or other programs. Because the objectivity and scope of university education are what makes it preferable to narrow, pragmatic training, however, the pressure and influence of business, industry, and government should not be allowed to color the academic aims and offerings of the university. Nor should any sponsored research be accepted that is not open, objective, and free from any restraints on pursuing knowledge, wherever it may lead. The objectivity of knowledge thrives on openness in debate and the opportunity to examine and reexamine research. Neither student nor faculty research should deal with material the access to which is indefinitely restricted by government loyalty tests, corporate agreements, or arrangements with outside agencies whose operative authority supersedes the university's. The autonomous university should have nothing to hide from any portion of society. Each portion of the university should be academically accountable to the other portions in the sense that the work of each must be open for interaction with and evaluation by the others, thereby helping to enhance the quality of the whole. Outside observers who wish to question or evaluate any portion of the university in terms of the canons of knowledge should be able to do so. If a university accepts government and corporate contracts that limit access and direct its research, it undermines its claims to objectivity and autonomy.

Tax money provides the primary support of state institutions of higher learning. The needed amount of support is contingent on such

267

factors as the number of students to be educated, the level of education (the higher the degree, the more individualized the instruction, and so the more expensive it will be), the faculty's pay scale, the size of support staff required, the cost of building and maintaining the physical plant, the amount that is necessary to support research and to maintain and develop the library and similar facilities. On all these matters the university should make known and should justify its needs. The level at which its needs are taken care of may depend on how much money is available and on what competing demands there are on the tax dollar. Support of the autonomous university should never be contingent on the *political* acceptability of what any one of the university's faculty members teaches or writes in his professional capacity or on the extracurricular activities of faculty or students.

The extent to which a society contributes to its universities is indicative of the extent to which it appreciates the nature and importance of knowledge. At least part of the burden of the education of the taxpayer and of the members of the legislatures as to the worth of the university, its true function, and its value to society falls on the university itself and on its spokesmen.

The university is constantly open to threats from without and from within. Many universities can and should eliminate unjustifiable uses of authority. Despite the needed changes, however, the university's role as a haven for the objective development, preservation, and transmission of knowledge should not be sacrificed. A society can limit a university's ability to perform those functions; but society can do so only at its own peril.

Whether or not a society adopts objective-knowledge universities, however, this analysis can be taken as an example of how the different kinds of authority present in an institution can be differentiated and evaluated. Authority, autonomy, and accountability go together in a university. The argument can be generalized. Authority, if it is to be legitimate and if it is not to become authoritarianism, involves accountability. Accountability does not deny those in authority the right to make decisions, but it does deny them the right to do so arbitrarily and at the expense of those who are subject to their authority. Accountability need not be frequently invoked; but if it is never invoked, the discipline that it instills is apt to atrophy. Various bearers of authority may claim a certain autonomy, based on their expertise to perform a certain task. This may be justifiable, but it is still restricted by accountability.

The justifiable kinds and uses of authority in a university vary with the ends and the structure of the university in question. It is appropriate in any university, however, that conflicts of authority and disputes about authority be settled, not by force, but by reason.

12

Creativity and Authority

Creativity is an expression of an individual in his uniqueness. Its source is deep within each individual's personality, and its operation is shrouded in mystery. It is a private gift; yet its expression is public. Authoritarian regimes typically do not look favorably on creativity they do not control; democratic societies are often wary of anyone who is different from the majority of their citizens. Are creativity and authority compatible? There is good reason to think so. Within the creative process itself several types of authority can play a positive role. When developed, the creativity of some individuals tends to become an authoritative norm for others. And although the relation of political authority and creativity is complex, the two are not necessarily antithetical.

CREATIVITY AND DISCIPLINE

The term 'creativity' is used in many different ways. Some might call a spider weaving its web creative and its web the spider's creation. Others would not. Parents might consider their young child who paints a picture creative. Others would not. For some people, creativity is a personal characteristic, a potentiality, a power, or a disposition. For others, creativity is a process. For still others, creativity exists only in an original product.

Although the spider weaving its web can be called creative, it will always weave essentially the same pattern, as will all other spiders of the same kind. When compared with other spiders, no spider weaves such an original, distinctive, or different web that it will influence other spiders to imitate it. This aspect of creativity pertains most appropriately to human experience. A child might show originality in a painting or drawing: he produces something that he has never seen

270

before, or he reproduces in a different way what he has seen. But unless what he produces is stikingly different from what other children of a comparable age produce, his originality is based on a comparison with what he himself has previously done, not on a comparison with the products of all mankind.

Creativity thus designates originality not only in a productive process but also in comparison to some base. Within that comparison we can distinguish degrees of creativity. The originality of a genius is measured against the base of general human activity, or at least of human activity in a given historical and cultural setting.

Although creativity can be expressed in a variety of ways and in any field of human endeavor, for the sake of simplicity we can consider four pertinent areas: the area of everyday life, the area of artistic expression, the area of science and technology, and the area of intellectual activity that is generally designated as the humanities. Paradigms in the artistic and scientific realms are the clearest and easiest to exemplify. In the artistic realm a painter who starts a new movement or school and whose work and style are imitated demonstrates creative genius. Lesser artists, who follow in his footsteps and produce good works of art, are creative and demonstrate creativity to a significant but lesser degree. In the realm of science a Newton or an Einstein sets the model for creative activity. Their original conceptions of the world of physics open up new possibilities and set new parameters within which those of lesser, though still significant, creative ability work, filling in the pieces and details. Philosophers have functioned similarly. Plato, Aristotle, Aquinas, Hegel, Marx, and Wittgenstein have forged new ways of philosophizing; followers have adopted their methods and have continued their work.

Although in a sense everyone can be creative in his own way and to some degree—even if it be the forming of sentences that he has never heard before—not everyone can be a Newton, an Aristotle, or a Picasso. Many psychological and sociological theories attempt to explain genius and creativity. For our present purposes it suffices to say that to produce a work of exceptional creativity, the producer must have more than ordinary ability, perception, intelligence, imagination, or whatever else is necessary for the production of such originality. It is not obvious that in the realm of everyday life special training is needed for such creative expression; even in the arts it is not clear how much training is needed for great originality to express itself. Yet it is beyond doubt that to be original in the the realm of modern science one must know science, just as in mathematics one

271

must know mathematics. In some realms, training is necessary for originality and creativity.

Creativity and authority in the realm of everyday life are frequently so commonplace as to be ignored. At some point a human being invented the wheel; some other human being discovered how to cook food; another tried to smoke tobacco. Others developed ways of constructing clothing. Manners, dress, furniture, ways of sitting and sleeping, and innumerable other aspects of everyday life were at one time new, inventive, and creative. We learn them as we grow up, and we take them for granted. They are so natural to us that we never question them. They bear the imprint of the authority of tradition. We are aware of the creative dresser, the hair stylist, and the trend setter. Sometimes such a person has a flair for the dramatic, the different, the unusual. Such creativity is often followed by others who have less flair and much less success. The trend setters are creative and become exemplary authorities in the matter of dress, hair style, or way of life. People who become such authorities typically do not imitate others; their style is authentically theirs—a fact that is often difficult for the imitator to grasp, because the imitation lacks the authenticity of the original. The authority of authenticity challenges and partially transforms the authority of tradition.

The authority of tradition in everyday life is extremely strong; it is enforced by the ordinary people who submit to it without thinking and who look upon those who do not submit as deviants, iconoclasts, or subverters of society. To some extent they are. By accepting the authority of tradition, we are freed from having constantly to decide how to act and what to do in each new situation. By following what everyone else does, we can save our energy for other kinds of activities, some of which may be creative. The authority of tradition serves a role in everyday life. The authority also allows for change. Some trend setters are accepted, and changes are thus introduced. The authority of tradition allows for this as well. Tradition also provides the backdrop against which one can be creative in everyday life by being different, unique, or authentic. Without such a background we would have chaos, and we would not be able to separate the creative from the unintelligible. Both creativity and authority hide in everyday life because they are not dramatic and do not produce any immediately perceived profound changes. The accumulation of individual creativity in everyday life, however, forms the kind of life that we lead as a society, and the kind that we authoritatively pass on to those who come after us.

The authority of tradition similarly serves as the backdrop against which we judge the great dramatic examples of creativity in the arts, sciences, and humanities. The creative genius or the innovator is different and innovative only against the background of the ordinary and accepted.

The authority of tradition also confirms, for the ordinary person or for a society, who the great creative talents of the past were. It stamps those people and their works as accepted. We have already seen that we can always ask why we should accept the authority of tradition. If we can give no good reason for accepting it, we may challenge it or react against it. But as a de facto form of authority it is pervasive and carries great weight. The authority of tradition operates without the need for justification, and those who would defy it have the onus of demonstrating the correctness of their position. In a dynamic society, tradition is open to innovation. Even if it seems to change slowly, it changes constantly and most often in response to creative activity that catches the imagination of a significant group. The relation between creativity and the authority of tradition is a reciprocal one. The two are mutually related, and both need each other.

Although we often think of creativity only in connection with the genius and the important innovator, everyone can be creative to some degree. This insight infuses some theories of education that attempt to foster, protect, and develop the spontaneity of children, which some theoreticians equate with creativity. Not all spontaneity, however, is creative. Unless creativity is channeled and disciplined, it is not likely to result in any creative activity or product. The channeling and disciplining that take place in schools often crush rather than foster any creativity that a child may have, because tradition imposes a heavy weight on all those who are subject to it, and the authority of tradition and of those who teach it may overwhelm the children who are forced to submit to it. Yet the relation of epistemic and exemplary authority to creativity can be a positive one.

Allowing genius to develop freely does not necessarily foster its development. An authoritarian teacher may object to any signs of creativity. But the genius must learn the field in which he is to work just as anyone else must. Unless he is willing to submit to the discipline of learning, he will not master what he has to know in order to do truly creative and original work. The discipline provided by authority is an initial guide to any field. The young learn from those who know more than they do. The young need epistemic authorities; they also need exemplary models in order to know how to carry on activities in any field.

A paradox of learning is that effective positive freedom, which consists in the power and the abilty to achieve the goals that one chooses for oneself, can often be attained only by going through a period of what one feels to be bondage. To produce any significant human advance requires control over one's powers. Only by initially submitting to a teacher and ultimately to the field itself—to rhythm, tone, and pitch if one is a musician; to paints, colors, textures, design, and composition if one is a painter; to logic, argument, and abstract thought if one is a philosopher—does one gain discipline in any field. One's talents must be honed, no matter how great they are. Undisciplined talent does not achieve great results. The period of submission to an epistemic authority—doing what he says, learning what he prescribes, struggling with problems he sets—is necessary in order to attain freedom in any area. Only then can one break the barriers of tradition and the constraints of established authority in a field. Free genius without control can run rampant. Freedom with discipline can turn creative genius into a creative force capable of yielding something new and productive. By initially submitting to authority, one will no longer need authority but will be able to work on one's own. One can challenge existing authorities that misuse their authority. The final paradox is that the one who successfully challenges authority usually ends up himself becoming an authority.

Some educational theorists who object to the use of authority even in primary schools fail to understand the function that epistemic and exemplary authorities can serve. They also often fail to realize that children need to channel, harness, and control their creativity and spontaneity if they wish to use it productively. These theorists rightly note, however, that many creative children enter school only to have their creativity, not channeled, but squelched; these children emerge repressed and stultified. Such results stem, not from the use of authority, but from the misuse of it—the authoritarian use of the operative authority that a teacher has.

If it is obvious that one must know mathematics before being able to do creative work in mathematics and that one must know physics in order to do creative work there, it is no less true that one must have mastered the techniques of painting before one can be a truly creative painter. Creativity and nonexecutive authority are clearly compatible.

In those areas in which training is necessary for creative achievement, native ability is not enough. Creative talent must in these cases be fostered; an authoritarian parent, teacher, or ruler can keep it from flourishing. Early promise, however, is not a necessary condition for later creativity, nor can anyone predict who will make a significant breakthrough in any area. By its very nature, creativity of a high order frequently refuses to follow past patterns. The bright student who quickly masters a field may never break out of it. Someone who is outide of the mainstream of accepted and acceptable practice often makes the major contributions to a field. But even they require training and can gain by submission to authority. Creativity and executive authority can be compatible, even though executive authority may at times preclude the development or expression of creativity.

If some native ability is a prerequisite for creative activity of a significant degree, then obviously it cannot be commanded. It makes no sense for anyone in authority to command someone who does not have the requisite ability to be original or creative. Although training and education may have as one of their purposes the enabling of individuals to give maximum expression to the creative potential within them, no one can effectively be commanded to do more than he is capable of doing.

It is also impossible for someone who has imperative executive authority effectively to command a person who has creative talent to produce a new paradigm, a new style, or a new vogue, if by this we mean telling him what paradigm to produce. To command a new product in any detail is to produce it. And if the one who is giving the command had already produced it in sufficient detail to command it, the creative talents of the one who is being commanded would not be required. In this case only the less creative talents of the competent craftsman, imitator, or follower would be necessary.

The relation of creativity and executive authority is an ambiguous one. An effective teacher might use his operative authority to command a student to carry out certain tasks, with the aim of developing the child's creative potential. Although creativity cannot be commanded and although authoritarianism may preclude the development or expression of creativity, those who have executive authority frequently have commanded the creative genius to produce works of art or to turn his mind to the solution of a particular problem. To do so is not to produce the art or to solve the problem but simply to know what task is to be solved. Creativity need not be entirely free. It can be constrained; works can be commissioned for certain purposes. Patrons need not be totally indifferent to what a creative artist produces, and they may direct and channel creative energy in certain directions, even if they cannot predict the outcome.

275

Nor is the negative relation between executive authority and creativity always to be lamented, because creativity does not necessarily improve human welfare. Not all innovation is progressive, and not all change is for the best. Genius can be creative in the realm of evil as well as in realms that foster human well-being. The creativity of the evil genius is rightly kept in check by politico-legal executive authority.

THE AUTHORITY OF CREATIVITY

Creativity does not consist simply of adding new pieces to an established view, theory, position, or trend. Although a building-block theory of knowledge suggests that truth is something that is discovered and to which we simply add new pieces, this is clearly not the case in some areas, and we can question whether it is the case in any area. The realm of art provides the clearest example. One mode of artistic expression, one kind of painting, or one genre of writing does not preclude other kinds of painting or other genres. One style is no more or less true than another, even though it may be more or less representative of nature. Creative genius may inspire, or it may repel; but styles and techniques are not true or false.

This may seem less applicable to the realm of science. Yet here, too, Einstein did not show that Newton's theory was false and his own true. The terms true and false are not the appropriate ones to apply to this case. Many recent philosophers have argued persuasively that scientific hypotheses, laws, and claims are theory laden. Obviously, some scientific theories are more useful, account for more of the data, and have fewer difficulties than others; but very few people believe that we have reached the last stage of scientific knowledge, that there is no more room for another Copernicus or Einstein. That we cannot see what a new creative breakthrough in science would look like is no surprise: for before the creative step is taken, it cannot be foreseen. We can know what a new theoretical breakthrough might do in the sense of knowing what problems it might solve; but to know how it would solve them is to know the new theory. In science, as in art, there is no reason to think that our theories are true in the sense that we know the universe as it is in itself. We have not reached the limits of our creative representations of nature; we can expect new paradigms; and we can anticipate that creative, original, and revolutionary theories will replace our present ones.

276

If the history of philosophy is any indication of what might happen in the future, there will probably still be Platonists and Aristotelians. These lines of thought have withstood the changes of fashion for more than two thousand years; they will probably still have some advocates many years hence. It is more difficult to predict that there will still be Kantians, Hegelians, or Wittgensteinians. The absence of any new, different, or original philosophy over the next several hundred years would be surprising however. But philosophical systems and approaches, like art and scientific theories, are neither true nor false. They involve interpretation, insight, new ways of looking at reality, new ways of participating in it. To know and to theorize is to interact with reality. This view presupposes that reality is not objectively somewhere outside of us, waiting to be found. In finding it we in part interpret it. Many philosophers from many different persuasions, including both Marxists and phenomenologists, share this insight.

The creative genius sets a tone, starts a new trend, and serves as a model for others; it is clear that he is an authority for them. This is the case whether we are concerned with the arts, science, the humanities, or everyday life. A Leonardo in art, a Newton in physics, a Plato in philosophy, a Gandhi in the realm of morality—all draw about them followers and imitators, who continue their work or continue in the line that they initiated. In none of these cases, however, does the authority relationship entail the right to command or any obligation of obedience on the part of the followers. They may decide to do as the authority says, but not because of any obligation coming from position, contract, or formal organizational relations.

How a creative genius becomes an authority differs in each of the four realms. The scientist addresses himself primarily to fellow scientists and proposes a theory, which he must demonstrate is fruitful. The demonstration must be logically persuasive, not simply the utterance of a propounder of the theory. Only after some degree of confirmation do those who are competent to judge accept what he says. Their acceptance certifies him as an authority for others—that is, for those who are not competent to judge on their own but who have some reason to believe the endorsement of those in the field. When there is great division in a field, those outside of the field do not know whom to believe. Historically, those who are dominant in a field have tended to organize, to become offically recognized by government or other parts of society, and to establish themselves as the ones who are to be believed in that field. Because of their competence, they are given positions in which they may exercise not only epistemic or exemplary authority but executive authority as well. They are given the power of office, positions of importance in organizing the field, in writing and publishing the authoritative works, and in advising those in public life to whom such knowledge is useful. In short, they become institutionalized. The next genius, the creative individual who challenges the accepted views and ideas, must then battle those who hold the entrenched position. It is not unusual for the creative individual to be ignored or not to be accepted by his peers in his own time. The truly creative individual in any field threatens those who have spent their lives and have built their careers developing, promoting, and defending the previous views. The authority of the recognized experts outweighs the authority of the innovator, who must prove to skeptical peers the worth of his new theories. The more he threatens the established beliefs and ways of doing things, the more he will be resisted. He can expect a better reception from those who are newer in the field and have less authority or prestige to lose by recognizing or following his achievements.

The same is true in the realm of art. The artist receives his authority not only from other artists but more often from the critics. If he is hailed as a creative genius by the critics and is so accepted by them, he wields more authority among the general populace than he would otherwise. Often, however, a truly creative artistic talent is criticized or ignored by critics who fail to appreciate him, only to have others discover him later. Whether an artist is an authority in his own lifetime or not makes little difference as far as those who imitate him and work in his style are concerned, for it is the work of the creative genius that inspires them, not his discussion about art. Just as scientists can wield power as authorities whose orders are followed because of their positions, so the critics, the official guardians of taste, the art historians, and others who are similarly placed can wield power and impede the reception accorded to the next innovator.

Creative discoveries are not temporary, even if they are innovative only at a certain time. The followers of the great artist, creator, and thinker work within his style and take him as an exemplary model to follow. In every field once a new, creative breakthrough has been accepted and its development is in process, it and its exponents take on an authority in the particular field which serves as a barrier to further innovation and creativity outside the current phase. Sometimes a creative genius is ahead of his time and is not recognized;

others are not prepared to follow and develop where he has led. The authority of entrenched ideas and trends stifles new ideas and trends.

GOVERNMENT AND CREATIVITY

We have considered as our paradigm the creative activity of the individual genius; but there are social dimensions out of which such figures come. Some periods and cultures foster more creativity than others. Also, not all creativity is individual; it may be collective or social. A disputed theory of creativity holds that social complexes explain the creativity of individuals and that the creative process is an ongoing one which simply finds its clear expression in individual figures; this theory has a certain strength. Although individual creativity cannot be denied, the social aspect of creativity needs further explanation and exploration.

The creative artistic force of the Middle Ages found expression in magnificent cathedrals. They are the creation of many individuals, working together, borrowing from each other, refining and simplifying and creating together. Architects, stonecutters, sculptors, painters, and a host of other craftsmen worked together to produce the final product. Those who were in charge directed workers and built according to plans or blueprints, which frequently changed as the original workers and planners died and were replaced during succeeding generations. In such projects we can see the need for operative executive authority, the right of those in charge to give orders to those below, and the need to have orders followed. Those who follow orders and are subordinate to those in authority may or may not themselves be creative. They may simply be laborers who are following the directions needed in order to lift stones or to move dirt. They may, however, be creative sculptors, carving statutes to fill niches according to some overall plan. Such authority is in no way destructive of creativity; in fact it is an essential part of a cooperative creative endeavor.

Large works, such as cathedrals, require the creativity of many individuals. There must be some overall design and concept if the whole is to form a unity. And many unskilled and relatively uncreative persons may be involved in the joint undertaking. However, the complex example of a cathedral as a creative work requires analysis if one is to sort out the creative elements. Some choose to put the emphasis on the person or persons who discovered the art of

279

vaulting; others focus on the architect and his conception as a whole; others look to the spirit of the age. The example shows that creativity may be found in a joint endeavor, but it does not deny the creativity of individuals.

Certain places and periods are more creative than others. The fifth century B.C. in Greece, the thirteenth century in Europe, and the Renaissance in Italy stand out as periods of exceptional creativity, as do the period between the world wars in Vienna and the turn of the century in Paris. Does creativity flourish because of government and the conditions it creates, or in spite of these?

Social creativity manifests itself in creativity in two basic ways. In one model the political order allows and encourages the development of creativity in the various areas of social life. The political order actively promotes and fosters the arts, sciences, and creativity in all domains, without directing them. Or the government may simply create conditions of sufficient stability, affluence, and freedom so that the creative energies of the people find outlets in endeavors of their own choosing. In the other model, government itself has a creative image of society, which embodies a creative approach towards authority. The government need not stifle creativity when pursuing particular areas. Governmental authority may affect individual creativity either positively or negatively.

Creativity in government (which falls under the category of creativity in everyday life) may be of several types. The laws and traditions of a country that bind a creative leader restrict the scope for originality and creative rule for fear of what an absolute ruler might do. The laws that restrict the harm that a poor ruler can do also restrict the good that the creative ruler can achieve. The kind of creativity in government that corresponds to the revolutions in art, literature, music, philosophy, or physics is possible under conditions of political revolution. Otherwise the entrenched powers of the established authority stifle radical, new, and possibly threatening changes. The more creative the changes, the more they differ from what has been previously accepted.

Creativity in government is best exemplified by governments whose creative leaders are unrestricted or by countries in which revolt has just occurred. Society has suffered such abuses from unrestricted leaders that many societies have chosen to restrict the kinds of activities the government can engage in and the violence that it can do to individual citizens in the name of creativity. After a revolution creativity takes on various forms. After the American

Revolution the Constitutional Convention produced a document that was in many ways a creative product, which other countries chose to emulate. Similarly, the Russian Revolution opened up the possibility of a new form of government and a new economic system, which other societies have also taken as a model. This type of creativity, however, is creativity by government in the realm of government and is different from a government as the chief social architect, seeking to mold society as its creative product, even if this is put in terms of leading the society to some new goal. Society is not the tool or product of its leaders, and the legitimate authority of government does not extend to using people as means to achieve its ends. The socialist government started under Tito in Yugoslavia attempted to develop socialist self-management in government and worker self-management in industry. It was a creative approach to governmental and social organization, and it fired the imagination of many theorists outside of Yugoslavia. As this example shows, however, even such a creative social experiment tends to repress any creativity not in accord with the overall plan.

A government that orchestrates all of the aspects of social development—as Stalin did in the Soviet Union—falls prey to the difficulty of not having the needed expertise to recognize and properly channel the creative work in all realms. In the Soviet Union the period of the early 1920s was often one of innovation, experimentation, debate, and creativity. It was followed by the repressive Stalinist period, in which socialist realism was demanded of writers, painters, and musicians. The party dictated the truths that were to be held, and it intervened to establish its control over all areas of learning, including that of science. The harm done to those fields took years to repair. Under Mao the Chinese experienced similar harm to their universities, to the arts and letters. In both cases, political authority was used in order to enforce doctrines that were believed to be true. Political authority either was substituted for epistemic authority or sought to become epistemic by force. Such cases demonstrate a misunderstanding of the nature of the various forms of authority and their proper function and justification.

A government is in a difficult position with respect to nonpolitical creativity. We have noted that creativity cannot be commanded. A government may wish to foster creativity in all areas of life in the belief that this is a way in which mankind develops and the society prospers; but it frequently cannot know who is the creative individual or group who is deserving of support. Government officials are not usually experts in the arts, sciences, or humanities. If they wish to foster these areas, they must rely on acknowledged authorities; but if they do so, they may empower those who are most threatened by true creative advances, who paradoxically are those who are best qualified to judge.

The situation is only exacerbated when a government identifies itself with or adopts an official art style, philosophy, or scientific view. It is one thing for a government to attempt to foster creativity in all realms. It is quite another for leaders of a government to consider themselves authorities in all realms of human endeavor. In general, the more closely a government identifies itself with any of the nongovernmental realms, the more likely it is that it will squash, prevent, and preclude the growth of creative, innovative development. For if the governmental leaders are not expert in those areas, they will tend to see creative innovation as poor science, art, or philosophy or as a threat to their own power.

The building-block view of knowledge and of development is frequently held by those outside a field. If that view is held by those who have the power to enforce the accepted position and to preclude the development or dissemination of alternatives, we can expect either that creativity will be suppressed or that it will go unrecognized and unappreciated. In either case the society is poorer than it would have been if the creativity had been allowed to flourish.

Creativity, if socially desirable, is best fostered by a government that does not identify itself with any particular position in the arts, sciences, philosophy, or other humanities. Those who are in a position to know and judge on the basis of the merits of the case may fail to appreciate the great creative innovator; but they and those in the field who have the least to lose are in a better position than governments are to decide what is worthwhile and what is not in a field.

Governments are not typically epistemic authorities in a particular field, nor are they exemplary authorities in most fields. They have great executive power. But most fields develop better and more fruitfully when those who know the fields argue, debate, and develop ideas, theories, and methodologies. A government that places its executive authority behind any given theory is using its executive authority improperly or is making epistemic authorities into executive authorites within the field. Any such activity misconstrues any field of knowledge or of artistic development. Operative authority may be granted to the masters and teachers in such areas with respect to those who wish to learn and who willingly submit to their guidance; but executive imperative authority, especially politico-legal authority, has no place in these realms.

Only a society open to change can hope to benefit from its creative members. Such openness, however, may take its toll in social order and, possibly, in social harmony. In the last analysis each society must determine how much creativity it really wants and how much disruption it is willing to bear in order to achieve creative advances.

Creative developments frequently build on the past and its creations; the position that underlines the new emphasizes the necessity for openness to what is new. The more closely political and other kinds of executive authority have linked themselves with the prevailing trends, philosophical views, or scientific theories, the less likely are they to be open to new developments.

Creativity has its own authority of authenticity. The more open and progressive a society and the less a state uses its authority to control nongovernmental areas, the more that society is likely to enjoy not only the fruits of its own creative citizens but also the fruits of human creativity generally.

13

Conclusion

Each generation must rethink the justification of authority. Some of the changes our generation has made in American authority structures have been salutary and are a positive development of some basic American traditions. Some changes have been pernicious and have spread seeds of discontent, which ripen on the soil not of reason but of confusion and demagoguery.

The American colonies were a refuge for those who were seeking religious freedom. The Revolution represented a drive for economic and political freedom from England. Throughout its development America has cherished freedom. Freedom has had a prominent place in American ideology. For millions of immigrants the Statue of Liberty has symbolized the freedom they had not enjoyed in their own lands. Yet those who yearned for freedom recognized the necessity for the rule of law. The Constitution stands as an enduring achievement of the early years of the United States. It balanced and limited the authority of the branches of government, and through the Bill of Rights, it protected the individual from the illegitimate intrusion of government into the lives of its citizens.

Freedom and authority achieved a balance in the United States Constitution. But the tension of freedom and authority is a continuing struggle which no document can eliminate. Those who exercise authority are constantly tempted to overstep its legitimate bounds. The defense of individual freedom requires constant vigilance. The difficulty of balancing freedom and authority stems from the paradox that freedom is often maximized when it is protected by law and therefore by authority.

We have seen that authority is a complex phenomenon. There are various kinds and types of authority, and it is always found intertwined in some social context. Attacks on it as a whole or any defense that approaches authority as if it were all of the same kind will be simplistic, distorted, and illegitimate. If we are interested in rational evaluation, we should keep straight the kinds and types of authority and the principles of justification and limitation that are applicable to particular issues or events. Some authority *is* justifiable. Both in theory and in fact we can separate the legitimate use of some types of authority from their illegitimate use.

Authority in American life has frequently been seen as appropriate in the public realm but as limited in the private realm. As applied to political authority, the view is generally sound. To allow political authority to control the private realm—religion, morality, and conscience; the search for knowledge, creativity, and individual spontaneity—is to justify totalitarianism in government. We have traditionally resisted government encroachment into the private realm. Yet some kind of authority is appropriate and legitimate there—though not the authority of government. The key to an appropriate defense against totalitarianism is not to argue against all authority but to distinguish among the kinds and forms of authority and to allow only those that are appropriate for the activity involved. My defense of authority throughout has been minimalist, not in the sense of defending a minimal state, but in the sense of justifying authority only to the extent that it is required in order to achieve the ends one wishes to attain. In the political realm, this may require a good deal more than a minimal state. Those who are free to determine what they wish the state to do for them must be willing to give the state the authority to do what they require and must allow it to be sufficiently large and powerful to accomplish the ends they assign it. The danger is that government may slip beyond the control of the people and that those in government may do what they want to the people, rather than what the people want. Such an abuse of authority, however, is not an automatic function of size, nor is it a legitimate reason for preventing people from using the state to achieve the ends they desire.

The revolt against authority in the United States during the 1960s and 1970s, though often misplaced, has in some ways been salutary. It forced many people to look at traditional, accepted, and sometimes encrusted structures of authority. In some instances, protests led to changes. Alternative forms of organization were envisaged, elaborated, and sometimes implemented. Increase in population density has in some ways reduced the individual's effective freedom of action. The massive growth of government and of corporations has increased the use of authority and has multiplied the opportunities for abusing it. Any attempt to reduce the size of either the government or corporations to that of the eighteenth century is as utopian as is the platform of anarchism. Yet the need for authority in such structures does not preclude our freedom to choose our own lives and destinies.

We need to accept and acknowledge only as much authority as is necessary for us to achieve our individual and our collective ends. The tension of freedom and of authority, however, is only one of the tensions we face. A second is the tension of equality and authority. A third is the tension between individuality and authority. In both the past and the present the first has received the most attention in the United States. Our ideology champions not only freedom but also equality and individuality, and the relation of these things to authority raises problems we have not squarely faced. The age of rugged individualism is past, and reality has effectively shown us the limits of the myth of individualism. The myth of collectivism is an alternative that has never had much appeal to Americans, but respect for the human person should be joined with recognition that human beings are social creatures and that outside of society they are but abstractions. Society implies authority; however, the freedom implied by personhood must temper it. The task is to combine them effectively in community. The means to accomplish this task is the effective use of the principle of authority from below. So far, democracy provides the best hope for a fruitful mix of authority and freedom.

The distinction between epistemic authority and political authority reinforces the American tradition of openness. If an epistemic authority has no right to demand belief of what he says, a political authority has no right to demand belief of any dogmas or doctrines or to demand belief of the correctness or justifiability of actions. The distinction between epistemic authority and executive political authority provides a bulwark for resisting state-imposed truth and rationality and justifies holding the government accountable for its actions and policies.

Americans have chosen to follow the authority of rules of their own making, insofar as the process of representative government leads to this result. Authority is always context laden. Not only the frontier and the opportunities that are provided by a new and open land but also America's history and its European heritage helped form the structures of authority that have emerged. Sometimes, the structures are not adequate, no longer fit, and must be changed.

Sometimes, abuses prevent the proper application of these structures. Sometimes, changing conditions demand corresponding changes, which may not be made until long after they have become appropriate.

There are, however, countercurrents. The authoritarianism of government is one danger; entrenched views are another. But the dogmatism of the incompetent presents a more subtle danger in the pursuit of equality.

The doctrine of democracy places its trust in the people, who tend to be distrustful of elitism of any sort. Because the doctrine of equality in law and equality of opportunity is so commonly accepted as a right for all, some people confuse these rights with equality on all levels and in all realms. Some consequently attack competence as elitism and sow distrust of the competence that is needed if a democratic society is to function successfully. Some reduce justice to equality; they consider equality of treatment and opportunity the same as equality of merit and competence. This endangers social, artistic, scientific, and all other forms of human progress and innovation. Competence authority and epistemic authority are justified because of real differences between the skills and knowledge in some and the absence of such skills and knowledge in others. To deny this difference is to limit the possibilities of the less skillful to learn what will benefit them.

The enormous growth in knowledge during the last decades has brought with it a number of paradoxes. The advance in knowledge undermines people's faith in the ability of anyone to know enough to govern well. It also erodes the faith that is necessary in order for the authority of competence to be accepted. At the same time the growth in knowledge leads to innovations that require more competence and more specialized knowledge. We then need more epistemic authorities, since there are more areas in which most of us know little. The complexity of society and the exponential growth of knowledge leads to an even greater need for education. Also, attainment of education fits poorly with the views of those who champion equality of results, rather than equality of opportunity. They see the need for education and competence as one more instance of elitism or as one more attempt at manipulation of the less competent for the benefit of the elite.

America did not traditionally guarantee equality of results. It guaranteed equality before the law and equality of opportunity. It has not always achieved the former, though such equality continues to be an ideal. Equality of opportunity is a more subtle and elusive goal. Opportunity drew millions of immigrants: America offered opportunities that were not available in their own countries. Not everyone who came to the United States prospered; few of those who did well struck it rich. But some did; and most were better off than they had been before.

The ideas that all should have enough to live and that society should provide for those who are unable to care for themselves have become part of our beliefs. The idea that all should succeed is a goal that some people feel should also become part of our tradition. Yet equality of opportunity does not yield equality of outcome. A fair race is one in which all have an equal chance because all run under the same conditions. But some runners have better muscle structure than others, some train harder, and some are willing to endure more pain in the effort to win. In the end, the race determines which runner is the fastest. One wins; the others do not. Equality of opportunity, in this sense, is incompatible with equality of results, as well as with equality in all aspects of the runners' physique, development, or temperament.

Those who attack authority in the name of equality confuse various aspects and kinds of authority. Political equality is compatible with elected representatives and political leaders; economic equality of opportunity is compatible with operative authority within a firm or business. Equal respect for persons is compatible with authority of competence, which acknowledges that some people are better at certain tasks than others are, and with epistemic authority, which grants that some people know more than others do. Students who know as much as teachers no longer need teachers. But popular vote does not determine factual knowledge and conceptual relations; nor does each person who has an equal right to vote determine what is true.

The third tension is between individuality and authority. The rugged individualism of a frontier society is less appropriate in today's complex, highly technical society. The individualism championed in an earlier version of American ideology no longer fits comfortably; yet the ideology remains. The resulting conflicts of authority and individualism are intertwined with and exacerbate both the conflicts between authority and freedom and between authority and equality. Mutual interdependence has in great part replaced individualism. As individuals we rarely know how to produce the necessities of life, much less the large variety of goods we take for granted as part of our daily lives. Specialization has led to an increased dependence on those who serve as competence and epistemic authorities for us; and it has made us more interdependent. The structures of the economy tie us more closely to one another as we abandon individual modes and adopt social modes of production. Communication and transportation networks bind us together even more closely. Inventions are now typically the breakthroughs of teams of scientists and engineers in areas that are targeted for investigation and experimentation. The list goes on endlessly. However, the myth of individualism—the individual standing alone, apart from society—is still part of the American ideology. It does not square well with the authority required by complex interactions and joint enterprises.

The levels of moral development described by Jean Piaget and Lawrence Kohlberg can be paralleled at least conceptually with respect to authority. In the first stage, one is simply subject to authority and accepts it uncritically. In the second, authority is seen as conventional and is accepted as such. It is equated with law and order and is accepted because others accept it and because tradition supports it. In the third and rationally critical phase, authority is examined reflectively on its own merits and is accepted as being justified or is rejected as being illegitimate.

The defense of democracy as a means by which one controls one's own future, instead of having it controlled by authority, may apply to other countries. If those people feel they are being dominated and exploited by others and if they view that authority as authoritarianism, the arguments that defend action against such authority can lead to justified revolt. The anticolonial rebellions exemplify this. The potential for other explosions is always present.

But since authority is always found in a social context, we cannot transport any argument about the justifications and limitations of authority from one society to another without considering the differing conditions and structures in which authority is found. Although I have argued against a paternalistic justification of political authority in the United States, it does not follow that all people everywhere are prepared for democratic self-governance. That paternalism is limited within the American family does not deny the fact that in some traditional cultures paternalism is accepted and is perhaps justified. We no longer recognize the tradition of parents' choosing the mates for their children as a legitimate function of paternal authority; but this argument against the practice may not be persuasive or applicable in all societies. Much of my analysis implicitly presupposes that adult human beings are able to reason, to link causes and consequences, to foresee the consequences of actions, and to be sufficiently informed about their own interests and well-being that they can govern themselves. If these conditions are not fulfilled, then some sort of paternalism might be justified. Whether any people are indeed so childlike as to require a paternalistic government is debatable. But if we acknowledge that most adults are able to decide for themselves what sort of government they wish, those who believe that people should have the right to choose cannot at the same time think it is their duty to force all people to choose the same way. The latter position assumes that there is only one right way for all rational people to choose: this is a dubious and unproven assumption.

The discussion of authority in much of this book has focused on the United States, its institutions, and its network of authority. Though the distinctions and principles can be applied to other societies, there are limits to their general application on a world-wide level. For since authority is always found in particular contexts, it is a function of a system. It is an internal concept. On the world level there is no effective international political or legal authority. Nations for practical purposes exist in something like Hobbes's state of nature, living in mutual fear. As more of them acquire nuclear weapons, they approach more closely to the position of equality in which each can mortally wound anyone else. Nations do engage in some joint activities, and they do acknowledge some operative authority. But subjected nations feel the unjust discrepancy between factual inequality and dependence, as well as the absence of world community, despite the essential brotherhood of mankind.

Political authority is accepted routinely and is challenged only for cause. Its legitimacy is presumed, and the burden of proof is on the dissenter. This is political authority as seen by those who are subject to it. But what if such authority divides people to their detriment? Or what if people freely make a poor choice? If they are not allowed to choose poorly, they are not free, and they are coercively subject to someone else's will, even if for their own best interests. This is an illegitimate use of authority.

Authority, in all of its forms and functions, with its justification and limitations, is only one part of the concrete reality in which we find our social lives embedded. Clarity about authority is necessary in order to evaluate the basis and legitimacy of our acceptance of it. Although authority poses a central social and political problem, it is

290

intertwined with questions of justice and, more broadly, of morality. In many specific instances authority cannot be evaluated without considering these questions, as well as pertinent facts. Theory can take us only so far.

Crises of authority are a function of changing conditions. The constant evaluation of accepted authority is the condition of our freedom as individuals and as a society. The tension between authority and freedom is a continuing one. At times, authority dominates; at other times, freedom does. The enemy, however, is not authority but the abuse of authority.

Bibliographic Essay

1. INTRODUCTION. For a general bibliography on authority through 1973 see Richard T. De George, "Authority: A Bibliography," in R. Baine Harris, ed., *Authority: A Philosophical Analysis* (University: University of Alabama Press, 1976). A number of anthologies deal with authority in general, political authority, or some other aspect of authority. The function and limits of epistemic, moral, political, legal, and religious authority are discussed in *Authority*, edited by R. Baine Harris (above). The Nomos 1 volume, *Authority*, edited by Carl J. Friedrich (Cambridge: Harvard University Press, 1958; reprinted, Greenwood, 1981), contains a group of still-pertinent essays by C. W. Hendel, C. J. Friedrich, H. Arendt, B. de Jouvenal, and T. Parsons, among others. *Authority*, edited by Frederick Adelman (The Hague: Martinus Nijhoff, 1974), includes essays by J. M. Bochenski, John Wild, Bernard Lonergan, and Karl Rahner. *Proceedings of the Aristotelian Society*, supplementary volume 32 (1958), contains a "Symposium: Authority," with papers by R. S. Peters, P. Winch, and A. Duncan-Jones. The articles by Peters and Winch are reprinted in Anthony Quinton, editor, *Political Philosophy* (London: Oxford, 1967).

2. THE CONCEPT OF AUTHORITY. A number of books and articles deal with authority in general. Carl J. Friedrich, in *Tradition and Authority* (London: Macmillan, 1972), argues that authority is the capacity for reasoned elaboration. Yves Simon, in *A General Theory of Authority* (Notre Dame, Ind.: University of Notre Dame Press, 1962) and in *Nature and Functions of Authority* (Milwaukee, Wisc.: Marquette University Press, 1940), claims that the essential function of authority is to assure unified action by a united multitude. Bertrand Russell discusses authority in *Authority and the Individual* (New York: Simon & Schuster, 1949), arguing that although security and government require centralized governmental control, progress requires the greatest scope of individual freedom compatible with social order. Peter Winch, in *Political Philosophy*, edited by Quinton (see above), defends the view that authority is an internal relation: for example, the authority of a

judge over me is understandable only within a legal system. Hannah Arendt, in "What Is Authority," in *Between Past and Future* (New York: Viking Press, 1968), pp. 91-141, maintains that authority rests on foundations that in the past gave it permanency and that an authoritarian government's source of authority is external force, which transcends the political order.

3. THE AUTHORITY OF KNOWLEDGE AND COMPETENCE. Epistemic authority is dealt with in a variety of ways. William P. Montague, in *The Ways of Knowing* (New York: Macmillan, 1925), chapter 1, "The Methods of Authoritarianism," makes the point that knowledge based on authority is the weakest kind. George Santayana, in *Dominations and Powers*, devotes two chapters ("Rational Authority" and "Rival Seats of Authority") to discussing the role of authority in knowledge. Paul Feyerabend, "Against Method: Outline of an Anarchistic Theory of Knowledge," in *Analyses of Theories and Methods of Physics and Psychology*, Minnesota Studies in the Philosophy of Science no. 4, edited by Michael Radner and Stephen Winokur (Minneapolis: University of Minnesota Press, 1970), attacks authority in knowledge. Georges Gurvitch, in *The Social Frameworks of Knowledge*, translated by Margaret A. Thompson and Kenneth H. Thompson (New York: Harper Torchbooks, 1972), deals with the social development of knowledge. Thomas S. Kuhn, *The Structure of Scientific Revolutions* (Chicago: University of Chicago Press, 1962; 2d ed., 1970), argues that shifts in paradigms are the basis of scientific revolutions. Stephen E. Toulmin, in *Human Understanding: The Collective Use and Evolution of Concepts* (Princeton, N.J.: Princeton University Press, 1972), develops the social aspect of knowledge and the role of authority. In *The Rise of Professionalism: A Sociological Analysis* (Berkeley: University of California Press, 1977), Magali Sarfatti Larson discusses the sociology of knowledge and the rise of the professions.

4. EXECUTIVE AUTHORITY. Max Weber's classic analysis in *Economy and Society: An Outline of Interpretive Sociology*, edited and with an introduction by Guenther Roth and Claus Wittich, translated by Ephraim Fischoff et alii, 3 volumes (New York: Bedminster Press, 1968), divides executive authority into legal-rational, traditional, and charismatic. His focus, however, is primarily on political authority. In "Authority" (see *Political Philosophy*, above, Quinton, ed.), R. S. Peters's 'In-authority' closely corresponds to 'executive authority'. An interesting work from a psychological perspective is Stanley Milgram, *Obedience to Authority* (New York: Harper & Row, 1974), which gives detailed responses to an experiment relating to executive authority. Shankar A. Yelaja, editor, *Authority and Social Work: Concept and Use* (Toronto: University of Toronto Press, 1971), is a collection of excerpts and papers that illustrate the use of executive authority in a wide variety of organizations and areas.

5. SOURCES, SYMBOLS, AND SYSTEMS OF AUTHORITY. Carl J. Friedrich, in *Tradition and Authority* (see above), underlines tradition as a source of authority, as does Hannah Arendt. Richard Sennett, in *Authority* (New York: Alfred A. Knopf, 1980), sees authority as one of four emotional bonds that bind society and emphasizes the fear of being deceived by authority. In their controversial study *The Authoritarian Personality*, T. W. Adorno, Else Frenkel-Brunswik, Daniel J. Levinson, and R. Nevitt Sanford (New York: W. W. Norton & Co., Inc., 1950) seek the psychological sources of ideology, but much of the work is applicable to authority as well. The church/state debate over the centuries constitutes the richest source of literature on the clash of systems of authority. Peter Meinhold's "Relations between Church and State in Europe," in *Freedom and Authority in the West*, edited with a foreword by George N. Shuster (Notre Dame, Ind., and London: University of Notre Dame Press, 1967), pp. 41-53, provides an accessible entry point. On symbols see Ernst Cassirer, *The Philosophy of Symbolic Forms*, translated by Ralph Manheim, 3 volumes (New Haven, Conn.: Yale University Press, 1953-57), which is a rich study of symbols in language, myth, and knowledge. Susanne K. Langer's *Philosophy in a New Key: A Study in the Symbolism of Reason, Rite and Art*, third edition (Cambridge: Harvard University Press, 1957), studies the transformation and logic of symbols in life and art. Umberto Eco, *A Theory of Semiotics* (Bloomington: Indiana University Press, 1976), provides the framework for an analysis of the symbols of authority—an analysis that has yet to be fully done.

6. FREEDOM, ANARCHISM, AND AUTHORITY. The literature on anarchism is very large. Two useful anthologies are *The Essential Works of Anarchism*, edited by Marshall S. Shatz (New York: Bantam Books, 1971), and *Patterns of Anarchy*, edited by Leonard I. Krimerman and Lewis C. Perry (New York: Anchor Books, 1966). The most extreme anarchist position is Max Stirner's, in *The Ego and His Own: The Case of the Individual against Authority*, edited by James J. Martin and translated by Steven B. Byington (Sun City, Calif.: Western World Review, 1982). *Bakunin on Anarchy*, edited, translated, and with an Introduction by Sam Dolgoff (New York: Vintage Books, 1971), is a good collection of Bakunin's writings. The most important contemporary anarchist is Daniel Guerin, *Anarchism: From Theory to Practice*, translated by Mary Klopper (New York: Monthly Review Press, 1970). Robert Paul Wolff's *In Defense of Anarchism* (New York: Harper Torchbooks, 1970) caused a stir, and many rose to respond, including Jeffrey H. Reiman, *In Defense of Political Philosophy: A Reply to Robert Paul Wolff's "In Defense of Anarchism"* (New York: Harper Torchbooks, 1972). Robert A. Dahl's *After the Revolution? Authority in a Good Society* (New Haven, Conn.: Yale University Press, 1970) is a good exposition of possible authority substitutes after the traditional type of government has been overthrown. Although he shows the limitations of

participatory democracy, he defends worker self-management. Murray N. Rothbard, *For a New Liberty* (New York: Macmillan, 1973), represents what is often called the anarchism of the right, which is often identified with libertarianism. *Anarchism* (Nomos 19), edited by J. Roland Pennock and John W. Chapman (New York: New York University Press, 1978), is a useful collection of contemporary essays and contains a good working bibliography. In opposition to the anarchists, many works claim that freedom and authority are interrelated, rather than in opposition. The position is argued, among others, by John Dewey, "Authority and Social Change," in the collection *Authority and the Individual* (Cambridge: Harvard University Press, 1937).

7. THE JUSTIFICATION OF POLITICAL AUTHORITY. The literature on political authority is vast. The historically important figures are Plato, Aristotle, Aquinas, Hobbes, Locke, Rousseau, and Hegel. Oscar and Mary F. Handlin, editors, *The Popular Sources of Political Authority: Documents on the Massachusetts Constitution of 1780* (Cambridge: Belknap Press of Harvard University Press, 1966), is a useful collection of documents. Max Weber's classification of authority into legal-rational, traditional, and charismatic is extremely influential. Thomas McPherson, *Political Obligation* (London: Routledge & Kegan Paul; New York: Humanities Press, 1967), and D. Raphael, *Problems of Political Philosophy* (New York: Praeger, 1970, chap. 3: "Sovereignty, Power and Authority," and chap. 5: "Liberty and Authority"), present helpful analyses, starting with authority as the right to issue commands and to have them obeyed. Kurt Baier's "The Justification of Governmental Authority," *Journal of Philosophy* 69 (1972): 700–716, defines authority and two conditions (the normative and the explanatory) that, if satisfied, yield authority. He emphasizes that compliance with authority must benefit the subjects as a class. Michael D. Bayles, *Principles of Legislation: The Uses of Political Authority* (Detroit, Mich.: Wayne State University Press, 1978), argues that the contemporary loss of confidence in political authority stems from citizens' discontent with the policies that governments pursue. Richard E. Flathman, *The Practice of Political Authority: Authority and the Authoritative* (Chicago: University of Chicago Press, 1980), is a good analytic study; ultimately, it is a defense of political authority.

8. OPERATIVE AUTHORITY AND THE MARKETPLACE. The liberal tradition generally argues for the absence of governmental authority in the marketplace. The laissez-faire doctrine has its roots in Mill's *On Liberty* and finds an extreme defense in Murray Rothbard (see above). The defense of worker self-management constitutes another approach to the issues, for which Robert Dahl argues in *After the Revolution?* (above). A classic work on organizational theory is Herbert A. Simon, *Administrative Behavior*, second

edition (New York: Macmillan Co., 1958). Amitai Etzioni, *A Comparative Analysis of Complex Organizations*, revised and enlarged edition (New York: Free Press, 1975), presents a systematic survey of organizations and includes an extensive bibliography on them. Robert L. Peabody, *Organizational Authority: Superior-Subordinate Relationships in Three Public Service Organizations* (New York: Atherton, 1964), presents a comparative sociological study of authority in organizations. Sanford M. Dornbusch and W. Richard Scott, *Evaluation and the Exercise of Authority* (San Francisco: Jossey Bass Publishers, 1977), is a sociological study of authority systems in formal organizations; it develops a model combining authorization, control, and evaluation.

9. MORALITY AND AUTHORITY. Contemporary philosophers, for the most part, assume the authority of morality and use morality to justify political authority. The source or ground of morality is widely contested, however, and has been throughout the history of modern philosophy. Kant and Mill supplied the most influential alternatives to a religiously based morality. Contemporary philosophers generally attack the use of authority in morals. Typical is C. Hendel's paper in *Authority* (Nomos 1; see above) and Richard B. Brandt, "The Use of Authority in Ethics," in his *Ethical Theory* (Englewood Cliffs, N.J.: Prentice-Hall, 1959). Elizabeth Anscombe, in "Authority in Morals," in *Problems of Authority*, edited by John Murray Todd (Baltimore, Md.: Helicon Press, 1962), pp. 179–88, argues that we learn morality by doing and that although we can rely on our own judgment, we can learn a great deal by believing public moral teaching. Jean Piaget, *The Moral Judgment of the Child* (London: Kegan Paul, Trench, Trubner & Co., 1932), and Lawrence Kohlberg, "Stages of Moral Development as a Basis for Moral Education," in *Moral Education: Interdisciplinary Approaches*, edited by C. M. Beck, B. S. Crittenden, and E. V. Sullivan (Toronto: University of Toronto Press, 1971), have been very influential in the growing and controversial field of moral education. The role of authority in such education and the authority of traditional morality are central issues in the controversy.

10. RELIGION AND AUTHORITY. Leslie S. Dewart's "Church and Authority," in his *Religion, Language and Truth* (New York: Herder & Herder, 1970), deals with authority in Catholicism, as does J. McKenzie's *Authority in the Church* (New York: Sheed & Ward, 1972). John Courtney Murray, in "Freedom, Authority, and Community," in *Freedom and Authority in the West*, edited by G. Shuster, (see above), pp. 11-23, applies three functions of authority (the unitive, the decisive, and the corrective) to the Catholic Church. Joseph M. Bochenski's *The Logic of Religion* (New York: New York University Press, 1965), pp. 162-73, deals with the logic of authority in religion. Robert H. Bryant's *The Bible's Authority Today* (Minneapolis, Minn.:

Augsburg Publishing House, 1968) provides a good overview of many contemporary positions.

11. THE UNIVERSITY AND AUTHORITY. Richard Stanley Peters, in *Authority, Responsibility, and Education* (New York: Eriksson-Taplinger Co., 1960), develops authority as the setting of standards and discusses different educational techniques, of which the use of authority is one. Kenneth Dean Benne, in chapters 1 and 5 of *A Conception of Authority: An Introductory Study* (New York: Columbia University Teachers College, 1943), pp. 1–28, 70–113, discusses pedagogical authority and the authority of the community in education. Burton R. Clark's "Faculty Authority," *Bulletin of the American Association of University Professors* 47 (1961): 293–302, presents a defense of that authority. Harold L. Hodgkinson and L. Richard Meeth, editors, in *Power and Authority: Transformation of Campus Governance* (San Francisco: Jossey-Bass, 1971), collect some essays that are representative of the views of the late 1960s. A classic statement is Karl Jaspers, *The Idea of the University*, edited by Karl W. Deutsch, Preface by Robert Ulich, and translated by H. A. T. Reiche and H. F. Vanderschmidt (Boston: Beacon Press, 1959).

12. CREATIVITY AND AUTHORITY. Arthur Koestler's *The Act of Creation* (London: Hutchinson & Co., 1964), begins with creativity in humor, develops it through the sage and the artist, and discusses habit and originality. It contains an extensive bibliography. A small but useful work with an annotated bibliography is George F. Kneller, *The Art and Science of Creativity* (New York: Holt, Rinehart & Winston, 1965). A good collection of classical excerpts and contemporary essays is *The Creativity Question*, edited by Albert Rothenberg and Carl R. Hausman (Durham, N.C.: Duke University Press, 1976), which also contains an extensive partially annotated bibliography. Elliott Jaques, in *Work, Creativity, and Social Justice* (London: Heinemann, 1970), argues that creativity in work finds its optimum condition for expression in a just environment. Robert G. Wesson, *State Systems: International Pluralism, Politics, and Culture* (New York: Free Press, 1978), is a study of the development of non-Western, Western, and world systems, with some attention to the political background of scientific and cultural creativity.

13. CONCLUSION. The attacks on authority that characterized the later 1960s and early 1970s provoked a number of contemporary studies and reflections on authority in America. A special issue of *Southern Journal of Philosophy* (volume 8, 1970) dedicated to the "Crisis of Authority," includes articles by Abraham Kaplan, E. Maynard Adams, and Iredell Jenkins. Robert Nisbet, *Twilight of Authority* (London: Oxford University Press, 1975), notes

that respect for authority has waned and that the traditional nonpolitical social institutions have lost much of their authority to the ever-growing centralized power of the state. The essays in *Authority in a Changing Society,* edited by Clifford Rhodes (London: Constable, 1969), attempt to face the challenges to authority in a large number of areas from religion to sport. *The Problem of Authority in America,* edited by John P. Diggins and Mark E. Kann (Philadelphia: Temple University Press, 1981), deals with the crisis of the legitimacy of authority in politics, literature, and psychology. Of course, the last word on authority in America has yet to be written.

Index

301

Index